THE**OASIS**OF INSANITY

THE STUDY & PURSUIT OF ACTING
AT THE **BEVERLY HILLS PLAYHOUSE**

THE OASIS OF INSANITY

THE STUDY & PURSUIT OF ACTING
AT THE BEVERLY HILLS PLAYHOUSE

BY ALLEN BARTON

Published by

Beverly Hills Playhouse

First electronic edition: July 2017, Version 1.0
First paperback edition: July 2017

Electronic edition ISBN-13: 978-0-9989968-2-0
Electronic edition ISBN-10: 0-9989968-2-3

Paperback edition ISBN-13: 978-0-9989968-0-6
Paperback edition ISBN-10: 0-9989968-0-7

For my family: Tiffany, Zoe, Reed and Henry

ACKNOWLEDGMENTS

I'd like to thank several people who gave valuable feedback—in forms both critical and encouraging—at various stages of writing this book: Fred Barton, Ruth Barton, Mia Christou, Art Cohan, Julie Glucksman, Melissa Hayden, Jay Huguley, Jimmy Lyons, Cameron Meyer (despite her Yale education), Adam Rotenberg, Samantha Sloyan, Brynn Thayer, Everette Wallin, Bailey Williams, Michael Yavnieli, and Robert Zimmerman.

In addition, to name the many BHP students, teachers, and staff members who along this weird journey have taught me, influenced me, helped me get through specific moments of crisis, or simply provided a form of oasis through their presence in my life at various stages – this would fill a book of its own. If you think you're on this list, you probably are, and thanks to you as well.

Contents

II Teaching: The Study And Pursuit of Acting   125

Preface

The Oasis of Insanity is presented in two parts: **Learning** and **Teaching**. Its world is that of the Beverly Hills Playhouse, one of the most renowned acting schools in Los Angeles. The BHP has been a training ground for thousands of actors over 40+ years, many of whom went on to make their indelible mark on "The Industry," and its current students continue in that tradition day in and day out. The BHP was founded and led for many of those 40+ years by Milton Katselas, a teacher of significant reputation and outsized personality. Milton was my mentor. Three months out of college, I tripped and fell into his school at the recommendation of a pretty girl, and eighteen years later I became its owner and principal teacher. The story of how that happened, of my apprenticeship with the mercurial and inspirational Katselas, comprises the first, **Learning** section. It's a rip-roaring good story, and while Katselas had many intense, close relationships with students and staff over years that predated my arrival, none was with the guy who ended up making it to the finish line to take over for him. None was with someone who worked as many different jobs from the bottom to the top of the organization, who also happens to be a writer, and so I'm thinking mine is as good a story to tell about him as any.

In becoming a teacher in my own right, ultimately tasked with carrying forward his legacy, I determined early on after his death that the BHP could not simply be a museum for Milton Katselas. The BHP headquarters on Robertson Blvd. in Beverly Hills was ill-suited to the role of mausoleum. The BHP is not inanimate. It's a living, breathing entity, active sixteen hours a day on most days, and like anything that is alive, it would inevitably need to evolve: new blood, new teachers, new ideas, a fresh, ongoing perspective on the ever-evolving world of the aspiring and professional actor in Los Angeles and elsewhere. That new perspective should honor Milton and his technique, and honor the unique culture of the BHP as he formed it, but should also be forward-looking and unconstrained by rigidity, dogma, or excessive nostalgia. Milton, the proud Greek-American, would often say himself that he wished Greece would blow up the Parthenon as a symbolic act of shedding what he considered a slavish devotion to its past. That is the spirit behind the essays of the **Teaching** section.

Taken as a whole, I hope *The Oasis of Insanity* charts an entertaining and informative atlas of the world of the actor, but not simply through the narrow, esoteric canyons of acting technique. I hope it presents the broader horizons of a journey taken by a young actor, director and writer under the guidance of Milton's unique mentorship, a journey through the often crazy world of Milton's Beverly Hills Playhouse, whereby the student became a teacher, the lessons learned became the lessons taught, Milton's BHP became my BHP. I hope it's an account both personal and practical, addressed not only to current and former BHP students, but to actors of all stripes, and as well to those who merely wish to understand better the actor's trip and the art of acting.

For the first "memoir" section of this book, wherein I describe twenty-odd episodes from my coming of age at the BHP, I have changed the names of a few players in that history. The purpose of this book is not to *dish*, but there were incidents and certain sequences of events that I felt were necessary to cover. Whatever I have included either had a significant impact on my learning process, is important to understanding BHP history, and/or revealed something interesting and vivid about Milton. Others who were at the BHP during the period 1990-2010 may or may not concur with my take on these events—real-life incidents, particularly in as volatile an environment as an acting school run by Milton Katselas, have as many versions as there are witnesses to them. But I don't want to be that memoirist who feels the need to cram laudatory adjectives before every proper name—it feels too often these days that everyone is bending over backwards in a highly self-conscious effort *not to offend*. Meanwhile, there's that great, unapologetic line in the Yasmina Reza play, *Art*: "The older I get, the more offensive I hope to become." I have always loved that line.

The fact is everyone mentioned in this book, Milton most of all, was part of a period of my life that formed who I came to be, and that impact was felt across the spectrum of good and bad feelings, and as I get older I in some way feel thankful for all of it. I'm not harboring grudges (except one—I'm definitely holding one precious grudge). The fact is I'd be happy to sit down to lunch with any of them (except that one guy) to rehash this vivid history, hopefully with the aid of a light alcoholic beverage or six. But at the same time, I remember giving Milton an early writing sample, an idea for a scene, and he called me a couple days later: "It needs some piss, some cum, a few shards of broken glass, a sprinkle of bitter herbs. Then you'll have something." So I've tried my best to balance that early advice with my not wanting readers who are new to this history to adopt any negative viewpoint on past BHP personalities who are currently alive, presumably well, and who have moved on to new and hopefully fulfilling "post-Milton" chapters of their lives.

Introduction

It's Tuesday afternoon, after 4pm. The driveway basketball court is small, using the half of the driveway that lies behind the gate—cars in front, basketball in back. I didn't often get this call. Not that I'm a terrible athlete—I play tennis religiously twice a week, and I'm probably better than could be expected at other sports, given I was never on a team, never played high school or college sports. I remember my freshman year at Harvard, one of my roommates was an Olympic-level competitive oarsman, and rowing crew was one of the few sports you could do at Harvard without ever having done it before. I had a brother-in-law who also rowed crew for Harvard back in his day, and at the Olympics, so I considered it all a "sign", and penciled my name in on a sheet of paper to row freshman light eights. And I wasn't bad. I got in the best shape of my life doing the "stadiums"—running up the seating section of Harvard Stadium, and then from the top of each section running down the small steps. Ouch. I couldn't walk after those afternoons, but it was still a good feeling. And the early mornings watching the sun rise over the Charles River…They didn't suck. On the posted time/strength tests, my name was solidly middle-of-the-pack, until around November, when everyone below me on that list had already dropped out of the program. I followed shortly thereafter. The Hasty Pudding Theatricals needed a pianist for their small pit orchestra ("the band"), and I was determined to get that job. So, I left the musty confines of Newell Boathouse and rowing crew for the musty confines of the old Hasty Pudding Theatre and playing piano for rehearsals and performances of a famous college drag show. I had done this, playing piano for the school musicals, since I was 14, and watching the rehearsals, quietly, day after day, observing the communication between directors, choreographers, actors and the tech crew—this served to be the quite unintentional foundation of my later training.

Back to the basketball court. I didn't often get this call, because Milton had a regular crew for his twice-weekly two-on-two half-court basketball games. Michael #1. Michael #2. Mark. Todd. David. Rick. There were plenty of them. If I got the call, it meant a bunch of people had been called and were unavailable, a fact that would very likely make the host more ornery than perhaps even usual.

Milton Katselas was very serious about his 2-on-2 basketball games. They took place Tuesdays and Thursdays at 4:30pm without fail, and often Saturday afternoons after he taught his renowned masterclass in the mornings. The three invited players would show up early, let themselves in through the driveway gate, and start warming up, perhaps with some uneasy banter about the goings on at the Beverly Hills Playhouse, the acting school Milton founded and still oversaw as owner and its legendary teaching presence. You wouldn't want to speak too loudly about any of it, because if Milton came out and heard you, he'd take up whatever topic was at hand and you'd find yourself with a 10-point list of actions to take, not just to handle the situation, but to improve whatever weakness existed within you that was part of why the problem existed in the first place. Better to speak *sotto voce*. If spirits amongst players were high before he showed up, there was always a darker undercurrent that would emerge when Milton made his appearance, exiting the side door from his office onto the court, wearing sweat clothes and saying little, if anything. Chatter would subside and a quiet ritual of warmup shots would unfold for a couple minutes before the game began.

Rule number one: Milton wins. Period. This didn't mean that anyone was expected to throw the game. It was just a fact. Milton wins. It was his court, and he had this absurd hook-shot that he could hit with 90% accuracy from anywhere. And while Milton could be physical in his play, he would also take harsh exception to physical defense against him. So his team would win almost every game, and if there was some disturbance in the space-time continuum and the other team won, it was not something you wanted to celebrate. No high fives. Suppress those smiles. Milton would simply take the ball angrily and start a new game, winning it 11-2 before returning inside his house after an hour without much further comment.

So here I was, teamed up with Michael #2, against Milton and Michael #1. At some point during the game, I took the ball to start play after a score, with Milton defending me. I saw a bit of space to my left and darted past him, drove to the basket and scored a layup. Silence. I got the ball again to restart play. I passed to Michael #2, he passed back to me and I made the same move to my left. Drove to the basket and scored another layup. Milton took the ball and slammed it to the ground before bouncing it to me for another restart.

Knowing better than to try the same move a third time, I just passed to Michael #2 and walked forward into the court.

"No," Milton said sharply. "No. You take it out."

Michael #2 passed the ball back to me, and I stood there not quite knowing what to do. Michael #2 just shrugged the shrug that said, *You're on your own, man.*

"Try it again," Milton said.

"What?"

"Try it again. Make that move again."

I smiled, thinking perhaps he was just joking. Nope.

"Make the move again. Try for the layup. Go ahead."

I half-heartedly dribbled out and tried to move to my left. Milton threw his body into me, launching me into the side of his house, after which I crumpled to the ground. My left arm was scraped and bleeding from the impact. I looked up, a bit dazed.

"My foul," he said.

Fast forward. It had been years since Milton was last able to play basketball—complications from a nasty diabetic foot infection brought that chapter to a close. But now, in late October of 2008, the entire world of the Beverly Hills Playhouse was turned upside down, because on a Friday afternoon, Milton passed away at 75 from a heart attack he suffered three days prior. He'd gone to the bedroom of his Alfred St. home to rest, and at some point one of the two guys who were almost always with him to assist, drive, cook, etc. looked in on him and saw something was wrong. It was too late—he had probably been in arrest for 5-10 minutes, and even with the arrival of the paramedics and quick transport to the ER at Cedars-Sinai down the street, he never regained consciousness, there was no brain activity, nothing. As the ER doc said when I arrived there 90 minutes later, "He's critical and extremely grave." They were able to keep him on life support for three days, but it was just a matter of who made the decision, and when. Technically, per his legal documents, I was to make that decision, but I knew I couldn't make it on my own without his family and his longtime girlfriend (hereafter to be known as "MG") agreeing as well. That agreement finally came on Friday morning. While waiting for Milton's brother Tasso to arrive at the hospital, I met with MG and Gary Grossman, Milton's long-time producer and loyal BHP soldier, in the lobby area of the seventh floor of the Saperstein tower at Cedars. As we spoke of the situation and what was to come that day, we all craned our ears at some weird sound we were picking up. Was the critical care tower now playing *muzak?* Impossible. Gary searched his pockets and found his iPhone, and it was playing "Life is!" from Milton's favorite musical, *Zorba.* I shit you not. There's no way that phone could have just "pocket dialed" its way through the many keystrokes necessary to find that song in the library and start playing it. So we took this as a sign that Milton was fucking with us still, somewhat mischievously (he hated technology— never owned his own cell phone or computer), and thus was telling us the decision was the right one, and he was ready.

The palliative care team came in at 3:30pm, and Gary, MG and I stood by Milton while they did their work. It didn't take long, and that was that. I had been at the BHP eighteen years by that moment, fully sixteen of those were spent in almost daily contact with Milton. And at that moment, I was split by two equal sensations: Fear and Relief. At age 40 I was now the majority owner of the BHP, and responsible for what would happen from that day forward to keep it going, which was going to be a daunting task, more so particularly in the next four years to come than I could even anticipate.

But what was with the relief? At different times of any day over the last few years, this was my mentor, my boss, my friend, and to a certain extent a father figure for me. *Relief?* This was very strange. But I would be willing to bet that those who spent time with him outside his always brilliantly executed teaching, or who worked for him—they might understand it. Some may have felt it themselves. Such was the dichotomy of Milton Katselas.

His teaching talent wasn't to be questioned, and he could be exceedingly charming and generous in his good moods. But this select group will also know well the essential question we all suffered through on a continual basis: *To communicate, or not to communicate? That was the question.* Because if you communicated the wrong thing to him, or at the wrong time, or in the wrong way, he could unleash a Mediterranean temper so horrific that it would suppress any future desire to communicate the right thing at the right time, in the right way, even if you were certain as to what that would be. There is a long line of personal assistants, who, when they reached the end of the road, took off and when I say we never heard from them again, I mean…*Gone*. This select group would know well the adrenaline-surging phone calls, taking place often as early as 7am or late as midnight. You'd be able to tell often in the first three seconds whether it would be a good call or not—his mood would be reflected in his greeting immediately. Good: "Hey, man, what's the latest?" Or, often, yelled at full volume across his art studio in Los Feliz, at his assistant holding the phone, who would then parrot Milton's words to you. Something like this:

MILTON (Screaming in the background, clear as day, mad as hell): Ask him where the fuck are the stats!

ASSISTANT: Milton would like to know where are the stats?

ME: Which stats?

ASSISTANT (back to Milton): He's asking which stats?

MILTON (Screaming): Which fucking stats does he think I'm talking about?

ASSISTANT: Milton is asking which fucking stats do you think he's talking about?

ME: Well, either financial stats or incoming interviews? Could be either. I don't remember him asking for a report.

ASSISTANT: He says it could be either financial or incoming interviews? He doesn't remember you asking for it.

MILTON (Screaming): THE FUCKING STATS. I don't give a shit which stats. I shouldn't have to ask for it. Financial. Interview. I haven't gotten them. They're linked. One is linked to the other. The stats. WHERE ARE THEY?

ASSISTANT: Milton thinks these are all linked, he's just wondering…

MILTON (Screaming): What is he doing today at 2pm?

ASSISTANT: Milton would like to know what you're doing today at 2pm.

ME: My guess is I'm canceling whatever it is to meet with him.

ASSISTANT: His guess is he's meeting with you.

MILTON: DAMNED FUCKING RIGHT HE IS. My house. Tell him to bring the stats. All of them.

ASSISTANT: Did you get that?

ME: Yup.

Click.

I had thousands of calls with Milton, and a lot of them went down like that. And I'll tell you, I write that dialogue, and I don't miss it. Not one word of it. I miss the man sometimes for sure, but I don't miss working for him. I don't miss the phone calls. Back before cell phones came to dominate, I had the landline in my apartment programmed to give a special *"RING-RING…RIIIINNG"* pattern when Milton was calling from his caller-ID blocked house. To this day, the *"SOUND-SOUND…SOUNNNNND"* rhythm surges my adrenaline.

In the weeks following his death, the story about his slamming me up against his house in the basketball game came up. There were a couple of memorial services outside the confines of his theaters—one at Celebrity Centre, which was the Church of Scientology's artist sanctuary on Franklin & Bronson (yes, I will be addressing this topic in a later chapter), and another, larger memorial at the Directors Guild of America. I was to speak at both of them, and I wanted to tell that story, along with another far more positive one about something amazing Milton did for me as I prepped a piano recital years before in 1994. (That story too follows later.) I wanted to show both sides of his personality, the mercurial and the generous, and the basketball story always got a good laugh from anyone who knew him.

However, both MG and Irene Dirmann, his longtime close friend, who had run the BHP for Milton as its iron-willed, Margaret Thatcher-like Executive Director for a dozen years or so until 1995, determined that the basketball story would cast him in a negative light and thus was unsuitable. MG and Irene were really in charge of the message and tone, and somewhat the logistics of these services, and so I acquiesced, telling just the one "good Milton" story. But it struck me as so classic, so much of what we all needed to move past, and quickly: Protecting him, managing people's perception of him, soothing him, sucking up to him, trying to win his approval, even posthumously...I told the basketball story privately in the many conversations that took place after his passing, along with the fact that I had been banned from repeating it in public. And while it shouldn't have been a big deal, I resented that I wasn't "allowed" to tell the story at the services. I thought, "C'mon, let's tell the story of this man. The real guy. The good, bad, the ugly and the exceptional." Part of the idea for this book was born at that moment.

In the years since, I've grown to have more confidence in my own convictions, and the voice to proclaim them. I managed somehow to steer the BHP through the turbulent waters of the time after Milton's death. I tried to honor everything I thought was the bedrock of what made the BHP special as an acting school, namely Milton's distinctive approach to talking about acting, while also removing the cultural aspects I felt were negative, largely associated with that same guy's very difficult personality and its impact on that culture. In 2009, I started a blog to express my thoughts on the study and pursuit of acting, which was a huge mental obstacle itself: *How dare anyone in this joint have a thought about acting without it being Milton's thought?* Such are the trials of studying with a master and then being out on your own.

It was only years later that I finally arrived at the title of "The Oasis of Insanity." Originally the title came from a class I taught at some point, wherein I was critiquing an actor, and if memory serves, he was bitching and moaning about his career, the doubts, the fears, and all the rest of it—the stuff people in the performing arts deal with practically every day, if not every hour, while imagining there is some "normal" life out there that they are really quite stupid, quite insane, not to have chosen. After a while, I brushed his complaining aside, and said something along these lines: "Listen. I've known you a long time. You love this. You love acting. You think it's insane, and maybe it is, but you love it. And you know damned well you have no place sitting in some florescent-lit office, typing or filing or programming a mobile app. If you did that, you know you would be miserable, and this theatre would become your oasis, instead of the symbol of a bad choice. So let's look at it that way now, take pride in choosing 'the path less traveled by.' Maybe this is simply where you belong, and it comes with its own doubts and fears, but that place you imagine, the so-called 'normal life,' has its own unique doubts and fears. Ultimately the oasis is located where you love what you do. We're all sitting here in an oasis of insanity."

It was just an extemporaneous thought, but as soon as I said it, I remember turning to the class, saying, "That's a pretty good title for a book about this place." So from when I was a 22-year-old who tripped and fell into the BHP on the advice of a pretty girl, to the 30-year-old who became the CFO of the BHP, then at 35-years-old the CEO, then at 40-years-old the owner, and since then…The BHP has been that oasis for me. I've essentially loved every second of it, and I still do. Milton was the epicenter of it all, and the unique experience of studying and working with him, in equal parts insane and inspirational —it was part of the oasis.

A few years after his death, I was teaching class on a Tuesday night as usual, and did my impression of Milton and how he might handle a situation. I turned in my chair to the class to catch the eye of those who would know, and was struck by two impressions at the same time: There were maybe five people there who would have seen him teach personally, and "it" had started to happen: There were fewer and fewer students currently at the school he founded who had ever met him. *Weird.* But the second impression: "Hey, this room is chock full of actors who clearly don't care that he isn't around. They're here because the place has value for them right now, based on the teaching happening right now." That was me, doing that teaching. In that moment I realized I had come in with an apologetic chip on my shoulder for a long time: "I'm sorry I'm not Milton, I'm gonna bring my best, I think it's pretty good, but, uh…It's not going to be him." It was bullshit. And Milton himself would never have tolerated such a chip in me. And in some way I thus arrived at my own moment of knowing I was the teacher there, no apologies needed.

Back in 2007, Milton had started teaching again during the week. He was always there for his master class on Saturday mornings, but for the weekday nighttime advanced classes, he had been scarce for many years, showing up now and again for a specific scene with a specific actor, often not even taking his chair, but standing at the side of the room and delivering his critique from there, before walking out. There were a range of substitute teachers who handled the vast bulk of the teaching duties during those years. But earlier in 2007, one of those subs, Gary Imhoff, had himself taken off rather dramatically. He called me one Saturday morning to say that the afternoon Musical Theatre class he had created and taught for years, well, it wouldn't be meeting that day because he had essentially absconded with it, no one would be there, they would all be meeting at some other theatre he had rented, and by the way, *seeya later*. That was the last gesture in a very long story between Milton and Imhoff, and it left a hole in the teaching schedule twice a week for the night-time advanced level classes. Milton picked up that slack personally, much to everyone's surprise and elation. He didn't just stand at the side of the room. He came in, sat down, and did the whole night, 3-4 hours of it. He did exercises, he met new people. And because he was there for four hours at a time, he couldn't just be that S.O.B. who showed up here and there, bellowed his dissatisfaction, and then left. Everyone got to see that far gentler, witty, charming, crazily generous man who yinned his Greek temper's yang.

What we didn't know was that he was beginning to fade. There was the weight loss. The recurring cough. I would receive calls from his number-one assistant Richard Shirley, just saying, "We're out of town." One time, a strange number called my cell phone—it ended up being Milton. Curious, I Googled the phone number, and it was a cancer treatment center in Arizona. There were weeks he was completely out of commission, barely communicating, and when I did hear from him he sounded awful. One morning he arrived to teach his Saturday master class, and was so wobbly from nausea that he couldn't enter the theatre. I and a couple of the students who helped run the class stood around the courtyard as he wandered a bit, taking several minute-long pauses to bend over. After fifteen minutes of this, he just willed himself into the room to teach. And we all never said a word about it. As all this started to occur, he asked that I show up when he was teaching, in case he needed to take off for not feeling well or getting tired. We then had a co-teaching deal going for 18 months before he passed away. Along the way, I remember three moments that forever changed my trajectory and confidence as a teacher:

1. The first time Milton was going to critique a scene that was repeated on notes I gave when he wasn't there. This was

a perilous moment I had observed many times as a student and "executive" in the classes before I started teaching. You could always tell if Milton disagreed with the original notes, no matter how politic he would be about it, and sometimes he wasn't politic in the least. Frankly, it was pretty clear he disagreed with his substitute teachers' notes more often than not. I stood in the back of the theatre and felt completely nauseated. I thought the scene was much better, but what would he think about it? He gave nothing away, asking many questions of each actor, about the scene, about the notes they received…Five minutes. Ten minutes of these questions. Finally: "Well. I thought it was just terrific. Excellent…" I practically passed out behind the seats.

2. In 2008, I directed a production of *Rabbit Hole* that was extremely well received, and ran with great houses for three full months or something. Milton's style was never to come to an actual performance, but rather to get his own preview before the show opened, so he could give his notes and hopefully improve the product before the audience came. So it was with *Rabbit Hole*, and I remember thinking we were on a good track because he didn't offer any corrections on the direction. He just argued with the playwright in absentia: "You think that kid is right when he says there are other versions of all of us in these multiple universes? Because I'm telling you, there isn't another me." Anyway, one night in class he was looking for someone who was absent, and the Stage Manager told him the student was missing because he was "directing a film." Milton freaked: "He's not directing a fucking film. Kazan directed film. Sidney Lumet directed film. This guy is not directing a fucking film. Directing isn't just picking up a fucking camera and press 'record.' You guys don't know what directing is." Pause. He looked at me. "Who here has seen *Rabbit Hole*?" We had just opened a couple weeks before, so maybe a third of the class had seen it by that time—their hands went up. Milton continued: "Allen Barton is a director." Holy shit. THAT was "high cotton," as my southern college roommate used to say.

3. Finally, in the fall of 2008, after several more occasions where he appreciated the work done by actors on my notes, there was a night he took off early. After his last critique, around 9:30pm, he would usually turn to the class and say, "And I now leave you in the capable hands of Allen Barton." But on this particular night, when he had seen another repeat on my notes, he offered that sentence, and as the class broke and people started blithely chatting and moving about, he halted them: "Hey. HEY. LISTEN UP." The chatter stopped. People came back into the theatre. He continued, "And when I say the capable hands of Allen Barton, I mean *the capable fucking hands of Allen Barton.*" And everyone applauded. Stunned, I walked out with him, and I thanked him for the comment. He grabbed my arm and held it tight as we walked to his car: "You're doing great. You're really teaching. And it's influenced by me, without you trying to be me. And don't try to be me, because I'm the only me. You just keep being you."

When I write *that* dialogue, I miss the guy a lot. I can only hope that I balance, in my way, both the toughness and the generosity with the students in my era as he did in his.

Every writer has his or her doubts as they churn out the pages, and certainly the process of treading on the hallowed ground walked by Milton and the many colorful personalities of the BHP—this has generated a tremor or five during the writing process. But those are the same fears that every actor or performer has, and I think part of the duty of a teacher is to lead by example, to blow past that doubting bullshit. So here goes.

PART I

Learning: Milton, Me & The BHP

First Night

I shouldn't be here. I'm in an alley off of Vermont Avenue, south of Franklin, and it's November, it's dark, a bit cold. There's a button that would indicate a buzzer of some sort, and I press it. Nothing. *Go home. This is nuts. People like you do not take "acting class." People like you went to arguably the finest university in the world. People like you do whatever it is that Harvard graduates do. Make some goddamned money. Win a Nobel.* I knock on the metal-sheathed door. *Go home. Now. Turn around. Just…leave! Who gives a shit what Sibel said. You're so fucking pathetic. When are you going to…There's been some mistake, and there is no class here. Clearly I've been given the wrong—*

"Hey." The door had opened, a young guy looked out.

"Yeah. I guess I'm supposed to start class tonight?"

"What's your name?"

"Allen. Barton. Last name Barton. First name—"

"Yeah. Cool. I'm Jimmy. C'mon in."

I'm ushered in to a small "lobby" space. Then through a side door to a theatre, where I see people on stage setting up furniture and boxes and such, and we walk behind the stadium-style seating section to another door, and through it into an office. I will end up spending roughly one bazillion hours in this office, in this theatre, the Skylight Theatre, over the next 25+ years. The other bazillion was spent at the headquarters of the Beverly Hills Playhouse on Robertson Boulevard in Beverly Hills, a building I will end up owning, and where I was the day before, interviewing for this stupid fucking acting class, and if I were just a bit quicker on the draw, a bit quicker to listen to my instincts, less in love with Sibel, I'd have turned around a minute before this and I'd have been on my way home to my first floor apartment at Fountain and Gardner, doing something productive, like…who the hell knows? My first three months in LA had gone by quickly, but consisted mostly of my working an office temp job at Disney Feature Animation, and sitting around the apartment watching the latest news from Operation Desert Storm.

The truly ridiculous thing about this moment was that I had moved to Los Angeles largely to get *away* from Sibel. I had fallen for her, completely unrequited, in my sophomore year at Harvard when I music directed a production of *Godspell* at the Agassi Theatre. And utterly fallen I remained, through junior year, when she starred in another production I music directed, *Little Shop of Horrors*. And disastrously, epically fallen I remained through my senior year, when she had already graduated and moved to New York to pursue acting. Somewhere in the haze of misery, I figured that Los Angeles might provide the necessary distance. If I moved to New York, I'd likely pine over her in close proximity all over again, and I'd end up a drug addict, self-methicating in my studio tent under a bridge somewhere. Los Angeles. It's warmer there anyway, and I was making this decision during a particularly brutal Boston winter. *Los Angeles.* Yeah. I always had a notion about California. Four years earlier, I was going to apply to Stanford for college, but my mother shot that down rather simply: "You will *not* be applying to Stanford." Maybe now was my moment.

And so after graduation, and a summer spent in my hometown of nearby Lexington, painting the house for some spare cash, I moved out west with my brother Fred, who was starting his first year at the USC masters program for film music composition. There were several other Harvard types out there chasing show business, including my new (platonic) roommate Heather Gunn, the future longtime dramaturge for the Center Theatre Group, Pier Carlo Talenti, the future successful playwright Jonathan Tolins, and others…It was a gang. Shortly after arriving, a bunch of us got together, and that was the night I was told that Sibel was in Los Angeles. "Visiting?" I asked. Oh no. No, no, no. She had moved out there with her boyfriend in the time since I had decided the 3,000 miles distance between Los Angeles and Newsibel-Yorksibel would be beneficial to me. Would I like her number? *Sure. Yeah. Sure. I'd like her number.*

About two miles. That's how far her apartment was from the one I'd just moved into. Three thousand had turned into…*Two miles.* Exercising immediate and immense self-control, I saw her as often as I could, which really wasn't that much, given we were "just friends" and all, but it was through Sibel that I heard more about this place called the Beverly Hills Playhouse. She and Jonathan Tolins were both studying there, with some teacher named Al Mancini. I never even heard the name Milton Katselas until I interviewed to study there a few months later, and I didn't care. At the interview, I fast-talked my way into the Intermediate level, even though I'd basically zero official training. But the interviewer went along with my argument that my background of watching actors for countless hours as rehearsal pianist and music director—this qualified me for the Intermediate level, which is where this guy Mancini taught, and that's where Sibel was…Ha! And then, a rare moment of sanity: *Had I moved all this way, just to end up not only in the same school again with her, but the very same class? Was this a formula for my staying there and learning something? Could I please be just slightly less pathetic?* So instead of choosing her class with Mancini on Mondays and Wednesdays at the BHP on Robertson, I chose Mancini's Tuesday/Thursday class over at the Skylight Theatre in Los Feliz, which is where I found myself on a cool, November night in 1990, knocking on that metal-sheathed door, yammering neurotically to myself.

I don't remember what Jimmy Green said to me that night. But given that I took over his job six months later, and then did that same job for another ten years when I "moved up" to the Advanced level class two years later, given that I ended up delivering that speech probably a thousand times, I can retroactively guess that he gave me the basics on how this class was supposed to operate. *You've interviewed at the school, so you know it's a twice-a-week acting class, scene-study based. No frills. Class runs four hours, you're expected to stay the entire time. I'm the "stage manager," sort of like a stage manager on a play or first AD on a film set. I keep track of everything, and if you're going to miss class you call me, or if you have questions or problems or whatever. There are other class executives who help run things, and you'll meet them. Your teacher's name is Al Mancini. You should think about something you want to do first in class—can be a monologue or a scene, or you'll do one of our exercises. Who sent you here? Sibel. Yeah, I think I know her, she's in the other*

*class Al teaches. Here's a class list. Here's a thing on class policy—
pretty basic, just treat the class like you'd treat a professional job. What's
your telephone number? Here are your books that Milton wrote. He's
the guy who started the school. Okay, you know that—just checking.
So, that's about it —you can take a seat anywhere in the theatre and
we'll get going in a few minutes when Al gets here. I'll check in with
you at the end of class.*

I take my seat. A couple of people say hi to the new guy.
Class begins with the teacher's entrance, upon which everyone
applauds wildly. This offends my Boston-bred Yankee suspicion
of all group-level enthusiasm. *Something fishy here, clearly.* The
teacher, Al Mancini, is short, wiry, with dramatic white hair and
a clear, crisp voice. He wears a lot of his favorite color: yellow.
He drives an old yellow pick-up truck. He smokes the better part
of a pack of cigarettes during class, in the theatre, in front of us.
The first scene is from *The Only Game in Town*, and it features
two actors, one of whom is Michelle Clunie, who would go on
to have a decent career, and then much later to have a child by
her longtime friend, the filmmaker and producer Bryan Singer.
Michelle is a year younger than I am, maybe 21, and she is so
pretty. She takes her blouse off during the scene. My eyes pop out.
People do this in acting class? Maybe that's why they're so enthusiastic.
The scene finishes, and the actors receive a nice round of applause.
Al delivers his critique, and my life is done.

Firstly, that girl Michelle Clunie who popped my eyes out
within fifteen minutes of showing up at the theatre? She became
an early scene partner of mine, and then…my first Los Angeles
girlfriend! So. On that count alone, the BHP was basically a place
where *dreams came fucking true*, because Michelle was way out of
my league, and even though the relationship was short-lived and
a mess, it forced me out of Sibel-obsession for the first time in
three years.

But secondly, this critique. I had just come out of sixteen years
of the formal education system, and even though the previous
four at Harvard were the fanciest, they were also in many ways the
least engaging. That wasn't entirely Harvard's fault—I was just
overbaked, academically, and so I didn't put myself into the class
work, preferring my extracurricular theatre activities, playing
piano for the annual Hasty Pudding Show, hanging out with
smart friends over long meals in the dining hall, or imploring

them to blow off their school work to go see a movie. I in fact spent junior and senior years on academic probation, and was in full revolt on the requirement to write fixed page-length papers on this or that. I had quite a bad attitude, which I regret, given the extreme privilege of the opportunity to study there. If I had chosen an honors "concentration" and had to write a thesis, I really doubt I'd have made it out alive.

But now here I was, after all that, in a smallish theatre in Los Feliz, listening to this energetic Al Mancini character analyze the scene, and I was fascinated. He talked about psychology, both the characters' and the actors'—he placed it all in context of where these two actors had come in their work, the script and its demands, he was funny, perceptive, completely engaging. It seemed that everything he said in that critique, and for the rest of the night, could be related exactly to people I'd known, behaviors I'd seen, the stuff going on in the streets and at 7-11. It struck me, oddly, as the most relevant teaching experience I'd witnessed. I felt it completely relevant and applicable to my life. I came back two days later for my second class. Ditto.

Time came for my first scene, which was actually a mono-logue I found somewhere. It was something about a young man jilted by his girlfriend, and I decided to make him a writer, at his typewriter, trying to figure out what to say about it all as he typed. I remember on the day I was scheduled to perform, I felt nervous for hours beforehand, while working my latest temp job downtown. I'm sure it was quite mediocre at best. I finished, sat anxiously in a chair in front of the class, and Mancini looked at me for a few seconds at the beginning of the critique. Already this was new to me—I'd either been in the standard "lecture to dozens (or at Harvard, even hundreds) of students" format of normal school education, or piano lessons. And piano lessons are of course one-on-one, but there actually isn't that much eye con-tact…You play, they correct, you play, they correct…Here was this man, Al Mancini, sitting there, smoking a cigarette, just…*Looking at me*. Five seconds. Ten seconds. Finally, he spoke: "You're a musician."

"How'd you know that?"

He pointed to his own face. "The eyes, baby. The eyes." The class laughed. They were used to this kind of perception.

"Well, yeah. Classical pianist since I was four."

"I got that. I saw it. You know how?"

"How?"

"You have a bubble of humanity in you. The way you do this monologue. It has music. You like to find the music."

"Okay."

"Okay? It's probably better than okay, man. How long you been here in Los Angeles?"

"Just got here. Three months ago."

"You have a piano in your place?"

"Ha! No, no...I mean...Once I graduated, my parents were..."

"Graduated where?"

"Harvard."

"Shit, man."

"Yeah."

"Where you from?"

"Boston."

"Boston. Harvard. I'm getting the picture." He laughed. *At me? Or just...In front of me?*

"...So anyway, my parents had always paid for the piano lessons, so now, it's, you know...'Welcome to the world. Over to you.'"

"Catholic?"

"WASP."

"So what are you going to do about that?"

"About what?"

"About the piano in your place?"

"Uh..."

"Uh, what?"

"I don't know."

"Those are the only three words we don't allow."

"Okay." *What. Is. Happening?*

"We're not wild about 'okay' either. How about this: You get a piano in your place by the end of the month, or you're out of class."

"Like...Kicked out?"

"You got it, baby. Once a musician, always a musician. You can't not have a piano. I won't allow it. I have a piano in my place. Used to be, everyone did. You're good, right?"

"I guess, yeah."

"You guess? I don't like false modesty, myself. You'll play for us. You'll get a piano, you'll play for us."

So I got a piano, a piece of crap rental upright with 85 working keys. I didn't think I'd do that much with it, and on that count I would end up being very, very wrong. But I wanted to stay in class with Mancini, and those were the terms. Welcome to the Beverly Hills Playhouse.

CHAPTER 2

Who Is That Guy?

I didn't even know what Milton Katselas looked like until six months into my journey at the Beverly Hills Playhouse. I was enjoying immensely Al Mancini's class, I did a ton of scenes, Michelle Clunie was my friggin' girlfriend, and I had plugged into a community in Los Angeles that I liked, so…Milton who? Didn't know. Couldn't spell it. Didn't care.

One night Jimmy Green, the stage manager, came up to me on a break. "Al would like to see you in the office." *Oh shit. This is it. I've been found out as a fraud. That fast-talking justification about how my high-level music training and experience justified my placement in Intermediate class? Exposed as ridiculous. I can't believe I'm being kicked out of class. Well, I can believe it. This is…You see? This is what happens when you—*

"We're thinking of training you to be a Stage Manager," Al offered, after I sat down.

"Surenoproblemokayyeah." I was so relieved that he wasn't kicking me out, I'd have said yes to anything.

"Great! It's actually easy. If you have any organized kind of mind, it's easy. You take attendance. You keep track of everyone. You meet the new people. And you talk with students, help them resolve any issues they're having with the class." Al had this interesting way of slightly pronouncing a hard "g" in "ing" endings: *Having-guh…* "And I'm right here, I can help you out. Not like I'm on a mountain, somewhere. You just call me. You have my number?"

"Uh, no. You're giving me your number?"

"Yeah, baby. We're lovers, now. And, you'll get free class once you take over. Not a bad deal! Okay?" He shook my hand, I was dismissed, and that was it.

So I started shadowing Jimmy Green, learning the basics. And yes, if you have an organized mind, it helps. So a lot of it—keeping track of attendance, scene production, incoming new people, phone numbers, etc. —that was all a piece of cake for me. When I was a kid, I was the geek who actually loved shopping for school supplies and organizing my notebook before the first day of school. (In the Boston area in the 70s, this kind of nerd was referred to as a "Bowmar", pronounced BO-maaaaahhhhh. *Bowmar* referred to the eponymous calculator, the early ones before Texas Instruments came to dominate the cutting edge 1970s calculator field. I grew up with a lot of *Bahhton, you fuckin' BO-maaaaahhh. Ya going' to Hahvahd anyway, you smaht-ass fuckin' pussy!*) So it took this BO-maaaah all of an hour or two to have the "stage manager book" looking A+ perfect.

Early on after I took the position over, I was invited to a weekend training session that included all the stage managers from all the classes at the BHP, plus anyone who was being tapped for the position. It was at the Skylight Theatre, and the guy who led it was the "senior stage manager," at that moment Gary Imhoff. Gary was one of the teachers at the school, but helped out in this additional role, supervising the stage managers, handling any issues that seemed too intense for just a fellow student in a class to handle. Gary was short, with thick hair, a bright singer's voice, and sunny demeanor—a fellow Bostonian who had grown up near Lexington, in Acton. I had used him early in my Stage Manager duties, when two longtime actors in Al's class, who were dating each other, asked to see me during class one night. They told me, each for completely different reasons, that they needed to leave the class. I was stumped. Obviously they were leaving together, and there must have been some discussion between them about whatever they found upsetting or objectionable, as well as a designed strategy of presenting two completely different stories about it. They just blew their cover by approaching me within fifteen minutes of each other. I called Gary, and he came to the theatre one night to meet with them, though I wasn't in the room for it, and I don't think Gary ever shared the real reason, if he was able to get it from them. Getting to the real reason a student is leaving class is always one of the more challenging tasks in administering an acting school.

At some point during the weekend training, the side door to the parking lot opened, a beam of harsh afternoon sunlight streamed onto the stage, and a heavy-set man, six-foot, with a gray close-cropped beard and slightly longish gray hair took three steps into the theatre, upstage left. He struck an aggressive pose, as if he was in imminent danger, quickly darting his head left and right. He had a strong, booming voice. "Hey! Isn't this where they teach Scientology?!"

Everyone laughed. I had no idea who this person was.

"Watch out for those people! They're teaching you Scientology!"

What the…? I leaned to the person next to me, to ask who this rude, presumptuous person was, interrupting our meeting. *And what the hell is Scientology?* The man saw that, picked up on it instantly.

"Some people here are like, 'Who is that fucking guy?'" Huge laughter. And then he darted out of the theatre and slammed the door. And that's how I first saw Milton.

CHAPTER **3**

La Bohème

At some point early in my trip at BHP, Milton decided he wanted to direct a chunk of *La Bohème* as a workshop presentation at the Skylight Theatre, using professional opera singers. I didn't know much about it at all until word obviously reached him that there was a pianist in Al's intermediate class who might be able to handle rehearsal duties. I can't remember who called me to ask if I was willing to play piano for Milton's rehearsals, but I signed on, thanked Al for insisting I get a piano in my place, and reported to the Skylight Theatre some morning shortly thereafter. I brought with me my standard equipment for such a gig: music, coffee, bagel & cream cheese, and that day's *New York Times*. Milton was there, along with the singers he had found to work with, his assistant, a woman who served as the "musical director" (who was to end up seriously irritating me on a daily basis), and someone else to help move stuff around. I went up to the piano, which was parked downstage left, unwrapped my bagel, positioned my coffee safely, unfolded the paper and opened it up to check out the state of the world. I didn't notice that everyone had stopped talking as I did this. Half a minute went by.

"Hey."

I was oblivious.

"Hey. Bagel Man."

Nothing. Clueless.

"Hey, Bagel Man. Newspaper Man. Piano Guy. Hey!"

Light finally dawned on Marblehead, and I suddenly realized Milton was addressing me. *Did I miss a cue already? I didn't even hear them start working.* I brought my newspaper down suddenly, only to find everyone looking at me with full-on "Springtime for Hitler" shock on their faces. Milton was impassive.

"Sorry," I squeaked. "Were you talking to me?"

"No reading in rehearsal, man."

Realizing I must have made a terrible *faux pas*, my face flushed and I stammered, "So sorry. I didn't mean to…"

"No problem! No problem! Relax! Everyone relax!" he barked, with a humorous, put-on frantic energy. "Just checking you're not a reporter." He seemed not particularly ornery about having to correct me, but the others still stared at me. In the coming years, I was to become Milton's gofer whenever he worked on a project, and I looked back at myself in "Springtime for Hitler" horror at how I could have shown up in front of him as an Intermediate-level young student, and just chomped a bagel while reading the paper in his face at rehearsal. Besides the protocol violation of its coming off dismissive and casual, the fact is you really didn't want to miss any of it. The state of the world per the newspaper was the state of the world. Rehearsal was fucking *rehearsal*. His work with these professional singers was classic. The lead guy playing Rudolpho was a quintessential bitchy superior queen, and their battles could be formidable. Milton directed with an intensely physical style, and he was having these singers stand on boxes, move over there, roll over on the ground—all while singing. And this guy had a serial tic that involved bringing up his masters thesis on Puccini, so he would always protest with some "Milton, when I was working on my masters, this exact issue came up, and my research indicated…" Milton often just listened patiently to whatever paragraph of total crap would emerge from this guy, pause for a second, and then say, "Thanks. Listen, I need you to roll on the ground here during that part." He'd just repeat the command, relentless in his battles to get them to do what he wanted. My first lesson in directing: It's not necessarily about imparting understanding and bonhomie. The task is simply to figure out how to get other people to bring to life what is in your head.

Later in the process of *La Bohème*, Milton and I came to our first impasse. My second (and final) steady acting class girlfriend, Valerie, had invited me to go with her to France to visit her grandparents in Aix Les Bains, with an additional visit to Paris. This was going to be my first trip to Europe, we had set it up some months before, and it happened to fall during a critical rehearsal period when they were gearing up for performances. Milton secured a replacement for the time I was gone, but word was that he was pissed about it, and to punish me was going to replace me for the performances, even though I had been there every day for three months or whatever it had been. When I learned I wasn't to do the performances, I remember mouthing off to his assistant about it in fairly strong terms. Five minutes later, my phone rang.

"I hear you're pissed off at me?" Milton asked, gruffly.

"Pissed off, yeah. I don't know if it's at you, particularly."

"Well, I'm running the show, so if you're pissed off, it's probably at me."

"Okay, then I'm pissed off at you."

"Good. About what?"

"Replacing me."

"You're not going to be here, man. I didn't plan your fucking vacation. You did."

"But I'm going to be back in time for the performances."

"It's the last two weeks. I don't want to wonder who's there, I want some fucking certainty about it."

"But I'm the one who put in the work for three months, and then you give someone else the actual shows."

"Maybe I like the other pianist better."

"If that's true, then no problem. But I don't think it's true."

"You don't, huh?"

"No, I don't, because I don't think you found anyone who can play that music better than I can."

"Is that so?"

"I think so, yeah."

He chuckled. "Well, fine. You might be right. I get your point of view about it. It might go your way. But it might not."

Where I got the freakin' balls to talk to Milton like that at 23 years old, I have no idea—I think it was just because I truly felt it was a bullshit decision, I felt like all the work I had done was being ignored in retribution for something that was in place before I'd ever been called to rehearse. It went my way, until it didn't go my way. After the call, Milton apparently had told his people that he was fine with my playing for the performances, but either the communication wasn't copied, or it was covertly altered along the way by that damned musical director, who later professed not to have "understood" that Milton said that. She simply never followed up with me, assumed that I wasn't available, and when I found that out, after the run of performances, and confronted her, she feigned confusion about who was interested and available and who wasn't, which phone calls she had made or not made. It was this hare-brained passive aggressive bullshit that I had detected from the first rehearsal, and yet she was Milton's right-hand dame on the vocal work for this project. But Milton always did have a habit of collecting hare-brained passive-aggressive people around him—certainly not all, but enough to make this a recurring theme over the years. Perhaps it was this early direct confrontation, where I just spoke my mind to him, that helped cement what was to come with us. Maybe he saw that for whatever reason, I wasn't so scared of him that I wouldn't just talk to him straight.

When I got back from Paris, *La Bohème* was about to be performed, and Milton's assistant called.

"Milton asked me to use very exact phrasing with you, so I need to know you're listening to me."

"Okay. I'm listening."

"Milton would like to ask you the *favor* of coming to see *La Bohème* this weekend."

"Well, of course I'm coming to see it, I wasn't…It's not a favor. It was never that I wasn't going to see it."

I heard the assistant repeat what I said to Milton, who was monitoring the call. A mumbled back-and-forth between them, then, "Milton says he really appreciates it, and looks forward to seeing you there."

CHAPTER 4

I'm Gonna Fuck You Tonight

After about eighteen months in Al's class, and a full year of stage managing, it was time for me to "move up" to the Advanced level class. In that time, I had plugged in to the BHP administration more than most newer students—as stage manager, I knew my fellow stage managers from the other classes, I knew the administrators over at the headquarters building, Irene Dirmann and Joyce Wallace, and I'd worked with Milton enough during *La Bohème* to get his vibe, and we made our way through our own problem there. But I had never seen him teach. When I moved up, it was very intimidating. The Advanced level class, on Mondays and Wednesdays at the Skylight Theatre, was chock full of really impressive talent, including Kyle Chandler and others who would go on to make their mark in various ways. The age range was much wider, and I felt like a new kid all over again.

Jeffrey Tambor was Milton's substitute for that class, and for a good while, he was the only teacher I saw in the chair. And he was plenty for me. Jeffrey was freaking hilarious, and seemed appropriately "Advanced-level" tough. He had that great career cooking already— this was at the time he was breaking out as Hank Kingsley in *The Larry Sanders Show*. Jeffrey would end up having a tremendous impact on my view of what teaching could be, how every aspect of the good and bad that you had to communicate as a teacher could be merged with humor. As a student of Jeffrey, you could count on laughing for a good part of those four-hour classes. There were comebacks that would receive the same huge laugh twenty times a year. An actor would say something like, "I don't know what happened to that moment," and Jeffrey would reply, "I don't know what happened to my hair!" He and I would end up in frequent communication about administering that Monday-Wednesday Advanced class, with several phone calls a week, occasional meetings at his house, all for a period of several years. He helped me get my SAG card via doing extra work on *Larry Sanders*, and in general Jeffrey provided much needed balance—an approachable, funnier yin to Milton's mercurial yang. He was beloved by hundreds of students over his 20 years at BHP.

Eight years later, Jeffrey's sudden and permanent departure from the BHP, via a short Sunday morning phone call to Milton, without a word of subsequent explanation to the vast majority of the 150 or more students-of-the-moment who bowed at his altar, ripped a decently-sized hole in my life. I tried to call him, but he never answered. I lashed out in an angry letter to him that I immediately regretted having sent, and which of course went without reply, but shit—how many of those students, including me, had some form of "departing parent" trauma in their past, and then Jeffrey walked right in there and lit it up anew. It felt like a seriously cold betrayal of all that affection everyone had for him. That coldness was alien to me, though many who knew him better would tell me later it was a prominent background feature of his personality. Nonetheless, Milton had publicly anointed him as his successor. Everyone knew it must have been a complicated relationship, but upon its end, couldn't Jeffrey even just send a letter to the group, offer some acceptable explanation of why he had to leave, offer an encouraging word or two?

For sixteen years thereafter, I pictured some kind of bookend conversation with Jeffrey about those years, a conversation that I know now will likely never occur. There have been brief exchanges: A stilted one, outside a theatre in New York in 2005, where he had just done *Glengarry Glen Ross*. A short email exchange about such a possible conversation in 2013. A brief phone call in 2014, when I reached out to congratulate him for his work in the first season of *Transparent*, was rushed, cut off three times by poor signal, and just weird. He was fine —polite and warm. I was weird. By then, I had loaded the possible moment of a conversation with Jeffrey with fourteen years of *import*, and for him it was a call he made, one of many, while on a train to a PR event.

In his own memoir, Tambor is chilly on his time with Milton
at the BHP. In reading it, I felt an echo of the same hollowness as
the morning when Milton called to tell me Jeffrey had left. There
wasn't a word about his connection with the students of those
years, their adoration of him, the launch point it provided for
him to go off on his own as a teacher and lecturer, no mention
of any good feelings or lessons learned there. It felt perfunctory,
mostly a negative review of Milton's controlling nature, the cult
of personality, and its increasingly negative impact on Jeffrey's
life, until one morning he snapped, cut the cord, walked away.
Perhaps the lesson here for me is that as a teacher, you will never
be everything a student needs. Inevitably, the student will write a
story of the relationship, and you can't control it, and it's unlikely
you will be able to fulfill the demands made of the "teacher"
character in that story. The math of a single teacher working with
dozens of students, adding up to hundreds over the years—it just
won't work out.

But here I was in 1992, having just started with him, and I
remarked on it to a classmate, that I just thought Jeffrey was the
bomb. The classmate replied, "He ain't Milton." I was shocked,
pissed off, even. I couldn't picture what Milton would do to
deliver better teaching.

Then one night, as I walked up to the theatre, there was a
bit of tension outside with the classmates who were in charge of
procuring the teacher parking space. Instead of wrangling only
one space, they needed to reserve *two* . The rear entrance of the
theatre adjoins a metered city parking lot, and there was always
(and still is, as of this writing) a dance of death that occurred
between students trying to save a spot for Jeffrey and/or Milton, and pissed-off Los Feliz parking-space-seekers who insisted,
sometimes to the point of threatening physical violence, that you
couldn't just sit in a chair in the space to hold it for your *fucking
acting teacher*.

When Milton showed up most of the time, it was to see specific
work that had been lined up for him, usually a veteran student
who Milton had a specific interest in seeing. There would be all
manner of jockeying to get your scene up in the first or second
slot, before he'd take off for a late dinner, and sometimes bitter
disappointment in those whose scenes would immediately follow
his departure.

On this night, he'd come to see a scene, as well as a longtime student, Tom, do an audition exercise. In this exercise, an actor would bring in sides for an audition, maybe one that was coming up, though Milton's preference was for neutral sides unconnected to an actual potential job. As he explained, "I might tell you an opinion that is opposite their view of the part." What he really preferred was not to coach an *actual* audition, but to see how the actor behaved when they entered a room, how they handled the whole process in general. Other classmates would play the director, the casting person, etc., and the person doing the exercise would enter the room, greet them, deal with whatever they doled out during the audition. These other actors playing the "casting office" would often gild the lily, make it tough on the person doing the exercise (I've since eliminated that element most of the time, because it would often become a distraction from the proceedings). Tom performed the exercise, and then sat down for his critique, looking glum and angry.

"So," Milton began, "What gives?"

"I don't know, man."

"You don't know what?"

"Just…I don't know. These fucking auditions, I haven't booked in ages, and I feel like I give them everything. I don't know. I'm just frustrated by the whole deal." Exasperated sigh.

"Well, there are two problems: One is you don't quite under-stand this scene, in my view. You don't quite understand what's going on in the scene. That's relatively easy to fix. But there's a bigger problem. You know what that is?

Tom shrugged apathetically, in full actorsulk.

"The real problem is you're hostile." Silence. Milton contin-ued: "You're hostile. And that's going to change. Tonight." More silence, then: "I'm gonna fuck you tonight."

You could hear a pin drop. Milton detonated.

"I'M GONNA FUCK YOU TONIGHT. AND YOU'RE GONNA TAKE MY FUCK. OR I'M GONNA GET ME ANOTHER PUSSY TO FUCK."

So this was Milton the teacher. Not much different from Milton the director of *La Bohème* rehearsals. And that's when I laughed. Unfortunately for me, in a room of fifty people, there was exactly one person who laughed. Several intimidating faces turned to look at me. *You're dead, kid. You're fucking dead.* Milton turned in his chair.

"Who just laughed?"

CUT TO:

INT. LEXINGTON HIGH SCHOOL, LEXINGTON, MA, 1986, DAY

Senior math class. Bored students die slowly under the electrifying teaching skills of a bored math teacher. Sitting to the front, a bespectacled Bomaaahh. Behind him, cool guys are up to shenanigans. One of them has some of those 'bang-pops,' miniature fire crackers that make a small pop simply by throwing them against a hard surface. He taps the Bomaaahh on the shoulder and hands him one of the bang-pops, motions for him to throw it at the chalkboard as the teacher is writing. Not wanting to be a 'fuckin' pussy, Bahhton!', the Bomaahh chooses his moment as the teacher turns to the chalkboard, and he rises up to throw it. His aim this afternoon is brilliant. It lands exactly in the middle of the circle that the teacher has just drawn with chalk, and makes a loud POP! The teacher launches into the air, with a petrified, mangled yell, and immediately grabs his heart. Did we mention he'd had a heart attack earlier in the year? Yeah. So he's grabbing his chest, face turning bright red, and turns to the class.

TEACHER

WHO DID THAT? WHO JUST DID THAT?

The Bomaahh, terrified, slowly raises his hand, and the teacher is utterly shocked.

TEACHER

You?!

CUT TO:

INT. SKYLIGHT THEATRE, LOS ANGELES, CA, 1992, NIGHT

"Who laughed?" Milton repeated, ominously.

"Uh...I did." I raised my hand from the back row.

"You? Why did you laugh?"

"Because…Uh…I just thought it was funny, you know…You're gonna fuck him, or…you know…get another pussy…I just…Thought it was a funny way of expressing a sort of unqualified intention, to…you know…get him to change…." Crickets. Utter silence.

"You're right, it is funny." He looked around the room. "He's right. It's funny. Why are you all looking so goddamned serious?" A swell of relieved laughter washed over the class. Milton turned back to Tom, and spent at least another 30-45 minutes with him, using practically every tool in his clearly stocked shed to get him to move towards a sense of confidence and optimism about his talent, his career, his future auditions. By the end of it, I realized why that classmate had said to me when I praised Jeffrey, "He's not Milton." It wasn't a knock on Jeffrey at all. No one was Milton. He brought in this whole "master" aura, and worked it to his advantage, and he had earned it by being extremely perceptive and absolutely willing to use force, temper, witchcraft, manipulation…anything—in the service of teaching. It was a brilliant performance against a clearly very discouraged and somewhat haunted individual.

Milton departed after this exercise, and Jeffrey took over the teacher's chair, muttering loud enough for us to hear, and to laugh encouragingly: "Icanstillteachanactingclass, Icanstillteachanactingclass, Icanstillteachanactingclass…"

CHAPTER **5**

Acknowledgment's Price

A week after the "I'm Gonna Fuck You Tonight" critique, Milton
came back, and sat in front of the class. He had a letter he wanted
to read. It was a letter from him to the class, saying, in effect,
"Dear Class, I thought my work last week with Tom and with the
other scene was first-rate teaching, and yet I didn't hear from any
of you. Not one. Not one acknowledgment. And I think that's
fucked." The reading of a letter was the only time I ever saw him
do that, but this was a constantly recurring theme that was very
specific to studying and working with Milton: *Did you properly
acknowledge him?* I never stopped my struggle with this "lesson."
His point of view was mainly that the failure to acknowledge
him was somehow a failure to acknowledge *yourself*. It was based
in low self-esteem. You think you're shit, you don't deserve his
teaching, or you think you couldn't do what he did, you couldn't
effect the change within yourself that he could with others, but
you're *wrong*. You *can* do those things. So his going apeshit
on getting praised was really his going apeshit on your own
lack of self-esteem and self-determinism, because if that was all
ship-shape, you'd be far more open to communicate freely and
positively to others about their good work. Starting with him.
Okayyyyy.

But let's face it: that's a pretty tough psychological road for
people to follow, the logic is porous and bumpy, and once you
arrive, the final doorway to the lesson always involved you getting
hammered in an unpleasant way about the failure to acknowledge
him. The pass phrase for the door to this Great Lesson about
yourself was, "Stroke Milton's Ego." That didn't mean that was

the only thing you got when you went through the doorway, but he certainly wouldn't change the sign over the door, would he? In fact, he could be a serious dick about it. And then there were the times that his neediness in the area of acknowledgment seemed, well, just needy, and attached to no such lesson whatsoever.

Fast forward a year later. I performed a scene from *They're Playing Our Song*, with classmates Lise Simms and Christian Lyon. Milton had passed through the theater during one of our rehearsals, and offered a couple comments. It wasn't significant input—my memory is that he asked a question or two and then went on his way. The scene *killed*. We killed it. Standing ovation. Tambor opened up the critique for comments from the class, which in BHP tradition is done only when something very obviously positive has occurred, and we want to ensure everyone knows it. Ours was the last scene of the night, and it always feels good to end class on a high note. We fielded compliments from our classmates, and I was flying high. The theatre phone rang. Had to be Milton. I answered it.

"Skylight."

"Yeah. How'd the scene go?"

"Fantastic. Standing ovation. Jeffrey opened up the critique."

"Oh yeah?"

"Yeah, we killed it." I couldn't wait to hear his congratulations. Instead:

"Did you mention my helping you out with the scene?"

"Uh…No."

"Why not?"

"I, uh…I don't know. I guess…You just…"

"I just what?"

"I didn't think…" Flying high, and now crashing to the ground.

"I just came into your rehearsal and asked you some key questions, is what I remember." He sounded totally irritated, bordering on pissed off.

"Okay."

"Okay, what?"

"I didn't think—it's not like you ran the rehearsal. It was kind of incidental contact."

"So you're saying no one in that class knows my contribution to this scene that killed in class?"

"I guess not."

"Who's still there? Is anyone still there?"

"There are a few people still left the green room."

"Tell them."

"Right now?"

"Is there another time? Put me on hold. Come back and tell me what they said."

I put the phone down, opened up the door between the office and the green room. I didn't tell anyone about Milton helping with the scene. I walked out, took another compliment or two, waited two minutes, and returned to the office, picked the phone back up.

"Hey—you there?"

"Sure, man. I'm here. Did you tell them?"

"Yeah, I told the few people who were here how you helped out."

"What did they say?"

"They were like, you know…'Wow!'"

"Good. And maybe you start next class with an announcement that I helped out on that scene, so everyone else knows."

"Will do." I hung up the phone dejected, resentful, crushed. What the fuck point was there to this conversation? What possible lesson was there? I just couldn't imagine, nor can I now all these years later, a teacher listening to a young student reporting a success like that and insisting the moment be about the teacher's contribution, rather than the student's success. I could find no lesson there, other than in this highly disagreeable aspect of Milton's personality.

This kind of unpleasantness led people simply to want to avoid his neediness, and its nearby Greek temper. *Anything* to avoid his temper! How do you avoid his temper? Suck up. And so emerged this ritual, structured pattern, occurring more times than I could possibly count: 1. Milton gives the class shit about not properly acknowledging him or his work. 2. People raise their hands and it's mea culpa, one after the other: *You're right Milton, you're brilliant Milton, I don't know why I can't say it, Milton, it's clearly because in some way I hate myself, Milton…* 3. A flood of letters hits Milton's mailbox at the school, with more mea culpas. Over time, many students just adopted a proactive "Suck Up" defensive tactic, so anytime Milton did anything, it yielded a Biblical flood of over-the-top compliments and acknowledgments, and I'm not above saying some of those were mine. It just wasn't worth the trouble to tell the truth sometimes, to say, "You know, I'm usually a fan of your directing work, but this one just didn't do it for me." I had seen others who had tried that very line, and they were annihilated by him, often in public. To my mind this all effected a cult of personality around him that went beyond mere loyalty to a good teacher.

Even as I became more and more embedded in the BHP culture, the personality cult was an aspect that troubled me. It would require a gymnastic level of mental gamesmanship to work it out, sometimes. Quite literally the last time I saw Milton alive, it was at an event for the publication of his *Acting Class* book, on which I had worked with him practically every day for the last year of his life. He and I had personally gone through every word, the structure of the book, its flow...all of it from scratch. It was a huge project. That release event was on a Saturday afternoon, at Skylight Books in Los Feliz. Sunday morning, I knew I should call him to acknowledge the event, the book, our work together. And I didn't. I flinched on it, not because I lacked friggin' self-esteem, not because I didn't value the work—he and I had created it together, it was mine as much as his. But even after sixteen years, I chafed at the requirement. *I'll do it tomorrow —Monday morning, a work morning.* And then I didn't again, but only because I was busy with something—I think a pediatrician appointment for my daughter. Now it was Monday afternoon. *If I call him now, I'll probably get some shit for not having called earlier. Monday afternoon is exactly too late and has an "I know I should have called by now and so I'm doing it now even though I don't want to" feel about it. That's gonna raise his ire for sure. Never in the mood for that. Hmmm. I'll now just have to revise the whole strategy, and I'll see him Tuesday night when I meet him on the sidewalk before class, because he wouldn't pick a fight with me in person right before we go in to teach a class, and that's the perfect time to slip in the acknowledgment without getting any extra crap about it.* See? This went on all the time. And I'll bet you a fair amount of money I'm not the only one who would do these gymnastics.

As it turned out, he had his fatal heart attack that Tuesday afternoon.

So for me, as I've now become the teacher, the lesson has modified: Acknowledge someone, and be timely and sincere about it because you never know—life and death are capricious little fuckers. In addition: if you learn to acknowledge the good work of someone right in front of you, when it's easy, you'll be better at acknowledging the work of people who are much harder to reach, but who may really be able to help you professionally. That's a simple lesson that doesn't involve the introverting psychological stuff that can clog up a lot of good teaching. And if as a teacher, you fail to get the acknowledgment you think you're due? Tough luck. It will never be worth the possible negative blowback from confronting someone about it, and the result will likely be that you'll come off as an incredibly needy dickhead.

I keep all my old letters, if I wrote them on the computer. Here's the letter from my 24-yo self to Milton, after the "I'm gonna fuck you tonight" critique and followup:

Milton,

Pursuant to your having hauled our asses last night in class, I'm writing this letter, which has been on my mind to write since *La Bohème* drew to a close.

After we talked on your car phone that time, I had a gut feeling that, because I wasn't going to be playing the performances, you felt I had become very down on the whole project. This feeling was prompted by your request that I do you the "favor" of coming to see the performances; I felt as if you thought I would have boycotted the opera as a demonstration of my pissed-off-ness or something. I never had any such intention, and I just want to say that what you did with those singers over those months really blew my mind. Really. Every time I listened to Matthew quote his fucking masters thesis on Puccini to you, I wanted literally to puke—he was the personification of every reason I decided not to go to Juilliard (instead I went to Harvard—a different breed of horror house as it turns out, but a horror house all the same). During the rehearsal process, my psyche was a boxing ring in which fought two combatants:

in the blue trunks was your directing and the inspiration it instilled in me, and in the red trunks was my frustration at the singers' resistance and my unspoken differences with Pat about technical matters and how best to help the singers and you fulfill your vision. The frustration was stronger than it should have been because I felt as though I should keep my trap shut and do my job rather than say anything to anyone about what was going on with me. It's a tough line to walk, but I've learned to walk it better.

Obviously, the Greek in the blue trunks won the battle, and I kept blowing off work so I could listen to you, watch Roberto and Raphael soak you up, and play Elyssa's aria until the year 2035. I tried, as much as I was able to in my position of lowly rehearsal pianist, to be a silent partner and cheering section for what you were doing. Again, the changes you effected in those singers and, more importantly, the way in which you effected those changes, consistently blew me away, and taught me tons about dealing with people. That is why it was so disappointing to me that after being part of all that, and getting your blessing to play the performances, I should hear Pat on the other end of the phone saying, "What? You wanted to play the performances? I thought you didn't want to…oh, that was Jon who didn't want to." Pow!—a strong jab from the fighter in the red trunks. It was small mixup on the part of a music director dealing with tons of details, a paramount detail to the pianists involved.

This low grade stupidity, however, became even less important recently, when I finally got to see you teach in class, an event I'd been awaiting eagerly for some time. For some reason I'd expected to see something different from what I had seen at the Skylight two or three mornings a week. When I realized that it was the same—a little tougher, because people weren't so new to what you were doing —I also truly realized what a gift the previous five months had been. It was like free class. I was earning my keep at the piano, but I need to thank you as much as S. needed to when you gave him three months class for free. Thanks.

—*Regards, Allen*

The week after he received this letter, Milton sought me out on a break during class, and grabbed my arm, much as he did 16 years later in the month before he died, and leaned in to me: "Yours was the best letter I got, man."

CHAPTER 6

My First MK Critique

The moment had arrived for the first scene I would be performing for Milton's critique. How did I know that Milton would be critiquing my scene? Because one of my scene partners was his girlfriend, MG. That's all that was needed. The other partner was another senior member of the class, Peter Allas. We were doing *Green Card*, and I was playing the dull boyfriend of the Andie MacDowell character, played by MG of course, with Peter doing the Gerard Depardieu role.

Along the way during rehearsals, I already thought I had blown my brief BHP journey sky high. As I was still relatively early in my studies, I thought it was beneficial to have dinner or something with scene partners, get to know them, particularly if we were going to be playing a relationship that had any intimacy or long standing per the script. But let's face it, most social engagement between actors working on scenes is purely voluntary, borne of the desire to make friends and, well, be social, and we mustn't leave out the standard worldwide eternal interest in acting class hookups. You can always justify this social interaction as beneficial to "the work," but it's crap. Nowadays I hardly ever socialize with new people with whom I'm working as writer or director—we just work. I don't care what they do outside rehearsal, and I never assign "chemistry" events, the way actors sometimes talk about: "We're playing husband and wife, so, you know—we went out on a date together to nail that chemistry." Yeah. Right. Tip: Even if you're not hot for each other, it's pointless for acting.

But being young and clueless, I went out with MG to have dinner at some health food joint in Beverly Hills as part of the rehearsals for *Green Card*. MG at that time was near 35 years old, pretty, tall, WASPy, high cheek bones and short hair, a Palos Verdes girl who had married and divorced young. I didn't know much about her, past the fact she was Milton's girlfriend, and as such enjoyed privileged status in the class —she came and went as she pleased, and often when we saw her walking up the parking lot to the theatre, that was an early sign Milton was indeed teaching that night. She left whenever Milton left. Stage Managers didn't talk to her about attendance or scene production—she was isolated from any "normal" communication the class might have with a student. Because of her relationship with Milton, people were generally nervous around her, and she didn't exactly go out of her way to neutralize that feeling. Even so, she and I ended up being quite close for many years—a relationship merited by actually growing to like each other and our varying circle of friends over the years, and by its being an absolute requirement of my continued work for Milton at higher and higher levels. It would simply have been impossible to keep arm's length from MG, or disdain her, while staying close with Milton. She was the de facto wife of the boss, even though they were unmarried, lived separately and Milton had other relationships here and there— she was his "main squeeze," and that was that. I would end up being charged with directly managing her affairs, whether it was getting something fixed at her house, paying her bills, or financial meetings to go over her budget. But again, despite the perils of dealing with MG, we liked each other. Milton would end up directing the two of us in a scene from *Manhattan* that was presented to all the classes on two different occasions in the 1997-1998 range, and we stayed close all the way until after Milton's death, when his disastrous estate plan blew up, and forced MG and me into opposing corners, lawyered up, glaring, fighting for our lives. As of this writing, I haven't seen or talked with her in seven years.

Right now it's 1992, and I'm 24, she's 35, she's the girlfriend of this Milton character that I am coming to know, and I'm thinking there must be some really cool story about how they ended up in a relationship together, some cool story that everyone knows, and I don't because I'm new to the class and missed it, some cool story about how they're both painters, or he met her directing a play. And so, to elicit this really cool story that I know she must want to tell, because everyone must know it, I ask, "So, how did you and Milton end up together, anyhow?" Her face turned to stone.

"I don't know, Allen. Why don't you ask Milton? I'm sure he'd be happy to divulge the details of his personal life to you."

Blood: running cold. Stomach: cramped. Breath: short. I stammered something apologetic in response, and we small-talked our way awkwardly through the rest of this awful healthy meal. I drove home, convinced that by the time I arrived, there would be a voicemail from Milton on my machine (no cell phones yet), asking to call him back, and that's when he'd kick me out in a screaming fit for trespassing on the matter of his and MG's relationship. I walked in the door: no message. I showed up for the next rehearsal: nothing. No mention of it. Bullet dodged.

The scene went okay. It was a bit of a mess. At some point Peter was supposed to encourage my exit from the apartment, and somehow we ended up locking horns, and it got out of control and he literally threw me through the portable doorway that is a common set piece—a fully functioning doorway that has wheels attached so you can move it around. He pushed me, I caught the side of the doorway on my way out, and the whole unit tipped over onto me, cutting my head. Yeah. So. The scene wrapped up and we sit before Milton, who indicated I should speak first.

"Yeah, well, the door fell on my head, so, that wasn't ideal," I began.

"We were here for that." Laughter from the class. Milton continued, "You know you had your part in that, right?"

"Oh yeah, I'm not trying to—" *Yeah, I probably was trying to…*

"You had your part. You understand?"

"Right." *I can't blame Peter? Shit…*

"You've been waiting for this moment, right? I'm the teacher you've been waiting for, right?"

"Uh huh." *Jeffrey is sitting right over there, I hope he doesn't feel slighted…*

"Go on. What about this role?"

"Well he's a device I mean the cliche of the boring boyfriend who's just waiting to have some charismatic French guy come along and steal his girlfriend and so while I understood that the script kind of mandated that I be this total square I resented the device and wanted to do something along the lines of being not quite so boring and yet still serve up what the story—" Blabbering. Uncontrolled blabbering. Total spaz, with a bleeding head. Milton listened for maybe twenty seconds, then raised his hand.

"Why are you talking so much?"

"I…uh…" Silence for a few seconds. I was short circuited.

"You talk like you don't expect people to listen to you." *Gonnnnnng.* "Why wouldn't someone listen to you? You seem like a bright enough guy to me."

I told him about growing up the youngest of eight kids. At dinner, we had to ask permission to address each other, and the lazy Susan in the middle of the table was so far away from me, and I was so scared to talk, or ask, that to this very day I don't salt or pepper my food.

"Uh huh." He turned to the class. "What do you all think of this actor? For instance: *He is the worst actor I've ever seen.* Something like that…" Laughter. A few hands went up. Stuart Rogers, who would go on to open and run his own successful acting school and theatre company in North Hollywood, was the first to speak:

"He just seems like a very smart guy. A smart actor."

"One man's opinion. Any others?"

I don't remember who else spoke, or what they said. I don't remember what else Milton said, and it doesn't matter. His first line, "You talk like you don't expect people to listen to you—why wouldn't someone listen to you?" was enough. It was a sentence that has come to my mind countless times over the years, at those moments when I wonder whether I should speak at all, whether it's worth it, whether anyone will really listen. To this day, I can occasionally get butterflies before teaching a class. That universal voice of doubt, whispering in my ear, "This is the night you're discovered for a fraud. You'll having nothing for these people. No insight. Zip." And just after that, Milton's admonition ensures I keep walking in to teach.

CHAPTER 7

Editor of Chief

The word had gone out to the classes that Milton was looking for someone who was good at editing or proofreading. He had Written Something. And it needed going over with a fine-tooth comb. I approached Milton's assistant, and explained I had been an editor for the high school paper way back when, and as well had been both assistant and managing editor of the *Let's Go* Travel series that is written by Harvard students. (I never did any of the traveling, but I spent two summers in—you guessed it—the musty basements of two different Harvard Yard dormitories editing the researchers' prose, and supervising groups of editors.)

I think partly because I was already someone known via my work on *La Bohème*, the article Milton had written was forwarded to me, albeit with some measure of secrecy and a verbal non-disclosure agreement. It was simply called "Blame," and it was an essay on how debilitating it was for the artist to submit to blame as a tactic for avoiding responsibility. He also prescribed a cure for this tidal, epic force in human relations, which was to *praise* the person instead. At the moment you wanted to kill them for whatever reason, find something to praise, "buy them a creampuff," and you'd find that the blame and hostility you felt would almost magically dissipate within you, all that beefed-up justification for how you felt would just drift away. It was a good article, and certainly valuable in terms of hitting a universal, daily, addictive drug for actors in particular: The notion that *that person over there fucked me over. That person over there is the reason I can't X, Y or Z.*

Unfortunately, while the message of the article was good, its execution was not. I blue-inked the shit out of this thing. There were grammar problems, spelling problems, organizational problems. I corrected, crossed out, and circled. I drew arrows indicating where to move whole paragraphs, suggested alternate wording and phrases, I wrote in the margins asking snarky questions and offering solutions so someone like me wouldn't ask those questions…I mean, this is what they wanted, right? If Milton is going to put something out there for all of the students, it should be as good as it can be, right?

Wrong. Milton apparently went apeshit. Who would dare blue-ink his writing like this? Who was this fucking kid? He just wanted it proofread, for chrissakes, not rewritten. He had called the office in a huff, and Irene Dirmann apparently told him she thought he should look again at what this presumptuous little shithead editor had offered, because she thought I might be on to something.

Meanwhile, ignorant of these goings-on, I was working at Macy's in the mall at Woodman and Riverside in the Valley. I worked in the Special Events department as an office guy, and I wasn't on the sales floor. I didn't have a direct phone number. I was barely an official employee— I got the job as a temp worker, and then proved valuable enough that Macy's decided to hire me, but it wasn't as if the position really existed. We were new to this location, barely had phones, and I was the barely-an-employee-with-barely-a-title, running the logistics of this recent office move. One afternoon, one of the new phone extensions I had hooked up rang near me. Hey, good news—the extensions are working! I picked it up.

"Special Events."

"Is this the guy with the blue pen?"

"Uh…Milton?"

"No, no. This is Dr. Schwartz. Your test results are in, and the news is, I'm afraid, not very good."

"How did you find me?"

"I'm a witch. I can find anyone. What are you doing tomorrow afternoon, say 3pm?"

"I think I'm supposed to be—"

"Good. We'll meet at my house to go over this article you so kindly drew all over. Call the office and they'll give you my address."

"Uh, Okay. 3pm tomorrow." *Why can't he give me his own address?*

"Right. And one more thing. Are you listening?"

"I am, yes."

"Be sure to bring your fucking blue pen." Click.

From then on, I edited practically every word Milton ever wrote. I eventually was put in charge of his correspondence, handling incoming mail and drafting responses that he would sign. In 1995, I was asked what I thought it would take, and how much time, to go over his book *Dreams Into Action* and make it suitable for publication, accessible to any reader. Up until that time, like his *Acting Class* book, it was just a collection of articles in nicely-made leather three-ring binders, targeted toward and available only to the students at the BHP. But Michael Viner at Dove Audio, whose wife Deborah Raffin used to study with Milton, wanted to publish the book, and I was to be the editor on that job with Milton. My estimate: 12 hours.

About nine months and several hundred hours of work later, the book was released in hardback. I had been the guinea pig for many of the lessons therein during that time. At one point, I drove up to his house for a work session, and he noticed my car, which at that point was a beat-up 1984 Volkswagen GTI with two broken wing-vent windows in the front doors and many other significant maladies.

"You like your car like that?" Milton asked, looking out the window at the GTI as I entered the house.

"Oh. Well. You know. Rent first, and all that."

"Uh huh."

We worked all morning, and then had lunch at his house, ordered in (or in later years, cooked by his personal chef). I looked out the window, and noticed my car was gone.

"Shit!"

"What?"

"My friggin' car is gone. That's not a tow zone!"

"Don't worry about it."

I got up to go outside, but Milton stopped me.

"I said don't worry about it. I took your car."

"Huh?"

Milton had had my car towed to a repair place he dealt with, to evaluate all its problems. He had taken the call during the morning, I heard him discuss the transmission, the brakes, the windows—but I hadn't realized it was about my own car rather than any of his. A couple days later, the car was returned to his house with new brakes, clutch, windows, motor mounts— everything that was obviously in need of fixing had been repaired. All on Milton.

"I can't have my editor driving a car like that," was his explanation.

But for all the fixing of my car because Milton felt "his editor" couldn't be seen driving a wreck, notably absent from the final book was any actual credit for me *as* the editor, which was the topic of a short conversation when I asked about it upon seeing the proof sheets. We were both nose-down, going over the galleys. I tried to be casual.

"I was just wondering, will there be any credit for me as…?"

"I don't think so, man." And that was that.

Upon publication, there was a completely overdone "release event" for the BHP students, held at a sound stage at Gower Studios. Class was cancelled on the night in question, all the students were summoned, and Milton drove up in a white limousine he rented for the 3-mile drive from his house. I made a few remarks to the crowd, mostly to joke about my 12-hour original estimate on the job. Then Teresa, who was one of the more forceful and charismatic BHP teachers, got up there to rally sales. This was always an aspect of Milton's operation that made me shrink in discomfort—the *selling the students* angle, whether it was his books, the occasional career seminars he would give, the exhibitions of his artwork…As a Stage Manager for the classes, I would end up having endless conversations with pissed-off students who didn't want to shell out extra for his book, or for his seminars, or a painting, who resented the hard-sell tactics and guilt-tripping that would be in play during these occasions. Teresa was up there exhorting each student to go buy *four* copies of Milton's book! There followed an insane push to buy the book, literally for the students to go call their relatives and friends in other states and have them buy the book, buy many copies of the book—the goal being to push it onto best-seller lists. All sorts of guerrilla operations were subsequently launched to reimburse people in various parts of the country for going into bookstores to ask for and purchase multiple copies of *Dreams Into Action*. Yuck.

Through a connection with his student Jolie Jones, who was famed music producer Quincy Jones' daughter, Milton landed an hour with Oprah Winfrey, along with some of his celebrity students over the years, such as Tony Danza and James Cromwell. I wasn't involved with this trip or the logistics, thank God. I remember watching in horror as Oprah tried to tee up Milton's entrance by asking the celebs softball questions regarding great teaching moments they benefited from—the idea being, of course, that Milton provided those moments. Cromwell described some earth-shattering moment of personal revelation, but then when Oprah asked him who who delivered it, he credited some east-Asian spiritual guide, not Milton! We all just sat there, slack-jawed. Oprah worked around it, and when Milton finally was brought on, he killed it, he did great, but he had to work against that bizarre moment. No matter—an appearance on Oprah was an appearance on Oprah, his book was being hawked by Oprah Fucking Winfrey, and so he broke the New York Times business best-seller list, and there was just a tremendous amount of traffic to come for the BHP and Milton, and I was heavily in the mix now as his editor, reader, and "handler of correspondence."

Over the next 12 years, there would be two more intensive projects to rewrite and then to release for publication his book *Acting Class*. The first re-write was to update the three-ring binders that were distributed to students, and the second, years later, was for the hardback publication of the book in 2008, again for Michael Viner at his new company, Phoenix Books. By that time, I had become so accustomed to writing in Milton's voice that our standard work-flow was essentially that I wrote for him, and *he* edited. I would draft or rewrite entire articles from scratch, and bring them to him and we'd go through it and he would change it from there. And for *Acting Class*, I finally received that credit as editor. Acting books don't get the hype that self-help books get, and in the 12 years since *Dreams Into Action*, Milton had mellowed out a bit, the personality cult had eased off, the BHP culture had already changed somewhat, I'd like to think partly due to my input, and so the release party this time was low key, no limousines, just a simple Q&A and signing event at Skylight Books, the Los Feliz bookstore he helped start, a mere three days before he left us.

After sixteen years of editing his articles, writing his letters, helping with his books, etc., it would be another year at least before the thought even occurred to me that I could possibly write something in my own voice.

CHAPTER 8

You Know What Late Means?

Upon arrival at Milton's house for one of my early editing meetings with him, I found the parking restricted for street cleaning, and it was one of those days where there simply was not a spot available but for three blocks away. As a result, I was six minutes late. I knocked on his door.

"You know what late means?" Milton asked me, upon opening it.

"Sorry, I had a problem with the—"

"IT MEANS 'FUCK YOU'!" Milton slammed the door shut. End of meeting.

CHAPTER 9

Bernardo

Ring-ring, rinnnnggggg. Ring-ring, rinnnggggg…

"Hello?"

"Yeaahhhh." This was drawn out. A full 1-2 second version of the word was a standard opening to a phone call with Milton. "Who's your piano teacher?"

"Right now?"

"No, ten years ago. Yeah, right now. Los Angeles. Right now."

"I don't have one."

"Why not?"

"My teacher in Boston passed away a year ago, and I just haven't…I can't afford it for one, and I'm just not plugged in to the scene here in Los Angeles."

"Good. Call over to the office, and tell them to get you the number for Bernardo Segall. He's a brilliant guy. Brazilian. Taught at USC for a while, I think. He did the music for me when I directed *Camino Real* with Pacino. He's a teacher. You set up some lessons, and I'll pay for the first five. How's that?"

"Uh…Shit. That's awesome."

"And if it works out, you let me know when the lessons are, and maybe I'll come watch. Even though I think he lives in the fucking Valley. But teachers should watch other teachers, and I don't get to do it very often. You know why?"

"Why?"

"Because if I'm in the room, who's going to fucking dare, right?"

"Right."

"Bernardo won't be intimidated. So you'll call over, get his number, let me know."

"Sure. I mean. Wow. Yeah!"

"You're welcome." *Click.*

I called over, got the number, called Bernardo, set up the first lesson through his wife, Beverly. Bernardo lived near Mulholland, just below it on a side street on the Valley side of the hill. He had something like six or ten dogs, all of whom barked ferociously upon anyone nearing the house, which was a relatively modest, un-renovated, open-floorpan ranch home of about 3,000 square feet. Bernardo was 80 years old, wore it like 90, and Beverly was half his age at most. Before the first lesson, I'd notified Milton of the time, and he told me to wait for him outside the house when I got there. And sure enough, right on time, Milton's black 1979 Mercedes 6.9 maneuvered down the narrow street. To this day I still can't believe he came for these lessons. I still barely knew Milton, and the more I got to know him over the next 15 years, the less likely it would seem that he'd drive over the hill and watch the piano lesson of some kid in class he barely knew, either. But there he was.

Bernardo forgot these appointments as often as he remembered them. So then picture a 25-year-old me hanging out with the legendary Milton Katselas in the driveway of a run-down ranch house under Mulholland, with ten dogs barking at us from behind the fence. Milton didn't like dogs.

"This fucking guy. He forgot again, didn't he?"

"Looks like it."

"You checked it? You confirmed with him?"

"Yesterday."

"Jesus, man."

"Yeah."

"Let's see if he comes. Maybe he's on his way," Milton would offer, hopefully.

We'd sit there, not much conversation. No Bernardo. The dogs barked. And barked. And barked.

"Fucking dogs, man."

"Yeah."

"You like dogs, though, right?"

"Not ones this noisy. But sure, yeah, I have a dog."

"What kind?"

"Labrador retriever."

"Those are nice dogs, right?"

"Yeah, it would take a lot to mess up a Labrador into a mean dog."

"I'm not a dog guy. Animals. Pets. Hate them."

"Uh huh." And we'd wait a few more minutes, then Milton would take off. No goodbyes or anything—he'd just start walking toward his car. As he got in, he would yell over his shoulder, "Keep letting me know."

When it worked out, it was fun. Bernardo didn't like my tone. For a while he'd have me play a single note with the proper arm weight and a certain kind of curled finger for which he advocated. I'd hit the note:

"That's not a tone!" I hit it again. "That's not a tone!"

Suddenly he'd be walking away from me, across the large living-dining area. *Where is he going?* Milton would watch, bemusedly. I hit the note.

"That's not a tone!" Bernardo repeated, as he walked into a bathroom and closed the door. I hit it again. "THAT'S A TONE!" he yelled, over the sound of his urinating.

We worked on Chopin's first Ballade, in G minor. He wanted the opening to be a dialogue, and he would make it up as we went along, in his Brazilian-accented lilt:

"That first phrase: Ya da da DA da da—dahh. dahh. Those first six notes, it's like this young man, saying, 'You know I love you true,' before the girl just shakes her head: dahh, dahh. Girl shakes her head. Play it again." I'd give it a shot. "No, this is a very halting young man. I want a confident young man. Again." I'd play again. "No, the girl is too strong. I want just…aloof. An aloof, beautiful girl, shaking her head. Is it a yes? It it a no? You can't figure it out with some women." I'd hear Milton guffawing on the couch at this stuff, and Bernardo and he would share glances and wink and nod and so forth.

Outside, after the lesson, Milton would ask if I understood what Bernardo was doing, and he'd explain, "He's doing what I do. He's getting you to answer the basic question: What's this scene about? What's this piece about? What's going on here? It's the same question. All the time." Often, a few hours after these lessons, Milton would talk about them in class, sometimes overtly, but sometimes just by quoting what Bernardo had told me that afternoon, and applying it to actors in pursuit of answering this question of *what's going on here?* Since early on, perhaps even my first critique, Milton had instructed me to put a piano in every scene.

"Every scene?"

"That's right."

"But this is a courtroom."

"So, the judge, he likes music. He's a Beethoven nut. He ordered a piano to be there, makes him feel better. He plays during the lunch breaks."

"It's a doctor's office."

"The doctor loves show tunes. He played them as a kid. I don't give a shit. Just put the fucking piano on stage."

So there would be a piano in every scene, and it wasn't so much that I was to contrive a reason to play in every scene, but he wanted the immediate connection to an object I felt I had command over, something connected to my confidence. After a certain lesson with Bernardo, which didn't go well, Milton stopped me outside before he got in his car: "You know, you don't have that trouble on stage."

"Huh?"

"That tension he's busting you on. You don't have it. You're at ease when you act in a way that you're not when you play. You know that?"

"Nope. I always assumed acting would be playing catch up to music forever."

"Maybe not. You got all those years playing piano, and that's leveraging your work as an actor. Maybe they feed each other. Each makes the other better."

"That would be good."

"That's what's happening, man." In the car, and off he went.

The free lessons expired after a while, but I knew I couldn't stop studying with Bernardo and protest poverty—Milton would have my head. So I struggled to pay them, but pay them I did. I was working that job down the street at the Macy's on Woodman and Riverside, and I'd take a 75-minute lunch to drive up the hill, have a 60-minute lesson, and then drive back for the afternoon shift. After Bernardo passed away, a year or so later, Beverly called me and referred me over to one of Bernardo's students, who was a teacher in her own right. Her name was Deborah Aitken, a tall, imperious brunette who taught out of Manhattan Beach. I ended up studying with her for six years or so. Milton wanted to meet her, and so at some point I arranged that the three of us would go out together to see some pianist at the Wilshire Ebell. Milton and Deborah had a weird vibe going—simultaneously flirtatious and hostile with each other. Neither suffered fools gladly. Neither played second fiddle. And that night, neither liked the pianist. So at intermission, we decided to walk out and go see flamenco dancing at El Cid instead. A week or so later, at the tail end of a phone call with Milton, he said, "Hey, by the way, I had a dream last night that I fucked your piano teacher, and it wasn't bad." *Okayyyyyy.*

But life is interesting, because one of Deborah's other advanced students was a young Korean UCLA undergrad named Jungmin Yu, who, like many Korean girls transplanted to the United States while young, went by an Americanized name, in this case Tiffany. Deborah would invite Tiffany to see runthroughs of programs when I was prepping for performances, and in 1997, after I spent much of the year recording my first CD, and thus found myself lacking in prepared "new" material for a recital, it was Deborah who recommended that Tiffany and I do a two-piano recital, which we did. We traded off solo works and then played the two-piano version of Ravel's *La Valse*. A week after that recital, Tiffany asked if I could be a fill-in platonic friend-date for her company Christmas party, because some other guy who was supposed to be the real date had bailed on her at the last second. *Sure. I'll go to your Christmas party.* Nineteen years later, as I'm writing this, our three kids have just fallen asleep in their rooms. That's a direct line from Milton offering to pay for some piano lessons in 1992, to my wife and family as they exist in 2016.

CHAPTER 10

VP of Stuff and Miscellany

After six months in the Advanced class on Monday and Wednesday nights, the class Stage Manager upped and quit the class. The administration wasn't quite prepped with a backup person, and I seized the opportunity for saving some money again via the free tuition you got for doing that job. I approached Milton one night in class:

"Hey, I understand you might need a Stage Manager for the class."

"Yeah, I guess. I'm sure they're on it."

"Well I just want to put my hat in the ring."

"Oh yeah?" he asked, bemusedly. I was 24. That was ridiculously young to become the lead executive of one of his vaunted Advanced classes.

"Yeah, I did it for Mancini for over a year. You can ask him, I think he thought I did a good job."

"Okay, man, I'll do that," he said, in the manner of someone who most definitely would *not* be doing that.

I assumed nothing would come of it, until a week later when I was indeed brought on as the Stage Manager. And in all its glorious decades, the BHP has never seen a Stage Manager with less presence or authority than I had at that moment. Picture this 24-year-old bespectacled *bomahhh* going up to veteran students, people who'd known Milton for years, had been in the class for years, and squeaking in a voice like a 13-year old: "Hi, I noticed you came in a little late tonight, and was just wondering—?" That's when the actor in question would laugh quietly and walk right past me, saying nothing. "Okay. I'll talk to you later on that!" I would say, losing more face.

But I'm nothing if not persistent, and I just kept showing up night after night, and bit by bit my consistent presence and my acting work in the class raised my standing. You had to earn that respect, just like anywhere else. Years go by and suddenly I'd been around longer than plenty of people in that class. I ended up Stage Managing the Monday-Wednesday Advanced class for *ten* years, all the way until I was made CEO of the joint in 2003.

You can learn a lot about acting from being in charge of actors in the way I was, keeping the class organized. You start to see the lies coming at you from fifteen feet away, before the actors open their mouths. You see how they hide what's really going on, you sense the internal conflicts and troubles, the resentments and the needs, the way small victories could transform them. I think you see more of what is really going on with an an actor *in toto* from this position as Stage Manager than even from the teacher's chair. But regardless, having this job was an amazing supplement to my education as an actor, director and eventual teacher.

It was from this job as Stage Manager of the Advanced level that I received a huge bulk of the knowledge and background from which I ended up running the school. Most teachers at the BHP during the Milton era were picked from his group of friends and longtime associates and/or students. But very few of them had ever worked for the organization, worked for the students before becoming responsible for teaching them. As a Stage Manager over those years, I must have had several thousand conversations, both short and long, with students of the school, often dealing with the trouble they encountered along the way. I saw which teaching styles yielded which complaints or accolades, I saw the troubles actors had outside the class, and what they were willing to tell me without being willing to tell the teacher. (And vice versa.) I saw which BHP policies seemed to match with the students' general willingness to participate in a group, and which seemed to strain the school-student relationship or even break it. Milton's personal approach with a student was always a wild-card, but I saw every sub who ever came into the class, how their varying styles and approaches would send student morale soaring and diving. Very few people have seen as many of the BHP teachers actually teach a class for hours at a time, month over month, year over year, while also being in communication with the students and class executives about how that teacher is doing, how the class is responding.

In 1992, Macy's filed for bankruptcy restructuring, and by early the next year, my handy, flexible job in the bowels of the store at Woodman and Riverside went kaput. I asked Milton if I could earn a dollar or two by helping out at the office. He assented, and I showed up one day, asking for something to do. "Alphabetize those student files!" I was ordered. Okay. I went to a pretty good school. I can alphabetize. I disappeared into the basement (I seem to have spent much of my life in musty environments, both corporate and theatrical), and showed up a couple hours later, with the student files alphabetized. "Wow! That kid sure can alphabetize!" was the stunned response. This was very exciting to the administration at that time—a little competence in the environment. Apparently other student actors had shown up here and there to help out, but had failed in the somehow undervalued "showing up" and "help out" departments.

From there, I became what I jokingly called "Vice President of Stuff and Miscellany." An acting school is in the personal communication business, but can suffer mightily in the area of "organized stuff." So I organized. Reorganized. Deleted. Cleaned out. Plugged in. Hooked up (equipment, that is). I ordered, picked up, and delivered. In January of 1994, when the Northridge earthquake rattled Los Angeles to its knees, I drove as early as I could from my apartment out by the beach to Beverly Hills to ensure the building was still standing. (I was also still taking class in Los Feliz, so you SoCal readers can imagine my getting from the Marina/Venice border to the Skylight Theatre in a city operating without the I-10 freeway, since it had collapsed between Fairfax and La Cienega.) From the "mail-room" on up, I got an in-depth view of how the entire organization was running, who was talking to whom about what and how, and I tried to coax it towards interaction with the coming technology revolution. I handled the acquisition of some high-tech *pagers*, and did the research on replacing our antiquated phone system.

As an all-purpose GoFer as well as his editor, I dealt with Milton a lot, in a wide variety of circumstances—teaching, directing, writing, working at his art studio, at his house. I was often in the rehearsals he held for various scenes he directed for class, or the occasional play outside—the last being *The Seagull* at Joe Stern's Matrix Theatre on Melrose Avenue. I took notes, ran errands, coordinated with Milton's assistant (the one job I never wanted) on his schedule or communication with actors and crew.

In 1994-1995 I was moving apartments constantly. My year at the beach, at the very end of Washington Blvd, above a restaurant, where I got to experience the Northridge Earthquake, and the dark rumbling collapse of the freeways in the distance, was over. I took over a house-sitting gig far further east on that same Washington Blvd, mid-city between Fairfax and La Brea. It was a street-level crazy industrial loft space that belonged to a classmate of mine and her director husband. The shower was outdoors, and the bed was up in a loft area under a skylight that let in the blinding search lights from hovering police helicopters several times a week—this was not a good area of town. I walked my dog by taking him out and begging him to do his business as fast as possible before my very white, Bostonian, bo-mahhh ass was noticed by too many local residents. I'd come out to my car in the morning to find that someone had stayed in it overnight, with the scraps of his or her no doubt second-hand McDonald's Happy Meal remaining as evidence! Awesome.

After a few months of that, I moved up to Sherman Oaks, to a house rented by two other classmates, one of whom had taken a gig in Hawaii. My eye, however, was on an apartment on the second floor of BHP's Robertson headquarters. One of the longtime tenants was leaving, and I had put my dibs in on taking it. Milton approved, and said he'd do a basic patch-and-paint to prepare for my arrival. Well. The guy doing the work was another advanced level student, Jim Gervasi, who happened to be also a contractor, skilled tradesman and former Sheriff. He figured out a way to blow out half the ceiling area up to the roofline, creating a small loft space to put a bed and some basic storage, with a steel-and-wood ladder that came down to the floor. He stripped the carpeting, refinished the floors, and exposed the brick along the outside wall. It ended up as a very cool, little 400-square-foot gem. I had to move out of my Sherman Oaks place a month before the apartment was ready, and spent that month sleeping on the dusty, unfinished floor of another recently vacated apartment down the hall at Robertson. But once it was ready and I moved into my first solo apartment, I stayed there for eight years. The day I moved in was a Saturday, and Milton wanted to check out Jim's work—he came up after teaching his class, and said, "This is fabulous. I wish I could get rid of everything and move in here instead."

I continued my various VP of Stuff & Miscellany duties, which were enhanced by my living in the building, so I was always available for this or that. Around 1996, a very bad management decision was made, namely that the mediocre receptionist at BHP would be a good candidate to run the finance office of the BHP. She would come in late, arms full with boxes of piping hot Chinese food, disappear into her office in the basement, with another girl who helped her out, and God knows what was going on. It all became bad enough that in 1997, the new CEO, Don Moss, ordered me on a special mission to Figure Out What Was Going On With the Finances. So I did. It was a mess. In sorting it out, I offered that if Milton paid me roughly what he was paying the two girls together to screw things up, he'd have a much cleaner operation. That deal went through, and I became the new "General Manager" (CFO). The Stuff & Miscellany days were over, and I was now part of the management team at the school. I brought on one of the more competent class finance executives, Gabi Wagner, to help me out, and for the last 20 years (as of this writing) she has handled tracking of student tuition payments, and together we've ensured the dollars and cents made sense, even as I took on additional responsibilities as the years went by.

Even though I had risen fairly quickly to that position, and had Stage Managed Milton's class for him for five years, I had never been invited to be part of his famed Saturday morning masterclass. This was the one class that he taught almost exclusively, and the various celebrities who would come to study at BHP were in this class, along with others who had known Milton for decades. One day, I happened to be in the office for some meltdown regarding the finances in that class. Milton generally just had one person assisting him in that class with attendance, the scene schedule, tuition collection, and audio recording his critiques. But the tuition payments were falling behind and after overhearing Milton lose his shit about it, I volunteered to take over that part of the job, in exchange for being able to audit the class. *Ding.* So for the next several years, I'd trundle down on

Saturday mornings from my cool apartment on the second floor to sit at the base of the stairs and track attendance and collect tuition. There were a lot of interesting personalities in that room, some of whom would insist they were kind of above the notion of, you know, *paying for class*. I had to deal with these special snowflakes' business managers and assistants in order to get the books straight. Milton was pretty infuriating on this point— he would take me apart for anyone who went more than a month or two without paying, calling me up to scream the handling I should implement ("Call so-and-so and tell them they can pay for class this Saturday morning or go fuck themselves!"). But, as was typical, he refused to be bad cop himself. When, inevitably, the non-paying student went to him to complain about me or the situation, Milton would suddenly wax charming, graciously accept their story, waive all past due amounts. This led to my having even less authority with that person next time around, and another inevitable blow-up with Milton down the road.

In late summer 2000, Don Moss' tenure as CEO ended dramatically (that was pretty much the only way any teacher or staff member's tenure ended). Milton wanted Gary Imhoff to take over. Gary didn't want the job, because he felt it would be too much responsibility to carry along with his heavy teaching load and on-going career as an actor and singer. Milton bullied him into it: He said if Gary was worried about too much responsibility, he could help with that, help Gary open up some time in his schedule. This "help" consisted of Milton calling Gary on certain mornings and telling him he wasn't teaching his class that morning— that a sub was covering the class. Gary got the message, didn't want the teaching duties reduced, and so he caved and took on the CEO job as well, with his wife Lauren taking over as Milton's personal assistant. That's a hell of a lot of daily Milton to absorb in one family, for sure, and during a difficult period, described more fully ahead in chapters *Hurricane Ponzi* and *ScientoloWAAHH?*

There had been a tremendous surge in enrollment in the late 90s, what with several visible celebrity students doing well, Milton's appearance on Oprah, and a thriving tech boom economy. So even though Jeffrey had resigned in 2000, dealing a heavy blow to the Advanced level, there was still a lot of influx, and to handle it, Milton started a new daytime advanced level class, which had the rather dubious start date of September 11, 2001.

That was the first morning of class, literally three hours after the terrorist attacks. He adopted this class and lavished it with personal attention, teaching it exclusively for 18 months. The only problem was that he lavished attention on the new class while utterly abandoning the night-time advanced classes, and it's not as if students didn't notice. Then he started a ridiculous war between the groups, showing up at night here and there to give the students truckloads of acrimonious shit for not coming to audit class on Tuesday and Thursday mornings to see him teach! You can imagine how that went over— students paying for "Milton's" nighttime Advanced class never seeing the guy, and then being yelled at for not showing up at some other time slot to watch him teach.

Some students attempted to follow his "instruction," showed up in the morning of the daytime class to watch, only to have Milton gruffly turn them down, because they had only done it after he asked, not of their own accord. And then if they accepted this "no," and went home, or didn't try again on another morning, this raised his ire all over again for their lack of *persistence*. When the student finally broke through to audit the class, well, they would inevitably want to *work* there as well, and request a transfer out of the night classes to get some undiluted Milton during the day. He literally robbed Peter to pay Paul. It was maddening, awful, and engendered massive ill will. This kind of infuriating gamesmanship with student loyalty was one of Milton's most destructive tendencies. Tambor's sudden departure had hit the nighttime classes like a bat over the head, and many veteran students there were unhappy that the vacuum was being filled not by Milton, but by a different and less popular substitute teacher. All this, while they were being harangued by Milton for not trying to break into his new morning class. The normally enthusiastic, positive vibe that had always been a hallmark of the nighttime advanced classes was turned to complete shit. Tambor went on to open his own class late in 2001, which led to several departures from BHP. So pretty much as soon as Milton's new daytime advanced class opened, representing the peak enrollment for the school, the numbers started crashing everywhere.

Gary's time as CEO was a pressure cooker, and to relieve some of that pressure on him, I took over many of the financial duties that up until then had still be retained by the CEO. I was now

fully part of the senior management team at the school, while
still running the Monday-Wednesday Advanced class, overseeing
the lower level classes in general, handling Milton's abundant
written correspondence, and being in charge of attendance and
finance for Milton's famed Saturday morning master class. Gary
lasted as CEO until 2003, when Milton—*ooops*— made a pass at
his wife. Oh yeah. This was during a period when Milton seemed
more incorrigible than usual in this area, which was leading to a
Scientology jihad against him rumbling in the distance. (More
on this ahead.) Then in addition, he suffered the foot infection
that put him in the hospital for a partial amputation and many
weeks of rehabilitation.

     None other than CEO emerita Irene Dirmann returned to Los
Angeles from Florida, to oversee Milton's rehab and help sort
out the management crisis at BHP. As part of that sort-out, I was
made CEO of the school. (Imhoff remained as teacher, though his
loyalty had clearly been mortally weakened by Milton's clumsy
attempt to move on his wife.) I was about to get married and
go on my honeymoon to Italy, and I remember Milton getting
ticked off that I wouldn't start immediately, like, the week of
my wedding. (Indeed, I was then to receive an angry phone
call *in Italy* about finding paperwork related to a car repair.) A
whopping 35 years old, I was the youngest ever to hold the post,
a fact that made me somewhat fearful, not to mention the added
fear of taking over at a moment of significant stress across the
organization. I told Milton I would only do the job if he was clear
as to my intention: To ensure that the BHP as a school and its
specified approach to acting would last for at least as long as I did
and hopefully beyond. And that would mean I had ideas, and I
wanted real input into staffing, culture, and the major decisions
ahead. I wanted more of a partnership vibe, while still granting
him his place as monarch while he was around. Milton, often in
the darkest and grumpiest of moods during his rehab, grunted
something vaguely unsentimental and dismissive, but I still think
he got the message. (And then I tried to squeak something about
my not wanting to have to fill out any approval paperwork for
time off, and he hung up on me. Welcome to the job.)

     Since 2003, including the last five years of Milton's life and
beyond, I've essentially held both CFO and CEO posts. Beyond
daily management duties and my regular weekly teaching nights,

I consider it my job to codify and protect the BHP Approach, which is a very specific body of information applied in a very specific way, and, like all communication about aesthetics, is easily messed up and alloyed with other information that has nothing to do with the BHP Approach. So another important function of mine is to standardize teacher training and its application to the classes, so the BHP doesn't represent a specific *personality*, but rather a specific *approach to acting*. The idea is that as best as we can, we take the individual talents and backgrounds and styles of our teachers, and create from that as uniform an experience for our students as possible, all tied to the approach that Milton had developed.

It's been a long and winding road since Mancini first pulled me into the office at the Skylight Theatre, and I, convinced I was about to be kicked out, spluttered "Yeah sure!" to his request that I help administer his single Intermediate class.

CHAPTER 11

Cars

Milton loved automobiles. He had four cars at the time I was coming up —the Mercedes 6.9, an old Jaguar, an old Toyota open-roofed SUV, and a convertible Saab 900—replaced at some point with a new Volvo C70 convertible, which he had specially made for him through a famous story he tells in *Dreams Into Action* about calling the head of Volvo and telling him about having worked with Liv Ullman. The older cars needed constant repair. He put more money into that damned Mercedes than it would have cost to buy two new ones. There would literally be 10-15 trips a year to the repair place in Westwood, and each repair was at least $500 if not far more. All the cars were registered in Nevada in some scheme to avoid California registration fees and insurance rates. It was ridiculous—we'd have to arrange guys to drive each car to Las Vegas each year to get smog-checked and registered, and some old friend of Milton's provided the mailing address. At some point I rose in the ranks enough to be able to put dibs on taking the Volvo convertible out to Vegas for the smog check. I was so excited, I left the top down for the whole drive, and by the time I checked into the hotel in Las Vegas, I practically passed out from sun stroke, sunburn, and borderline radiation poisoning. Tiffany just shook her head in bemused dismay at my predicament; our Vegas getaway turned into de facto hospice care.

Anyway, it saved not one red penny to do all this, when you factored in the cost of paying people to drive out there and get a hotel for the night, but Milton loved these schemes. He had a Pennsylvania drivers license with no photo, and he had a favorite story about being pulled over at some point in West Hollywood with Nevada plates and this sans-photo PA drivers license. The sheriff's deputy apparently looked at Milton, the NV registration and the PA license, and said, "I don't know what's going on here, and I'm not sure I want to. Just make sure you make a full stop next time," and let him go.

His Volvo was once involved in a minor fender-bender, and Milton insisted that I talk with the insurance company about replacing the engine.

"Milton, you were hit on your rear quarter panel."

"So?"

"So what does that have to do with your engine?"

"It's not running the same."

"Uh…"

"IT'S NOT RUNNING THE SAME. Don't fucking doubt me on it. Something's fucked up, and I want it replaced, and with the bigger engine." Of course, I would make no such demand of the insurance company, but made up stories along the way about how they were considering the matter, they were going to send someone special out to evaluate the car (he loved that), and just bit-by-bit I'd get the story of my efforts to line up with what everyone knew from Minute One: The insurance company wasn't going to replace his friggin' engine because of a fender-bender on his rear quarter panel.

Back when we were working on publication of *Dreams Into Action* in 1996, Milton insisted on my doing an exercise in fulfilling a dream, and had me go test drive a BMW 3-series sedan, because that was my dream car. My story of that is memorialized on the audio from the large seminar he conducted that year timed to the release of the book. He said he'd put money in escrow that at some point I'd have one. And he was right. A friend of mine sold me her used 325i which I drove for a while until it was totaled by a drunk driver while parked outside the BHP one night. And then, in one of the rare instances of Milton instantly approving a pay raise, I asked for a small bump in pay so that I could afford the lease of a new BMW 325 in 2004, and Milton was practically giddy when I brought the car by for him to take a look at.

In the middle of the worst financial crisis he ever faced, Milton bought a used Rolls Royce, and then later on, he became obsessed with the Mercedes G-500 SUV, which goes for around $100,000 or more. At one point he got a loaner, or rented one or something, and came 'round the Skylight on a night he wasn't teaching just to show me the car. He called on the theatre phone, instructed me to go out back, and there he was in the G-500. I practically had a heart attack, as he grinned and invited me to hop in the passenger side. He drove it around a couple blocks, flooring the accelerator and going on and on about how amazing this vehicle was. Dropping me back off at class, he asked, "So, what do you think?"

"Nice hunk of metal, Milton. No question." I must have had a dubious tone in my voice.

"Okay, okay, I got it, I got it," he replied gruffly, and drove off. Thank God he didn't buy one.

CHAPTER 12

Restaurants

Milton spent an inordinate amount of money on restaurants, and I was fortunate enough to be invited along here and there—for someone who lived mostly on tuna sandwiches and pasta in whatever shitty apartment I was renting, these meals were amazing. Order whatever I want? However much I want? Dessert, too? *Holy shit.* As the new kid on the block, I stayed quiet most of the time, but Milton had a regular entourage of guys who'd be along for these meals. The only women around would be MG, and whichever female friend or two was close to her at that time. Milton would sit, facing the door always ("Need to watch out for snipers"), generally not saying much.

When he taught in Los Feliz, he would often grab a bite to eat after teaching a couple scenes. Back when I was stage managing the class, the phone would ring in the office a few minutes after his departure, and I would pick up.

"Skylight."

"Yeaahhhhh. Want to grab some food with us?"

"Sure."

"The Thai place." This meant Sanamluang, on Hollywood and Kingsley. I still go to Sanamluang to this day.

"Great."

"You got someone to cover for you as Stage Manager for the rest of class?"

"Yeah."

"And some girls. We need some girls."

"Uh huh."

"So who are they gonna be?"

"Well…"

He would offer a couple names. Or, sometimes: "Who was that brunette in the second row, house left?" And I would go look out at the class to guess which attractive young woman he was talking about. My job was then to get their attention, literally during the critique of his designated substitute teacher, and whisper an invitation to go get Thai food with Milton.

At one point he and I were having lunch at Le Petit Bistro on La Cienega —I can't remember who else was with us. But a former student of his approached and offered a friendly greeting. Milton was polite in response, then the student asked, "So, are you still teaching and all?" This is like asking Picasso if he's still painting, Horowitz if he's still playing piano. Milton didn't flinch, no reaction, didn't miss a micro-beat:

"Nah, man, I gave it up." The former student was taken aback.

"Really?" he stammered.

"Yeah, I sold it."

"The Beverly Hills Playhouse?!"

"Yeah." Milton turned to me, and asked, "Who's teaching over there now?" I was too slow. Pathetic. Behind on the game. Milton prodded, "I can't remember, did the guy who bought it…?"

"I don't know," I offered weakly. "Wasn't it…?"

"Tony, right? Didn't he go by Tony?"

"Tony." *Phew*. Caught up. "Absolutely, yeah. He's running the whole thing now."

Milton turned back to the shocked former student. "Tony. He's doing it now." The student walked away, knowing nothing other than that some Tony person had purchased the BHP from Milton, who had apparently quit teaching.

He also had a favorite game of guessing the professions of other diners at the restaurant, often, as usual, with startling accuracy, which was verified by sending someone from Milton's table over to ask the stranger what they did for a living. If the report back was that the stranger in fact did *not* pursue the career Milton had guessed, he might respond with, "He's wrong," or, "Well, he's pursuing the wrong career."

During my time as CFO, the arrival of Milton's American Express bill was a monthly buzzkill to say the least. Often I would lose sleep on Milton's behalf because of his American Express bill. The restaurant tab was just thousands and thousands of dollars every month. In the old book of instructions for doing the CFO job, there were admonishments not to "let" Milton spend too much on restaurants, along with a hand-written note in the margin, "Nothing will stop him." As our CPA would later say to me, Milton was "unadvisable" on the matter of spending. The restaurant tab did slowly come down in the couple of years before his death, but I also think it was a function of his health. At some point he ordered up a light lunch from his cook during a meeting between us at his house, and said he'd rather go out to eat, but that the doctor had warned him that his diet was "sheer anarchy," and he had to start monitoring it.

CHAPTER 13

Do It Now. Or Later.

There was a year in there when the city of Los Angeles decided to demolish the old parking lot behind the Skylight Theatre, part of a renovation to double the number of spaces and upgrade the meters. For months it sat there as a pile of dirt, requiring one of the students to valet Milton's car to another location, and Milton would walk over the dirt and rocks to enter the back of the theatre. During the rainy season, it would be just a muddy catastrophe. He was so pissed off. Every week.

"What's going on with fixing this lot?"

"Well, it looks as if they're actually making some—"

"Call the mayor."

"Call...?"

"Get him on the phone. Now. Call the fucking mayor and get this project done. Let me know at the first break."

Or the lights in the lot would be out. Total darkness. Same thing: *Call the mayor. Get him to fix these lights. Let Milton know at the first break.*

This was a very typical M.O., and Milton prided himself on his motto for *Dreams Into Action*: Do it now! And when it was on someone else to get something done, particularly a staff member, he was absolutely unyielding and unreasonable on that point. *Call the mayor. Get it done.* Of course, no one could get the mayor on the phone, so there would be a good-faith effort to present a decent story there: *We called the Mayor's office, yes. I got one of the administrative assistants on the phone, and reported the issue. She said she would let the mayor know, and their office will get back to us with an update.* Then, as time went by, while you worked the actual angle, which was to contact the city's Street Lighting Department or what-have-you, you could kind of fudge a story of the update: *They're working as hard as they can, the Mayor's office contacted the Street Lighting Department, and they've said they're going to work a little harder because of our efforts*, and either the problem would be fixed or Milton's order would die out at some point, providing some breathing room before the next thing would piss him off, requiring that you get the President on the line.

Yet, when something was entirely up to him, he could be infuriating in his decision-making process. If you as a staff member needed his approval for something, it generally had to be written up in memo form for his weekly mail pack. Getting a simple checkmark next to your "Approved" option on the memo to him— whether for time off, or to do a necessary repair or upgrade—was arduous. Requests for raises? Ha! It was never *Do it Now* for a raise. So when a loyal staff member needed anything, *Do it Now* was a slogan subject to much discussion, and when Milton needed something, it was like Zeus himself had said it back in the days when gods walked the earth.

Anything expensive that wasn't a car, his house, a restaurant or his occasional travel plans to New York would be put on maximum delay mode. I remember the front door to the Robertson headquarters had gone completely wonky, and needed to be replaced. It wasn't just the door— the entire doorway needed to be replaced, refinished, new hardware and framing top to bottom. I couldn't get him to deal with it. I'd say, "The front door needs to be replaced," and he'd just reply, "No it doesn't." So then I'd have a temporary fix put in, but it would fail pretty quick, and I'd type up a new memo for Milton to approve replacement, and he'd simply return the memo, having checked the "Unapproved" option. Eventually, he'd open or close the door himself, and be like, "What the fuck is with this door?"

"This is why I keep saying it needs to be replaced," I'd reply.

"What do you mean you 'keep saying'?"

"I've asked three times for your approval to replace the door."

"No way, man."

"Yeah, I have."

"No you haven't. Not in any way that made an impact on me. This thing is totally fucked."

"Yeah, I know."

But then, as with any decision of this sort, *Do it Now* was not exactly the order of the day. A committee would be gathered to render various opinions on the matter. New door? Or rehabilitate the current door? Rehabilitation was part of his career concept, and should never be taken off the table. And who would rehabilitate it? A regular carpenter, or the positively the most expensive fabricator of fancy custom doors and shelves known to man? Get that guy over there, get his take on the matter. Should we install a small window in the door? And should the new and/or rehabilitated door be the same color? New color? Let's get samples of various colors. And the finish—gloss? Semi? Maybe a metal door! There was a door he once saw on a trip to India, it was to a temple of some sort, call so-and-so and see if he remembers the door Milton saw in India, maybe there's a photograph of it. No photo? Maybe call the temple, ask them to take a photo of it and send it to us, which temple was it? No phone number? Call the Prime Minister's office. This kind of thing could go on for weeks.

The front door wasn't replaced until after Milton died, when I was finally able to, you know, just order up a new door.

CHAPTER **14**

Tell Me About Bodhi

Ring-ring, rinnngggg. Ring-ring, rinnnngggg.

"Hello?"

"Yeaaaahh…Tell me about Bodhi."

His voice is low, calm. Too calm. I know right away this won't end well. He's heard something about Bodhi, and this call is to verify that information, with a subtextual correction of my handling of the matter: *Why didn't I tell him first? I'm too passive. He clearly has found out from someone else, probably MG, and it should have been from me…*

"Uh…What about him?" Have to pretend I don't know—otherwise it's a tacit admission of guilt about not telling him.

"Tell me about Bodhi." Exact repeated intonation. He knows I'm full of it.

I pretend to try to think of it. "Well…he booked a big TV job. He announced it last night in class."

"What'd he say about it?"

I'm so screwed. My heart rate ratchets up more. "Well, he made sure to credit Teresa, you know, for helping him buy some new clothes."

Teresa was on the teaching staff at BHP between 1994-1998. She was a force of nature, Jamaican-American, full-on New York attitude, always dressed in black, always a black car, hair drawn back tight and lots of makeup applied expertly. She had charm, temper and presence to rival Milton's. In fact, during these years, it would seem Milton was the only check on her clear ambition to become the dominant personality at the BHP. She had her own teen class outside the BHP, and funneled many students into her BHP class from there, and along with the late-90's huge spike in enrollment overall, this brought her intermediate class up to 80 people or something on the class list. "Largest intermediate class at the BHP" was a title she wore proudly. She also ran the student theatre company, The Theatre Group, which she helped create and ran as producer for a couple years in there, in parallel to Milton's own Camelot Artists. (A knockdown drag-out fight between Teresa and famed actress Doris Roberts, who directed one of the plays, was an all-time classic—two epic divas screaming bloody murder at each other until Doris dropped the mic and ended it with, "I'm too old, too successful, and too *rich* to put up with this shit from you!") Teresa sold artwork for Milton whenever he had an exhibition of his paintings, and was legendary for her sales numbers, and the pressure she would use—a high-octane blend of charm, persuasion and bullying—to achieve them. She was always surrounded by a posse of potent young male students who would do her bidding and seek her hard-won approval. Life around Teresa was never dull, that was for sure. As with Milton, it could go from hilarious to terrifying and back in all of twenty seconds.

For a couple of those years, she was also one of the subs, along with Tambor, for the nighttime advanced level classes, where she became quite infamous for her often controversial critiques. She would talk quite openly of students' physical appearance, once chastising a middle-aged actress in a critique that her poor choices in the scene were due in part to her jealousy regarding her young scene partner. "Look at her, Marilyn: She's beautiful." (Picture me at the side of the room, watching over it as the Stage Manager—blood washing from my face, already angling myself for the door to which I thought Marilyn would run first.) She was quite conversant on proper feminine tips for the women, and she cultivated a sense of being the school-wide Virility Evaluator for the guys—passing judgment both overtly and covertly on the male specimen. She could advocate in class for a very aggressive, colorful style of acting, even on material where it maybe wasn't so well-suited. Milton would occasionally come in and be pretty pissed off about it. There was a classic moment that actually began the end-trajectory for the Teresa era: *A Doll's House.* It was the situation where Milton came in on a repeat of the scene on her notes, though she wasn't there. She had ordered, in the name of some sense of color and passion in acting —*don't be boring, don't bow down to convention*—that the actor playing Krogstad should be stark naked and ranting in the most insane way to Nora. Milton saw the scene, and the critique mirrored the phone call I was involved in at the moment. He was very calm: "What were the notes?...Uh huh...Uh huh..." A couple minutes of this. Then, to the actress playing Nora: "And...Let me just ask you something: Why are you not running for your life? Why aren't you calling the cops?"

"Huh?" the actress replied, stumped.

"You have a naked man in your house. He came to your house naked. He seems to be very agitated. Why aren't you calling the cops?"

"Well...Uh...Teresa told us that..."

"I know what was said. You've been clear about that. I'm trying to talk to you about a little thing in acting that I call fucking 'logic.' What would you do, right now, today, if you opened the door to your apartment and found a screaming naked man there?"

"I'd..."

"Would you let him in?"

"No."

"Would you call the cops?"

"Probably."

Boom. "SO WHY THE FUCK ARE YOU ACTING DIFFER-ENTLY IN THE SCENE? WHY AREN'T YOU APPLYING THE SIMPLE LOGIC OF YOUR LIFE? WHY AREN'T YOU CALLING THE COPS? WHAT THE FUCK ARE YOU DOING LETTING HIM IN? YOU'RE PLAYING THIS SCENE WITH HIM, AND WE'RE ALL OUT HERE THINKING YOU'RE BOTH FUCKING CRAZY—HIM FOR BEING THE WEIRDEST MOST DISTURBED BANKER WE'VE EVER SEEN, LIKE, GET A FUCKING PADDY WAGON, PEOPLE, AND YOU FOR TRYING TO TALK WITH HIM!"

And that was just the beginning. Then he went off on the class: "And how is that you all sit here, listening to this critique, where a teacher advocates that a nineteenth century banker show up naked and screaming at this woman's home? How is that?"

No one knew what to do. Questioning the teacher on their notes just wasn't done. Everyone stared, silent. Milton wouldn't relent: "HOW IS THAT? I'd better see some hands. I need a fucking explanation."

And there followed a very interesting conversation about acting, integrity, about awareness. I was clocking the lessons fast: *If you're going to make a wild choice, make sure it's connected to the story and its logic. Don't just take the word of an authority figure—learn to think for yourself. And, in terms of inside baseball at the BHP: The substitutes here don't necessarily know what Milton is about. Teresa might be toast.* It was remarkable because he was absolutely blowing Teresa's critique of the scene into smithereens, and then annihilating the actors in the scene and all of us in class for even listening to and accepting such a critique. It was devastating for Teresa, and it didn't matter to him. If it meant saving the world from bad acting, from an illogical treatment of the scene—he'd have fired every teacher and thrown out every student. I'd never seen anything like it. After that scene, Milton started showing up again in class more frequently for quite a while. He felt the acting that he saw in the class simply wasn't up to spec, and that he needed to come in and clean it up. It was all quite specifically related to this scene in particular, as well as this phone call I was on. Teresa's ascendancy was reversed. She blew out of the BHP in a supernova of acrimony by the end of the year.

Back to my phone call. Bodhi.

"New clothes, huh? Tell me about that."

"Well, you know Teresa does these 'career consultations.'"

Milton affected weariness: "I don't know anything, man."

He knew. But this was a standard tactic of his, feigning ignorance and thus forcing further explication. He'd do it while teaching all the time. A scene from *Romeo and Juliet*. His first question: "So what's going on here? Who are these people?" And the actors would have to earn it all from scratch, understand and communicate the story from scratch, no assumptions. The Teresa "career consultations" were well known, and becoming a big problem—it wasn't appropriate for a teacher (other than Milton, of course) to use the BHP students as a marketplace for personal services outside the classes, and these consultations cost more than a month of class. Some students had complained to me they felt they got the short shrift—four hundred bucks for an hour in Teresa's apartment while she conducted business on the phone and tossed suggestions their way distractedly. Others were lavished with attention. It was an unfolding ethics disaster. Milton was torn by two of his worst attributes: that of coddling intolerable behavior in teachers who he felt he couldn't afford to alienate, and his own avarice. He was caught between banning these consultations, which he knew would damage his relationship with Teresa, and simply insisting he take a cut of the action. I had already advocated banning them in the strongest possible terms, but in vain.

I continued, needlessly: "She does these 'career consultations' and charges the students like $400 for it. And it can include how you're dressing, how you present yourself, that kind of thing."

"And Bodhi paid for one of these so-called 'career consultations,' says he got these new clothes, and that's how he booked a job on television?"

"I don't know that he was saying—"

"What do you think? Do you think he booked a job because of his new clothes? What kind of new clothes were these?"

"I don't know. I think a new suit was part of it."

"A new suit. You think that got him the job?"

"Probably not."

"Probably not?"

"Definitely not."

"What do you think may have contributed to Bodhi's wonderful television job?"

"Uh…"

Detonation. "HOW ABOUT A FEW YEARS OF MY BEING ON HIS ASS ABOUT HIS FUCKING ACTING? ABOUT HIS LIFE? ABOUT HIS ATTITUDE? ABOUT HIS CASTING? ABOUT HOW TO LOOK AT A FUCKING SCENE AND MAKE IT WORK? HOW ABOUT A HUNDRED OR MORE CRITIQUES BY EVERYONE WHO HAS TAUGHT FOR ME IN THESE CLASSES? YOU THINK THE ACTUAL STUDY OF ACTING HAD ANYTHING TO DO WITH IT?"

Stay calm. I'd learned that if you just stay calm, keep it a touch bored, that was the fastest way out…

"I think that probably had a lot to do with it."

"MORE THAN A FUCKING NEW SUIT?"

"Definitely."

Silence for five seconds.

"What is Bodhi's phone number?"

"It's—."

Click.

Ten years later, it was a few days after Milton's death, and we were having ad hoc memorial events within the BHP for the classes. Teresa came to one of those events, saw me outside in the parking lot, approached, touched my arm, and said, quite kindly and perceptively, "Oh, Allen. He was your father." I quietly lost my composure and had to spend a few minutes getting it back together before going inside to attempt charting the future.

CHAPTER 15

Every Finance Meeting I Ever Had With Milton

MILTON: What is this?

ALLEN: That's the profit-and-loss for the last quarter.

MILTON: What is that, "Profit and Loss"?

ALLEN: It's just a report, it tracks the income and expenses, and adds it all up.

MILTON: You always say that, and it sounds good, but I don't know what these numbers are.

ALLEN: This section is your income.

MILTON: Which section?

ALLEN: This one here.

MILTON: You're not doing this right. I'll show you how to do this.

Milton takes a yellow pad of lined paper and one of his $10-each Faber-Castell pencils, and writes, "Finance Meeting" with the date at the top of the page.

MILTON: So. What's the income?

ALLEN: This section. These numbers right here.

MILTON: I see.

He writes the word "Income," underlines it, then copies the numbers that are printed from my report, pretty much in the same order.

MILTON: First question for you. Don't kill me. I question everything. Income from what?

ALLEN: From all that you do.

MILTON: And what is that?

ALLEN: Primarily, you're an acting teacher and a landlord. You have some miscellaneous other income. Social security, all that.

MILTON: Really? A landlord? How's that?

ALLEN: Because you own the buildings.

MILTON: That's what this number is—"rental income"?

ALLEN: Right.

MILTON: Who pays me rent?

ALLEN: The company does, and a few individual tenants, like me.

MILTON: What company?

ALLEN: The school. Your company pays you rent to use your buildings.

MILTON: But that's all the same money.

ALLEN: It is in a sense, but it's good to break it down by business.

MILTON: I don't want to do that. I don't need to know what I pay myself for rent.

ALLEN: I thought you'd say that. So here's a second version of the same report, where I take that out.

Milton takes the new report. Looks at both, comparing numbers.

MILTON: Okay. So why are these numbers red now?

ALLEN: Those are the expenses of owning the buildings, without income.

MILTON: What expenses?

ALLEN: Mortgage, insurance, maintenance, property taxes.

MILTON: So according to this I'm losing a shitload of money.

ALLEN: No. It looks that way because I took out the rental income on this report.

MILTON: Why?

ALLEN: Because you said you didn't want to see money you paid yourself.

MILTON: So if I don't pay myself, I'm losing a shitload of money, is what you're saying?

ALLEN: I prefer just to look at each business individually. There are income and expense figures associated with each business. But on that second report, you'll see the profit from the school goes way up because I took out the rent it pays to you.

MILTON: You've lost me, man. Why is the profit larger?

ALLEN: Because I took out the rent expense. As if the school pays no rent for the theatres it uses.

MILTON: I don't want a fake report. I want the real expenses.

ALLEN: Then we'd have to use the first report I gave you.

Milton leans back in his chair, rubs his eyes.

MILTON: You don't think it's ridiculous that a man like myself, all that I've accomplished, this reputation, I'm supposedly this great teacher, and all I get is a lousy $1,000 a month?

ALLEN: That is not what you "get." That's specifically the cash you want each month.

MILTON: Cash is money, right?

ALLEN: It is.

MILTON: As far as I'm concerned, all this place pays me is $1,000 a month. It's nuts.

ALLEN: What you make is listed there, it's that number right there.

Milton leans over his desk, peers through his glasses to where I'm pointing.

MILTON: No fucking way, man. That's the gross?

ALLEN: That's the net.

MILTON: I'm sorry, my friend. You've lost me. Where is this money? I never see it. I see $1,000 a month.

ALLEN: Well it goes in the bank. It's in the bank, and we write checks against it to pay for your life. I assume you wouldn't want me putting it all into cash and dropping it on your desk.

MILTON: That sounds fantastic. Literally fantastic. I would want to see it. Please. Let me see what my hard work gets me.

ALLEN: But then you'd also have to pay your own bills.

MILTON: You can still pay the bills, just let me see the income.

ALLEN: I can't write checks against a pile of cash on your desk.

MILTON: So that number is the net. But at the bottom here, I guess this is what we save?

ALLEN: Right.

MILTON: That's practically nothing.

ALLEN: That's correct.

MILTON: Where did it all the money go?

ALLEN: You spent it.

MILTON: On what?

ALLEN: All this stuff here. This section is your expenses.

He turns back to the yellow pad, draws a line, and writes "Expenses."

MILTON: Alright. Restaurants. This says I spent $10,000 on restaurants. When?

ALLEN: In the first quarter. January to March.

MILTON: Three months.

ALLEN: Right.

MILTON: No way.

ALLEN: Well…

MILTON: Well, what? No fucking way I spent that much money. I'll bet you fifteen thousand that I didn't spend ten thousand. That's my mind. That's how I think. That gets me excited.

ALLEN: Well don't bet me, because you spent the ten thousand. Here's the breakdown.

MILTON: Breakdown of what?

ALLEN: Of your restaurant expenses.

MILTON: Not interested.

ALLEN: But—

MILTON: Not interested. Take your breakdown and fuck yourself with it. I want you literally to have sex with your fucking breakdown.

ALLEN: Okay.

MILTON: *Okay*, what? What do you mean *okay*? My whole life I don't know what it means. People stare at me, with that expression that you have right now, and say, "Okay, Milton," like I'm a crazy person. Is that a Beverly Hills Playhouse "okay"?

ALLEN: I don't know what it is. You're telling me you didn't spend $10,000 on restaurants, and I'm saying you did and here's the breakdown, and you say you're not interested and I should fuck myself with it. I guess I'm just acknowledging that sequence.

MILTON: "Acknowledging that sequence." You and your Ivy League, Harvard fucking bullshit, man. You don't understand money.

ALLEN: I think I do. It's just simple math. That's your own teaching: you wrote a chapter in your book called *Money is Real* where you lay it out—

Milton takes his glasses off, and throws them to his desk. But he has this amazing spin move he does with them, where he throws them down with a spin that takes the energy out of the collision with the desk. They never break. But this was the customary moment in meetings with Milton that anyone sitting in front of that desk would have been well advised to move a few inches back and contemplate beta blockers and heart medication, if not an entirely different existence than the one of being involved with this man.

MILTON: DON'T FUCKING QUOTE MY TEACHING TO ME, MAN, OR THIS MEETING IS OVER LIKE THAT. DON'T DO IT!

Breathe. Stay bored. Don't react.

ALLEN: I'm not trying to quote your teaching. Your teaching didn't invent arithmetic. But you use simple arithmetic when you talk to the students about money. Your own advice here to them is to pay attention to simple math, that money is very simple, very real, very much about basic arithmetic and keeping to a—

MILTON: Nah. It's not simple math, man. That's Harvard bullshit. Money is perception. Money is intention. Money is *ganas*. Money isn't what I fucking spend on restaurants. A man like myself shouldn't have to give a shit about taking people out to eat. If I'm using your logic, there's not a fucking movie that ever gets made, man. "Well, Mr. DeMille, we have this fantastic story, huge stars, exotic location, but there's a guy over in accounting, he went to Harvard, he says we can't do it because the catering might go over budget."

Nothing. There is no point in speaking. There is only quiet meditation and prayer.

MILTON: What are the stats?

ALLEN: Which stats?

MILTON: Students. New students. You're telling me I'm not allowed to eat. I have this big school, but all I get is $1,000 in cash each month, and I'm not allowed to eat. So get me some fucking students. What are the stats?

ALLEN: Here's the report of incoming new students.

MILTON: I don't get it. What is this?

ALLEN: These are the numbers of new students.

MILTON: What does that mean?

ALLEN: Someone who starts the school, who pays to start the school.

MILTON: For how long?

ALLEN: First quarter: January through March.

MILTON: No, how long do they stay? This doesn't make any sense unless I know how long they stay.

ALLEN: Well, that's infinitely variable.

MILTON: What the fuck does that mean? I'd rather you just give me that little "okay" from before.

ALLEN: It's impossible to know how long any new student will stay. Some might leave next week, some might be here in twenty years.

MILTON: Well, that's finally something interesting. What are the stats on how long people stay?

ALLEN: As an average? We don't keep those, it would be hard to—

MILTON: You should keep those. Those are the stats. That's a really important stat. You've got to break things down, man. Specifics. If we can keep them studying, maybe I can eat. How long do you think they stay?

ALLEN: It's really impossible to—

MILTON: What's impossible?

ALLEN: Because of leaves of absence. Most students will leave the school by not returning from a leave of absence, and at some point we consider they're gone. They rarely tell you they're leaving for good, and many probably don't intend to, but it ends up that way. The acting school business doesn't invite normal metrics, so it makes it very difficult to track the—

MILTON: How many LOAs don't return?

ALLEN: I don't know.

MILTON: That's a stat. That's an important stat. We should know that.

ALLEN: I'll try to figure out how to gather that information.

Milton's mind turns on something. Slight distraction.

MILTON: How is—- doing as a teacher?

ALLEN: I haven't seen him teach in a while. I assume he's doing—

MILTON: Don't assume anything, man. Not a fucking thing. He looked weird on Saturday morning. I looked over at him and he was just…blank. Nothing. Weird. You don't know anything?

ALLEN: I haven't talked with him.

MILTON: I didn't ask if you talked with him, I asked if you know anything.

ALLEN: I don't know anything that might be going on with him.

Milton picks up the telephone and dials—. He'll spend thirty minutes covering the teacher's life, romantic entanglements, career, health, diet and workout habits. Hangs up at last. Makes another call about what he wants for lunch.

MILTON: So where were we?

ALLEN: Incoming new students.

MILTON: Right. This is exhausting. You know those restaurants? Some of those, you were sitting there eating the meal, too, you know that, right?

ALLEN: Yes, I know that.

MILTON: Do you want to take that amount out? Because you benefited from that. How much of this supposed ten thousand in restaurant expenses includes Mr. Harvard enjoying a meal, tallying up the bill so he can throw it in my face in a meeting some time about how I spend too much fucking money?

ALLEN: If you want me to pay for my portion of the meals you buy, that's fine. I can buy my meals.

MILTON: Do you have someone telling you how much you spend?

ALLEN: I do. I do all this for myself, too. I make these reports and try to ensure I'm in the black as much as possible.

MILTON: In the black? That sounds bad. Isn't that losing money?

ALLEN: In the red is losing money. In the black is making money.

MILTON: Black doesn't seem right. It should be, "in the fucking yellow," man. "In the pink." Isn't that another saying?

ALLEN: Yeah, that means "all is good," as far as I know.

MILTON: So if you're in the pink, all is good, but if you lose money, you're in the red. That makes no sense.

ALLEN: You're onto something there.

MILTON: Let's pick this up some other time. This shit is fucking depressing to me.

CHAPTER **16**

Art Shows

Milton was a prolific painter, beginning this background career to his directing and teaching back in the 1960s, when he was inspired by a girlfriend at the time who was a painter. He would tell the story of his beginning with a 72-hour nonstop burst of creativity, and then winning a prize in his first competition. To my knowledge, his work was never exhibited in any museum, but occasionally he'd find a champion of his work in a gallery owner or art *macher* he'd come across. Kazuhito Yoshii, who ran The Yoshii Gallery in New York and Tokyo, displayed his work right alongside some famous painters in an exhibition called *Petits Formats* in 1999, and later on there were some exciting possibilities emerging from an association with the art dealer David Tunkl. (Until, that is, Milton walked out of Tunkl's office in a Greek huff because he made him wait outside during a phone call or something, thus blowing the arduously cultivated possibilities of that relationship into smithereens.)

By the time I came along, Milton had a 3,000-square-foot painting studio he rented adjacent to the Skylight Theatre, and every two or three years, Milton would do an art show, either renting a large gallery space somewhere in Los Angeles or using his gallery storefront at the BHP headquarters. As part of my Vice President of Stuff & Miscellany post, I'd be brought in for the moment of naming the pieces, which involved several of us—his assistant, me, whoever the current CEO was, Gary Grossman, and a few from his regular entourage, including his French hair stylist, Turkish actor friend, and Indian nutritionist, Rahul Patel. We'd walk from painting to painting, and Milton would stare at it, before finally intoning something like, "Sunset at Delphi." Or "Joking with Fellini." And everyone would nod immediately. *Yes, yes, "Sunset at Delphi," "Joking with Fellini"—these are perfect.* Rahul was always the most obsequious—he could literally start applauding at a certain idea for the name of a painting. Rahul was an *ideas man*. He was fully capable of saying something like, "Milton, this work is so brilliant you should take this art show on the road, and exhibit it in fifteen cities across the world! You will inspire the local artists, and we could do lectures and seminars!" Rahul would then point to someone else in the group: "And So-and-So should run that project!" This would necessitate up to half an hour to discuss fully the potential and logistics of whatever the absurd Rahul idea was, including the fact that So-and-So's face had gone white at the prospect of being put in charge of the worldwide Milton Katselas Painting and Lecture Tour. My job in this particular circus was merely to stand at the side, nod in agreement, write it all down, and turn these titles into numbered lists of the artwork for the salespeople. Then I was to make little title cards that I'd meticulously cut to a certain dimension, and affix to the wall by each painting. I actually loved this job, as it would involve my getting a few hours alone with the work. A single exhibition could include over a hundred pieces— paintings on canvas, paintings on large sections of reclaimed wood, sculptures, monotype prints, and much of it was very colorful, exciting work. I'm no expert, but I liked a lot of it. I'd bring a level, some mounting clay, and the cards, slowly going around to ensure all was *just so* before the opening. I did this job all the way through his last exhibition in 2008, when I had been CEO for five years and could easily have offloaded the task.

During opening week of an exhibition, Milton would call off a night for each Advanced class, and instead the class would meet at the gallery to get a personal walk through with Milton, to have a Q&A about the work. On the one hand, this was a perfectly acceptable "field trip," to get actors out of their notorious film/television myopia, and into a gallery to see other forms of artistic expression. On the other hand, it would have been better if occasionally these field trips were to see an artist who wasn't Milton himself! Because it wasn't just taking a night from class and having to walk through the gallery. The students would be called individually to schedule their own private walkthrough with a salesperson. They would be called multiple times. They would be followed up with. Milton not only didn't shy away in the slightest from the idea that students buy his work, they were sold *hard*. Probably 95% of total sales of his work throughout his career were from his own students and friends. The salespeople were often culled from the teachers and other staff, taking advantage of a natural desire in largely young students to please either the known salesperson or Milton by buying a painting. Milton would tell the story of being a broke, aspiring artist in New York and getting a couple Picasso drawings that he paid off over time —he felt this was an important lesson in valuing art and not being constrained by your own relative poverty from owning artwork that moved you. (After he died, we were presented with the news that those Picasso drawings were likely inauthentic.)

Milton's own work was pricey—$1,500-5,000 for most, and the larger works were even more expensive than that. He would facilitate irresponsible purchases by the students through allowing payment plans that would extend for years. Wealthier students and friends would always buy at least one, if not several, but many times I would witness a shaky-handed, heart's-a-pounding young student affixing a red dot on the title card of a painting he or she could not remotely afford to buy. (I myself affixed a shaky red dot on some of this work, far beyond my budget.) Later on I would be in charge of the art payment spreadsheets, and making the grinding, depressing phone calls to students, some of whom would have long since blown out of the classes, to get them to make good on these payments. Between the stratospheric out-of-pocket costs to rent the gallery, to frame and mount the pieces, cater the opening, and pay commissions-in-full on works that were bought on payment plans, these art shows would be huge money-losers up front, with only modest profit to be realized later on.

His last exhibition was source material for quite a fight between us. There was a disagreement about when it should occur. He wanted it to happen in April, but several of us disagreed, arguing that to open an art exhibition the same month as taxes were due wasn't such great timing, and he should wait until later. He went nuclear on all of us about it, which included a phone call to me during which he screamed and cursed that I, of all people, shouldn't be such an unsupportive shithead about his

work. It had been years and years and years of this behavior, and
that day, for whatever reason, I'd had enough. I remember I was
running a personal errand down in Torrance, and had stopped to
fill my car with gas. I stood there listening to him scream at me,
and as the pump clicked to a stop, something clicked within me
and I told him he could fuck off and I hung up. I'd never done
anything like that. That was 10am. And then I didn't answer
the phone. He called back. His assistant called back. A different
assistant called. The office called. And I just checked out for the
entire day, spending part of it writing him a letter, wherein I told
him he would likely not find many people on planet earth more
supportive than I of his life and his school, and yes, his other
artistic activities. I even wrote him of one plan I had for after he
died: that I would turn the Gallery storefront at the Robertson
building into an ongoing retrospective of his work, curated by
his art studio assistant, so that his work could be seen by whole
new generations of students and others we could promote to. If
sixteen years of working with him every day, now running his
school, and planning for the indefinite future all seemed so unsupportive of him, I didn't know what else to say. I delivered the
letter under the door to his house in the afternoon, and went to
a movie. We were supposed to teach together that night. After
"going dark" for nine hours, I figured I had made my point, and
showed up fifteen minutes early for class, as always, so I was
waiting for him on the sidewalk when he pulled up out front. He
got out, smiled, shook my hand, and said, "I knew you'd be here,
man." He never yelled at me again.

Some time after that, something odd happened. One morning
I drove up to the BHP for work, and found Milton and several
helpers in the Gallery storefront, with a small rental truck out
front. It would be highly unusual for him to show up at the
building without my knowing about it in advance. But there he
was, hanging an exhibition of work. The last show had wrapped
a while before that, so this was unrelated to any known project. I
poked my head in to say hello, but he wasn't very responsive, and
wasn't giving off a vibe of wanting other people around. What
was this about? As I walked through the courtyard up to my
office, I remembered my letter to him, with my idea about how
to use that space, and a chill ran down my spine.

He left after a few hours, locked the gallery door, and there wasn't a word to be said about it.

Weeks later he was gone. And in the year or two afterward, we tried my idea about that gallery being an ongoing retrospective of Katselas artwork. But in the ultimate irony, the idea failed because of Milton's own estate plan, which managed to place various interested parties in direct conflict with each other. In the Great Acrimonious Reckoning that was to come in order to settle that mess, I gave up control over his artwork, and all of Milton's paintings located at the BHP were removed.

CHAPTER 17

Be Sure To Talk About Me Around Town

Milton isn't happy with the vibe in the class. He watched and critiqued the first scene, but before he calls for the customary break, he sits in a chair on stage facing the class, and stares at us. A few moments go by.

"So what's going on?"

Nothing. Uncomfortable silence.

"Oh, that's great. I love silence. I love fear. I love everyone hoping someone else will speak up and take the pressure off. No one will take the pressure off. The pressure is on. Always."

More staring.

"Okay," he says, flatly.

Five seconds.

"Shit. Didn't work. My staff says that to me all the time. 'Okay.' I don't know what it means, but maybe, I was thinking, if I use it on you, it will make some sort of change. I see now it truly is just a piece of shit. *Okay.*"

Someone finally raises their hand, and Milton calls on him.

"Do you mean, like…You seem unhappy with something, and I'm not sure what it is."

"The energy in this room sucks," Milton replies.

"Okay," the student mistakenly answers.

"See? Piece of shit. I say, 'the energy sucks,' and you say, 'okay.' Okay the energy sucks? Okay you like it? Okay you don't like it? Okay you agree with me? Okay you disagree? Jesus. *I got that.* That's another one. I love that one: *I got that, Milton.* You got what? What exactly do you got? 'Okay,' what?"

"Okay, I understand now that you think the energy sucks."

"And you didn't know that before? Is that what you're saying?"

"No, it seemed like a normal class to me."

"Get some new eyeglasses. Check your hearing. Check your life. Check your perception. You all are going to be on sets, and you need to suss out what's going on around you. Is it going well? Is it tense? Does the director know what he's doing? Does he get along with the DP? Is the producer happy? What's going on? You need to know that."

"Okay," replies the student. The class laughs, finally, as does Milton.

"You," Milton says, pointing to another student. But there's confusion as to which student. "No, not you. *You.* No. No, not you. *You.* Yes. You. In the green. You."

The student in green finally gets it. "Me?"

"You. What's going on with you?"

"Uhhhhhhh…"

From there unfolds fifteen minutes on this student in green, who Milton has never met before, during which he does the usual "Milton sees your past!" routine, at which he was quite brilliant, where he picks out important elements of your past training, your relationship with your family, a baseline psychological profile— all with startling accuracy. By the end of this exercise, the student in green has probably cried at some point, admitted that he or she has exactly the passivity, fear or hostility that Milton has identified, and for the exact reasons he perceived, and the class is suitably awed and entertained at the exercise. The room has come alive somewhat.

"So, the room is different. You feel it? You need to feel that energy, both the bad side of it, and the good, and figure out when it's bad, how to make it good without my having to do it. Because I'm not always going to be here. If I come in again and feel that shitty energy, the apathy, the lack of attention, I'll just turn around and walk out of here. Class will be over, and you'll still pay. You understand?"

General assent from the class. But not from one new girl in the back row. She's got a face. In BHP lingo, if you "have a face," it's not an anatomical statement. It means your face has some expression, you're harboring some negative attitude, some judgment. Milton sees, it, and hones in.

"You, in the back. You understand?"

"I'm not sure."

Milton's mood turns dark again. An edge creeps into his voice: "If the energy in this room sucks, and I walk in, and I sense that it sucks, then I'm walking back out, class is over and you all still pay. Clear?"

"I don't think I should have to pay if there isn't going to be a class." Hey. She was new. She didn't know.

"I THINK YOU'LL PAY WHEN I FUCKING TELL YOU TO PAY. HOW'S THAT, HONEY?"

Tears. Instantaneous hysterics.

"Why are you yelling at me?"

"You don't like it? Leave. Leave now."

"I will leave! I'm leaving!" She starts to pack up her stuff.

"Good! Leave! How long you been in the class?"

"This is my first night!"

"Well, shit. That's the way it goes. Who interviewed you?"

"Jennifer."

"I see. Well, it's up to you."

"I'm leaving!" Full-on, victimized tears. Enemy-for-life tears.

"Well, get to it, then. You have your purse? Your whatever? In these situations, you want to make a clean exit, don't leave anything behind."

The young woman has made her way down the stairs and across the stage, reaching the sliding door upstage left at the Skylight Theatre. Milton gets her attention: "Hey. Hey! One more thing: *Be sure to talk about me around town.*" After she left, Milton signaled to one of the Stage Managers, and said, "Go see if you can catch up to her, talk to her." But she was long gone. So...one new student burned, along with any of her friends—wouldn't be a stretch to assume she wasn't going to recommend the place.

On the one hand, I'd look at incidents like that, and think to myself it was such a waste. He launched that volcanic Greek temper at her and she wasn't ready or acclimated, and so the BHP lost a new student and anyone she might ever refer. I thought,

The business is too tough to burn them like that. But the flip side also held an important lesson: He didn't care. He was going to be who he was, and he didn't care who said what to whom about it. There was an integrity to his own way and his own point of view. To see someone like Milton, who was so unapologetically himself, even when it was tough to take, was probably a more important lesson in the long run. I was to end up running the school, I think partly because my antennae were already tuned to the station called, "What works here? What draws students? What keeps them? How does this bizarre ecosystem function?" But the students who were not destined to run the joint got an equal lesson, because to say you're going to be a performing artist is to invite ridicule, doubt, mockery, both from within and from without. People always want you to move closer to what's "acceptable," nowadays more than ever. The tidal pull towards conformity, political correctness, and likability is a relentless force, and it must be resisted, in both teachers and their students. The willingness of Milton to acknowledge that his "way" was not always pretty, to acknowledge that people will gossip about it and he didn't care—that was a lesson on its own.

CHAPTER 18

The Goddess

As I watched the scene, I sensed something was wrong.

Directing had gone well for me. In 1996, I had watched a scene from *A Few Good Men*, the climactic courtroom confrontation between Kaffee and Colonel Jessup. It hadn't gone well, and there were a lot of moving parts in the scene when you added in the judge and other people you needed to bring it to life. For some reason, as I was listening to the critique, I thought to myself: "I know how this should go." I approached Milton on the break and asked if I could direct the repeat of the scene, and he seemed very positive about the idea.

The repeat under my direction killed. And I had a blast doing it. As the actors and I worked, generally very late at night because that was the only time everyone was available, there was a very clear realization on my part that directing was what I should be doing. It went back to Mancini's first comment to me on my first monologue as a student at BHP: "You like to find the music." There was something about directing that linked up with my musical instincts, and to the degree that I currently have a "style" as a director, and people say I do, it is based in this linkage.

Part of the process on this scene involved a separate meeting with the actor playing Kaffee, in order to help sort out some confidence and big-picture life issues that had been brought up by Milton in his critique. Milton loved that I had done that meeting, as he of course was well-known for renovating the entire lives of the student actors he directed. An actor in a scene being directed by Milton would often find their bills paid, their apartment cleaned, their car repaired, and in addition received intensive ad hoc counseling throughout by Milton on the major issues of their lives.

After the success with *A Few Good Men*, I became Mr. Fixit for scene repeats. I must have done dozens of them, where I came in after a critique and supervised the repeat of the scene. This was great training as I was able to work fast, with actors and a scene that already existed and just needed to be shaped. Almost all had gone really well, and I had built up a decent reputation and some degree of self-confidence about my work.

But tonight, I felt something was wrong. The scene was from *The Goddess* by Paddy Chayevsky, and it was off. The actress playing the religious mother was coming off too strongly righteous, maybe? I remember sitting in the back thinking…*this isn't good.* I had never had that feeling before.

Milton had come to see the scene. But he was doing one of his "stand at the side of the room" deals, where he let Tambor enter the theatre, take the teacher's chair, and receive the start-of-class applause, and then Milton snuck in through the back entrance and watched the scene from the side. Looking at him as he leaned forward on the railing, I noted he didn't look as if he was in a very good mood. I had observed previously that his "stand at the side of the room" impulse was usually based in not really wanting to be there, but showing up out of some sense of obligation. I was grateful to be on the list to whom he felt obligated, but the look on his face made me nervous.

The scene wrapped, and promptly received a standing ovation. Hmph. Maybe I was being too hard on myself. Maybe it worked after all! I took my seat on stage with the actors, in a slightly more hopeful frame of mind. After a few introductory remarks, which were neutral but leaning in the direction of validating the standing ovation, Jeffrey, per protocol, turned the critique over to Milton, who had remained impassive while leaning against the wall.

"Well," Milton began, taking a slight pause before continuing, "My first thought is that I could have spent this time having a good dinner."

Uh oh.

"But instead I'm here watching this scene. Apparently I'm in the minority, though. You all stood up. I'm curious. Why?"

The class stayed quiet.

"Maybe you didn't hear me. I'm wondering why you all stood up. You, there…" He indicated a classmate. "Why did you stand up?"

The classmate responded, nervously, "Well, I just thought the performances were, you know, really compelling."

"Check your vision. Get some eyeglasses. Who else? You." Another classmate into the frying pan.

"Allen has a really good touch as a director, and I thought—"

"Allen didn't have a good touch tonight, my friend."

"Okay."

"'Okay,' what? He didn't have it tonight. This isn't a good scene. I could have been having dinner."

I think he ripped another few people on an individual basis for having stood up for my scene, before ripping me a new one for the performances. The actress playing the religious mother was indeed too righteously indignant. He thought her daughter, the movie star, would never have wanted such a woman to stay, as the script indicated. It didn't make any sense. It didn't track moment to moment. It was, in a weird way, an echo of the annihilation of that scene from *A Doll's House,* where the "bold idea" for the acting choice strained all credibility. It was quite the smackdown. Being the Stage Manager as I was, I had to lead by example in taking it all with aplomb, don't look crushed or beaten, and I copped to having sensed the scene was off but not acting upon that intuition.

Milton cornered me on this. "When exactly did you have the intuition it wasn't working?" I didn't know. "When exactly did you have an intuition that it *was* working, then?" I didn't know that either. I had never felt it really was working. "That's your problem, man. You never knew it was working. You were faking it. You bought your own PR. See you later. I'm going to recuperate by having that dinner, even though you've spoiled my fucking mood."

From then on, I have tried to ensure that my own sense that the scene or play is working is intact fully before presenting it to an audience. That doesn't mean everyone will like it, that's an impossibility, but you have to be able to stand your ground on the choices and the performances. The director is the audience before the audience shows up. You have to love it first. You don't have much of a chance otherwise.

CHAPTER 19

Hurricane Ponzi

"You know I can hear that it's all gone, if that's what's true."

Milton said it simply, no drama, no threat, no fear, no nothing. I listened to him from my seat across from his desk, and next to me was Reed Slatkin. The year was 2000, and Milton had commenced a large project to buy the adjoining property to his house, demolish what was there, and double the size of his house. Milton wanted Reed to know why he was pulling significant money out of his account with Reed Slatkin Investments.

Reed would go down as one of the great con artists of the late 1990s, a Ponzi scheme operator who ripped off many people in L.A., many showbiz people, many Scientologists (since he passed himself off as one). At the time, years before Bernie Madoff took the crown, Reed Slatkin ran one of the biggest Ponzi schemes in American history. Hundreds of millions of dollars of fraud were involved. He had made one good bet on Earthlink at the beginning, and from there it was all total crookery. And right there in the middle of it all was Milton. And MG. And several longtime friends and associates. They were all in. Reed ultimately served around ten years in the penitentiary, and died of a heart attack not long after his release. I personally knew a fair number of people who wished far worse for him than this passive death.

I first heard of Slatkin when I took over the CFO position at the BHP. I saw these statements come in each quarter from Reed Slatkin Investments. They consisted of just a single heavy sheet of paper with his letterhead from an office in Santa Barbara, the date, and two figures: "Value of assets beginning (date)" and "Value of assets ending (date)." The latter figure was always 5-12% larger than the former, with astounding annual gains of 25-35%. That was it. No list of stocks or bonds or other holdings, or where all this money was kept, nothing like that. Just those two figures. I remember first seeing these "statements," and while I was far less knowledgable about general financial affairs and investments than I am now, I thought to myself, "Total bullshit." That was my first reaction. I recall even raising a skeptical question about them to whomever was CEO at that time, and I was rebuffed immediately. *Reed was a genius. Reed was an investment guru. Reed was going to ensure Milton died a rich man. Oh, if only one had sufficient assets to get them to Reed to manage!* And Milton had those assets—he had no fewer than four accounts with Reed, had transferred almost all his wealth to him. He even refinanced real estate and deposited *those* checks. He was disastrously all-in on this Reed Slatkin.

The reason these Ponzi schemes keep going for as long as they do, is that when you ask for a disbursement here or there, it actually shows up. And for many years I saw these checks show up for both Milton and MG. A letter would be drafted in Milton's name asking for a sum of money, he would sign, and we'd fax it over to Reed's office, and a week later a check would arrive in the mail, and everything was fine and dandy. MG's spending cash came in regular payments requested and received every quarter. So the mechanics of the scheme work just well enough, and the rest is all the psychology of belief, arrogance, and the club mentality: *You're in. You made it. You're one of the few who can get to him.* And look at those statements! My God, in another few years of this, you'll be worth a fortune! And he's a Scientologist to boot! One of those great, ethical and superior beings—my God, one barely needs a contract or verification of figures if you're dealing with a *Scientologist!* (Insert a photo of my vomiting here.)

And so it went, until it didn't. At some point in 2001, in the middle of the crash of tech stocks, I requested a disbursement from Reed, and nothing showed up. I called the office, and Reed actually answered. He sounded frantic, telling me, "Listen, tell Milton to look up what a 'hedge' investment is, or do it yourself and tell him. Everything's fine! I need to go!" But no check appeared. And no one answered the phone after that. There was a meeting about something else at Milton's house that week, and I let him know about the call, and that I hadn't been able to contact anyone since. Milton's face went slightly ashen, and he picked up the phone to call Irene Dirmann, who by then had moved to Clearwater, Florida. Irene retained her status as his number-one advisor, and, I believe, was the person who originally introduced Reed to Milton for the purposes of encouraging investment.

"Yeah, how are you?" Milton asked, upon Irene answering the phone. "Good. Listen, this is a little unpleasant what I have to say here, but Allen says he can't reach Reed Slatkin. Says he sent a check request last week, had one weird phone call, and hasn't heard anything since." He listened to her for a bit, as if she had some reasonable explanation —perhaps Reed had to go out of town? Family emergency? Milton took off his glasses, grabbed the bridge of his nose, and looked into the distance. "I think it's gone, Irene." You could hear Irene's voice protesting on her end, and he then forwarded her remarks to me: "She says, 'no way.'" I shrugged. This was *way* outside my pay grade, but I knew enough to know that if Reed Slatkin was a house of cards coming apart, we were sitting ducks, landfall for a life-altering shitstorm of epic proportions. I was trying to get my head around those ramifications even now before it was all confirmed.

"Irene, I think it's gone. Well…Alright, let me know." He hung up. "She's going to try to get a hold of him."

It didn't take long to realize the epic shitstorm was indeed upon us, Hurricane Reed's-a-Fucking-Ponzi-Criminal, Category 5. For those unfamiliar with the intricacies of being victimized by a Ponzi scheme, the whole notion of what you think you "had" with the crooked investment advisor becomes moot in a hot second. There are only two questions that count: How much money did you unwittingly feed into the fraud, and how much money can be proved you extracted? If you extracted more than you put in, then you are what's called a "net gainer," and the federal authorities in charge of the investigation will be coming after you for that net gain. If you put in more than you took out, you are a "net loser," and all you can do is pray that the forensic accountants discover actual, verifiable assets held by the Ponzi operator (typically zero to minimal), and some portion of those, along with the amounts now to be clawed back from the "net gainers" are all you will ever see, and it will take years to see anything. Net gainers will file bankruptcy. Net gainers will leave the country for exotic non-extraditable locales. Net gainers fight tooth and nail. Both net gainers and net losers commit suicide, or die of both sudden and chronic illness from stress. (Milton would have that disastrous foot infection two years later, at some point thereafter he was diagnosed with prostate cancer, and when I look back at it, was on a physical decline pretty much from 2001 until his death seven years later.) Everyone is capital "F" fucked.

Milton was a net gainer to the tune of middle-high six digits. MG was also a significant net gainer. I remember one of the early meetings about the unfolding fiasco, as we tried to get our heads around the chaos to ensue. Milton asked what I thought was going to happen.

"You're going to have to change your life, is what's going to happen."

"How do you mean that?"

"Well for one, you've been pulling money from Reed to cover budget shortfalls and to build this house. All of that is gone. You have to live purely on what money you earn annually, starting now. Secondly, they're going to come after you for the 'net gain' you made from Reed."

"What 'net gain'? It's all gone!"

I explained the net gainer/net loser deal, and how they were going to come after him.

"I didn't fucking know he was a crook! It's not my goddamned fault."

"It doesn't matter, Milton. It doesn't matter you didn't know. Reed effectively stole money from other people and gave it to you. You can't keep stolen money on the justification that you didn't know it was stolen."

"As far as I'm concerned, he stole $3M of my money."

"You never had $3M. That was just made up. All those statements were just made-up numbers. The only money you had was the money you gave him, and you pulled out more than you put in, and that's all that matters."

"What about MG?"

"MG needs to get a job."

"Why do you say that? Are they coming after her?"

"They will be, yes."

"I got MG into this. I told her to take her divorce settlement and give it to Reed."

"MG's a big girl. She let you do that. She can face reality."

"MG will not be getting a job."

"Why not? Might be good for her. She's a perfectly capable person."

"You don't understand a woman like that. It's not going to work. Her and a job."

"Then how is she going to live?"

"I'll handle that."

"So you're going to pay for her life, and yours, you're going to finish this house, and pay a huge settlement with the federal Slatkin bankruptcy trustee? How?"

Pause.

"You know what's going to change around here because of Reed Fucking Slatkin, Allen?"

"What?"

"NOTHING. THAT'S WHAT'S GOING TO CHANGE. NOTH-ING." The eyeglasses spun onto the surface of his desk.

"I don't know how that's possible."

"WATCH ME."

And watch I did. Because after the tide went out on the technology sector, and many were exposed for having no pants on, the tide came back, and it came back big: Real Estate. The big money flooded into real estate, and Milton rode that new bubble all the way from 2001 until his death. He bought MG's house at fair value, she lived off the proceeds of the sale, and eventually, she would have zero assets and declare bankruptcy in the face of the relentless Slatkin Trustee. Then he sold and/or refinanced everything he held in real estate to the tune of millions of dollars, paid the Trustee his net gain figure, paid MG's expenses directly, finished his house, and in fact changed almost nothing about his or MG's spending habits. He ran chronic huge deficits that were made up by refinancing the buildings again and again, riding the insane valuations and kooky no-doc loan approval processes. By 2003, I had become the CEO, and we effected a fair amount of cost-cutting on the business side, but he didn't relent personally. In the middle of the unfolding hurricane, while recovering from his partial foot amputation in 2003, Milton bought a used friggin'

Rolls Royce for $70,000. Irene was staying with him at the time, selflessly giving up weeks of her life to assist with his recovery, and when she called to notify me of this purchase, she humorously reported to him my reaction to this news: "Milton, he just gasped." Milton guffawed in the background. A couple years later, the Rolls was sold back to the dealer at a significant loss. Milton died in October of 2008, when the real estate bubble had just burst and the world seemed to be ending. The epic shitstorm he managed to postpone through reckless borrowing off the real estate was now coming hard for me, and would devour four years of my life.

Back to the Slatkin meeting, in 2000. Milton had said, "You know I can hear that's it all gone, if that's what's true." I remember looking to Reed Slatkin on my left. He looked directly at Milton, waited a good five seconds.

"It's all there, Milton. You have nothing to worry about."

CHAPTER **20**

Scientolo-wahh?

It's a word so loaded it can overwhelm everything in its vicinity: *Scientology*. I can say without the slightest reservation that the most irritating aspect of looking after Milton's legacy is his linkage to Scientology as his controversial belief system. To this day, some people —the number is falling, but still exists—reflexively want to associate the BHP with Scientology, and when I hear about it, I want to punch holes in the nearest wall, because I have done a lot to make known our *lack* of association, in fact our *enemy* status. The topic is so exasperating that I even envisioned a version of this book where I simply didn't mention it for fear of continuing, needlessly and inaccurately, its association with BHP. But I wanted to write an honest appraisal, detailed and inclusive of everything I encountered, and Scientology had its role to play there. Not many in Los Angeles have my history: knowing nothing about it, then a little, then a lot, becoming involved, becoming alarmed, then revulsed, and ultimately becoming a vocal critic and declared enemy of this so-called "Church," even writing an entire play, *Disconnection*, about it. If there are readers tangentially familiar with Milton's history, or former students who worry that this is in any way going to be an apologia on matters Scientological, read on.

Phase 1: Huh?

There were the odd terms. "Ethics Officer." Originally, the Stage Managers in class were called *Ethics Officers*. This was taken directly from Scientology organizations, where there was a person with a similar post, whose job was to ensure parishioners taking the courses were doing well. As an ethics officer, I was trained to handle students whom I observed to go up and down in their morale (who doesn't?, I think now…), or who got sick (who doesn't?…), or who seemed generally down and discouraged (who isn't, now and again, sometimes for good reason?). I was trained to implement a "handling" developed by Hubbard, who called this "roller-coaster" condition PTS, for potential trouble source. The PTS was a person, though the term could be used colloquially as both noun and adjective. If the PTS was connected to a critical person, a suppressive person, then they may start manifesting these very specific symptoms, and if you could help them spot the negative influence in their lives, coach them to handle the situation or disconnect from that person, then the PTS would improve in their outlook and stop getting sick, having accidents, feeling down, etc. But all these terms…*Ethics officer, PTS, Suppressive person, handle, disconnect, roller-coaster…*There is an entire language to learn, with hundreds of acronyms; my aptitude for learning was tapped and it would feel good to get all these definitions down and be able to speak like a native.

There was the weird obsession with "stats." What were the class statistics in enrollment, attendance, scene production? I was very good at basic organization and completely anal about keeping track of things, so it didn't bother me, particularly. Later on, however, as I moved into BHP management, Milton's constant drumming about the "stats" became the bane of my existence, as an acting school is a spectacularly ill-suited business for conventional tracking by statistics. All the "stats" stuff at BHP came from Hubbard's similar obsession, that all sane organizations ran by this rigorous system of stat-keeping, with various "conditions" applied to staff whose stats were down and not up. *If enrollment drops over the Christmas holiday, that is not normal, that is an aberration, that is the result of some asshole not keeping his stats up, of someone being "reasonable" (a negative adjective in the Scientology world) about holiday absences, and let's handle that guy, because only weaklings let the stats go down at Christmas…*At first, you think it kind of makes sense, and then after a while you realize it's 100% bullshit, and does nothing but make for miserable staff people who lie, manipulate, hide or do whatever it takes to make a "stat" seem higher than what it really is, just for fear of punishment. Milton had fortunately not adopted the system in total, but the word "stat" was heard at BHP more than I had ever heard it in my life prior, and a phone call from him asking about "stats" was one of the worst you could get. Milton would lose his shit each year about enrollment numbers over the holidays, and we'd be ordered to have adversarial conversations with students about why they wanted to take two weeks off from class to see their families. Ugh. To this very day, I never ask for "stats," I don't reward or punish a "stat trend" in any direction, and I shut the whole school down for two weeks over Christmas. It's all a lot less stressful, and we're doing just fine.

After having been a student at BHP for a while, I'd hear the word on the street: "That's the place where they teach Scientology." I think it depends on how you look at it. If you had a Jewish acting teacher, and he said to you, "I had a rabbi once that said to me blah blah, and I think that applies to you/to this situation/to this analysis of a scene," is that guy "teaching Judaism"? If the answer for you is yes, then yes, Milton occasionally taught Scientology. But most would say no, this kind of approach, common to all teaching, where the teacher tries to bring some sense of his or her truth to a student in whatever means available—this is not proselytizing for religion. The main thing Milton gave a shit about was good acting, and those that knew him I think would agree. But there was no doubt that the fact that he was a Scientologist led to others with a similar belief system being drawn to him as a teacher. Many of those students were real cheerleaders for the cause, which was a good part of the overall "cult vibe" that was subject to so much gossip and criticism.

Still, during this early phase for me at the BHP, I was quite open minded about it all. I enjoyed the environment and the people very much, and these Scientologists I got to know as teachers and staff people all seemed very on point, competent, and energetic. I read the famous *Time* magazine article, "The Cult of Greed," and didn't see in it anything I recognized as true about the people I was getting to know. It seemed so over-the-top, in fact, that I went and bought *Dianetics* and read the whole thing (which apparently no one actually does—even veteran Scientologists were like, "You did what?"). Then I read *Science of Survival*, which was Hubbard's treatise on what he called the "tone scale," a numerical scale of emotional tones that a person can exhibit, both chronically and acutely. He developed this whole chart of human behavior associated with various tone levels, and I must say it seemed entirely accurate. This was an important moment in my early curiosity phase, because at a very low tone level, he described just about every single behavioral and psychological trait of my then current girlfriend Valerie, who was driving me completely bonkers. He nailed her top to bottom. All of it. And I thought, "Well, I don't know everything about Hubbard or this Scientology stuff, but this book absolutely nails people and how they think and how they act." It was extremely predictive and accurate on it all.

That book led me to ask about doing more stuff at Celebrity Centre, which was the organization that catered to artists, delivering courses and "auditing" in a renovated, gaudy-but-grand old hotel building at the corner of Franklin and Bronson.

Phase 2: I'm In. Kinda?

I took a bunch of those courses, and after a while I felt pretty integrated into the Scientology club, without really calling myself one. And look, there are many worse activities a 20-something could be doing in Los Angeles than going to Celebrity Centre with a growing circle of friends who rarely drink or do drugs, spending quiet time in a course room, learning about the human mind and behavior and all that—the general area of self-improvement. There was a good piano in the lobby, and I enjoyed going there to practice, and the staff and public seemed to enjoy it as well. The courses there were not lecture-style education as I had experienced all the way through Harvard, but individually tailored, just you versus a checksheet of chapters to read and exercises to complete, and that appealed to me because I could move as fast as I was able or desired. Since I was under the umbrella of the BHP and Milton, I was treated well, probably far better than many who at that time showed up without this "protection." And I was just wired for a little more self-confidence than others, so if some annoying staff person insisted I go with him to some room to talk about doing more courses, I was able to say, "Nope. I'm going home now. See you later." It didn't bug me that much.

And, I got this shit for free! One of Milton's staff members, Joyce Wallace, was for many years his point person for all things Scientology, handling students who were also on course at Celebrity Centre, and generally consulting, advising and cajoling everyone in her surrogate maternal way. She was what was called a Field Staff Member, or FSM, and part of their compensation from the church is in the form of "training awards," essentially a system of points that the FSM could allocate for courses, either for themselves or people they were training.

I, as an up-and-coming ethics officer, was one of the beneficiaries of Joyce's training award points. Had I needed to spend my own money, I doubt I'd ever have done any courses, but for free? I was totally game. I did intensive courses on communication, courses on all the information behind "PTS Tech" (*technology* was the term used for all this information that Hubbard had developed and collated, commonly referred to as the *tech*), and an endless course on ethics called the Ethics Specialist Course. In addition, I would be a guinea pig for other students studying to be auditors, and I would be their "pre-clear" as they learned to deliver auditing sessions. I did an introductory course on how to use the e-meter. All this coursework would happen on the off-nights from class, but I was in my own class on Mondays and Wednesdays, and then on Tuesdays and Thursdays I'd often be in another BHP class—I was becoming an expert as a Stage Manager (let's leave "ethics officer" forever in the historical dustbin of vocabulary), and so I'd go into other classes to help out as well. My coursework was crammed into the nooks and crannies of my week, and some of these courses took months and months to get through.

I would go to the big Scientology events, and the holiday and summer anniversary "galas" at Celebrity Centre. The church had their own filmmaking unit, called Golden Era Productions (abbreviated colloquially to just *Gold*), and they started using me as an actor in their films. I did a ton of them, and they paid union wages, and the crew who worked those projects became friends as well—this included Marc Headley, who eventually left (escaped, really) and wrote the book *Blown For Good* that first popped my eyes out years later, after I'd disengaged. This acting work included going out on many occasions to the secretive international base two hours east of Los Angeles, and shooting on their huge sound stage there. As a musician, I was hired to go the Caribbean, where they operated their *Freewinds* ship, and I once spent an entire month down there playing classical piano during meals, reading very thick novels, completely unplugged from the world. I was "in" with the President's Office at Celebrity Centre, which was where the big name celebrities would hang out—they had their own entrance into the building, their own parking lot, all that. Being in general still young and clueless, I can confess now, and sheepishly, that the ego-stroking, the in-house celebrity thing, and the I'm-friends-with-the-realworld-celebs thing was attractive and felt good. It's completely embarrassing now, but at that time…Sigh. *Youth.*

But through all this period, which consisted of the years 1994-2000, I could only barely muster the thought that "I'm a Scientologist." I didn't grow up with any religion or Sunday School. I was not particularly into "self-help." I was able to say it only through a complicated mental process that went something like this: *I am an official Smug, Cynical New Englander with a fancy education, and thus I can't possibly be one of those people who belong to whatever this kooky fucking church is, most of whom I observe to lack much of…I mean, the family will be completely horrified. Anyone I ever knew prior to moving to Los Angeles would shake their heads in amazement and derision; I'd lose my bomahhhhh status and go to fuckin' cult membahhhh status in no time flat. So it cannot be. But hold on: My friends are by and large these people, my mentor is famous for it, and they're good people thus far by my direct observation. The courses are interesting for the most part, by my direct experience. I like hanging out there, and I love that damned piano in the lobby. It is seriously a very good piano. I get all this for free. And they even pay me union wages to act here and there. I have yet to see anything untoward, nor have I been treated in any unfair way. So. Shit. Am I a fucking pussy for not just saying it, then? I guess I am one? Kinda? Shit! No way! I am an official Smug Cynical New Englander…Round and round it went.*

Phase 3: There is something wrong here

After about seven years, around 2000-2001, there were several developments that sent me packing. Firstly, I had worked myself up to CFO and a top-level stage manager for the classes over several years, and woke up one day with a terrible realization: *Looking at the people at BHP who drive me nuts on a regular basis, almost every one of them is a Scientologist. Looking at the people I rely on in my life to provide some sanity, none of them is a Scientologist.* That was an interesting "cognition," to use the word favored inside the church. Your average Scientologist seemed fully as capable as anyone of being mad as a hatter, only they had this very specific and odd nomenclature for describing their common-as-dirt neurosis and other human failings. But having this "tech" gave them an air of superiority, as if having cool vocabulary about it all kept them above the common folk, the unenlightened, it absolved them of the inconvenient fact that they were in fact no better than anyone, as in *anyone*. The game seemed not to be about becoming a better person, or behaving more sanely, but rather a game of who could use this so-called pursuit of betterment, and its strange nomenclature, in a way that best advanced their position, their *feeling* of superiority.

Secondly, there was a significant and palpable culture shift in Scientology. I correlate it with the rise of Tom Cruise as the leading celebrity spokesperson for the Church, and his weird steely-eyed intensity about it became the way everyone started acting. Later there would be a big event where he was awarded some prize for being such an advocate for Scientology—and I didn't go. (I had started not wanting to go.) I ran into a fellow BHP student the week afterward, and asked her if she went, and what she got out of it. She answered, maniacally (of course): "What I got? I got that you need to get on the fucking train, people, and if you're not on the train, get the fuck off of it!" I was startled by her manner, and the message. I even remember thinking to myself, "I'm gonna get off your fucking train because I don't like you or your attitude about it."

The church began to interfere with the BHP in ways I found completely inappropriate. There was suddenly a problem with a chapter in Milton's *Acting Class* book called "How The Artist Does Under Attack and Suppression," where he basically gave his own take on what PTS information was, how it affected actors, and how he felt that learning about it, spotting it, and handling it, could be of benefit. But now from on high, it was deemed this chapter was somehow an alteration of what Hubbard intended, and you're not allowed to alter it, you're not allowed to talk about it, or write about it. All you could "ethically" do was to hand out little fucking pamphlets that were written and approved by the Church, and send people to the local organization for handling. Milton dutifully removed the chapter from his book.

There was an insane spike in the writing of "Knowledge Reports" on Milton and the BHP. A Knowledge Report was supposed to be a neutral, sane and evolved way of reporting any non-optimum situation, the idea being that if there was any parishioner or staff member who started collecting too many KRs, then the higher-ups would know perhaps there was a problem there, and they could use their infinite wisdom, kindness and humanity, and Hubbard's "tech," to handle the situation. But of course, the KR just became a petty, bitchy way of attacking Milton and the BHP for anything that pissed people off. One guy wrote a KR on us because he agreed to have a 6am rehearsal with a classmate for a scene, and that made him feel tired later on during his course at Celebrity Centre. This was the BHP's fault for our expecting actors to rehearse. Or, if one of our actors participated in some talent showcase that had sexual material in it, we'd get a KR that this student was engaged in unethical sexual activity for which we were responsible. Scientologists can be extremely puritanical about sex, although they're utterly hypocritical—celebrities by and large could get a pass, engage in pretty much any real-world behavior, make movies on any topic. Tom Cruise was shooting *Eyes Wide Shut* at the same time we were getting KRs about "unethical" scenes that had sexual content in class. (And, if any of them had actually read a more objective biography of Hubbard, perhaps they'd know something about his own questionable treatment of women.)

There were two young students whose mother had been "declared" suppressive by the church because she had left the church and liked to stand outside their buildings with placards and such. They asked that these students be dismissed from the BHP because they refused to "disconnect" from their own mother, and if we didn't comply, the church would ensure all Scientologists in good standing at the school "disconnect" from us. That was the straw that broke this particular camel's back—I was done. I stopped returning phone calls, stopped going, stopped it all. I wasn't ornery about it, but I just could no longer invest time and energy in any organization that promoted this crazy behavior, or held the point of view that motivated it. It sickened me. That ended my seven years of being involved directly. I returned happily to being a Smug Cynical New Englander through and through.

Phase Four: Milton under attack

In the late 1990s, the Scientology zeitgeist at the BHP reached its peak. Milton had released *Dreams Into Action* and appeared on the Oprah Winfrey show. He directed Jenna Elfman in a series of one-acts he wrote, and she had just won the Golden Globe Award for her work on *Dharma & Greg*. Jeffrey Tambor was teaching regularly, and was hot in *The Garry Shandling Show*, Anne Archer and Giovanni Ribisi were doing big movies, and Catherine Bell was starring in *JAG*. Jason Beghe, another successful actor and longtime BHP student, was brought into the church and pursued it avidly for a number of years. At some point even the temperamental BHP teacher, Teresa, was brought into the fold, and with the size of her personality, she became an intense cheerleader for the cause. With that number of celebrities going full rah-rah on the BHP, the classes were literally overflowing with students, and since many of our cheerleaders were Scientologists, the traffic between our students and Celebrity Centre was high. By high, I mean about 10-15%. That was the peak, and that included hardcore Scientologists all the way to people who dabbled with a quick course or two.

When the culture started to shift in 2000 to a kind of maniacal pursuit of Scientology's version of ethical purity, with Tom Cruise providing the leadership on *maniacal*, the era of Milton as an "opinion leader" in the church started to wane. Milton, who for decades had taken a fair amount of shit in the broader Los Angeles showbiz community for being a Scientologist, and for supposedly proselytizing for the church via the BHP, was suddenly taking heavy incoming fire—but now it was from the Scientology community for not being Scientological *enough*! He wouldn't go to the big church events. He didn't cheerlead for David Miscavige, the controversial head of the church. He was "stuck on the Bridge"— meaning he wasn't doing the necessary work to climb the delineated steps of enlightenment that Hubbard had called the Bridge to Total Freedom.

And, being an unmarried, red-blooded, heterosexual Greek man of a certain generation, Milton indulged in his share of womanizing, including with students at the BHP. He was a certified lady-killer, and I remember one of his old friends telling me he admired Milton as a young man for "fucking everything that moved." I personally observed plenty of female students flirting with him, and as the guy who handled his mail for many years, I personally read letters from said students to Milton, describing fantasies and egging him on—one even using the name of his book, *Dreams Into Action*, as a call to pay her some attention. I did not personally observe what Milton did about all of that, but I know there were plenty of interactions.

At that time, I didn't have many details. It was more that everyone knew Milton was a player, and it all fell under the general umbrella of "womanizing." I never had a big puritanical issue on Milton fucking around *per se*—I mean, an older charismatic man, a brilliant teacher and director, surrounded by beautiful young adult women, actresses no less, in constant proximity, with personal communication and the like? Eeeeeek! *I'm shocked, SHOCKED!* This shit has been happening for eons.

Where he really got in trouble was with his predilection for making passes at younger women who had shown no interest in him, no interest in a pass (many were happily married), and who were dismayed at the very least by his behavior. Many of these young women were themselves Scientologists, for whom Milton held a dual esteemed role as their teacher and as an "opinion leader"/Church veteran. The sordid details of how these passes would play out only hit me much later, usually via direct conversations with some of the women involved. I have seen significant tears flood their eyes, years later, as they told me separate but similar stories, which were clearly indicative of straight up, no-way-around-it sexual harassment and borderline predatory behavior, with Milton using his stature as a teacher and often a 40+ year age gap to manipulate 20-something-year-old women into bed. Older women seemed to handle it better; there was one I spoke with years later, who was 35 when Milton made his move, and her take went something like this: *Yeah, of course Milton made a pass at me, and you know what? I'm not sure I want to be in a world where charismatic Greek men don't make passes. If you're an adult, you handle the situation with some charm and some certainty about it—about what you're going to do or not going to do. I just looked him in the eye, real friendly and warm, and said, "Milton, you know this isn't going anywhere." He laughed, and that was that, and we were always fine. He'd make a remark here and there, and I'd parry it off.* It's more comfortable for me to align with this point of view, and infinitely less so to reconcile the teaching talents and many positive influences of my mentor with the hair-raising stories told to me by at least half a dozen younger women, who I'm sure are only representative of a greater number.

When his adventures in this area went awry, there could sometimes be a wave of gossip and recrimination in the class about it. He stopped teaching his treasured daytime Advanced class because of a pass-gone-wrong situation that blew up in his face. How many students left because of this activity? Unknown. How many potential students did he lose, because of this reputation? Unknowable. I asked him that question once, to get him to look at the larger implications of his behavior, but Milton was unrepentant. He greatly admired his mentor Elia Kazan, who did his own share of womanizing, and Milton told me he felt this was part of life, part of life in the business—that the chemistry, flirtation and sex was part of why a lot of people loved show business, and he was quite unapologetically part of that tradition. He would insist it never affected his teaching, saying in his characteristic vernacular, "No pussy will ever change the way I teach," but based on what I would come to hear after his death, several women would probably call that a significant lie. In any case, Milton seemed blind to how his reputation in these matters affected the bottom line that was so crucial to us, especially post-Reed Slatkin.

Within Scientology, there is a culture of "flowing power to power," which translates loosely into, "Protect people in power, because the good they do from that position outweighs the bad," or further: "Suck up to celebrities, indulge their behavior—they are the front people for this 'Church.'" During the period when Milton enjoyed his longtime status as an opinion leader, he was afforded significant "ethics protection," and a young woman's complaints about his behavior would likely hit a buzz saw of "What did *you* do to pull Milton's attention in?"—it was always put on the young woman for having been irresponsible. But as the zeitgeist moved away from Milton, a bigger celebrity was about to take him down.

It was 2004, and we had decided to start a BHP newsletter that we hoped to put out every quarter, with various items of school news, plus an interview with one of our students who had done well in the industry. The introductory issue was going to have an interview with Jenna Elfman, who was at that time the most visible celebrity associated with Milton and the BHP. The phone rang at my apartment, and it was Bodhi Elfman, Jenna's husband.

"Allen, it's Bodhi."

"Hi, Bodhi."

"Listen, Jenna and I are disconnecting from Milton and the BHP."

"Uh…What?"

"And we're telling you you can't print that interview with Jenna, as she no longer supports the BHP."

"Uh…Okay…"

"Did you print the newsletter?"

"No, it hasn't even…No, we're not even done with it."

"Because she can't be in it."

"Yeah, I'm getting that."

"And we're going to be telling everyone we know that we are disconnecting, and encouraging them to do the same thing."

"Bodhi, listen, what the hell is—"

"Because Milton is a fucking piece of shit, okay? You can tell him that for me. Is he there?"

"What?"

"IS HE THERE? ARE YOU THERE WITH MILTON? IS HE LISTENING?" Bodhi was screaming at me over the phone.

"Bodhi, you called me at my apartment. Milton is not here with me at my apartment. Milton doesn't come to my apartment."

"BECAUSE YOU CAN TELL HIM FOR ME I THINK HE'S A PIECE OF SHIT."

"Milton isn't here, Bodhi, you'll have to call and tell him yourself."

And so it began—the shot heard 'round Los Angeles. If Reed Slatkin had induced a financial shitstorm that we were still fighting to address, then Jenna Elfman led the "disconnection" shitstorm that would gravely affect the life of the BHP and Milton personally. In the ever-flowing stream of acrimonious gossip about Milton's advances toward Scientologist actresses, I believe one of the more unpleasant of those interactions had been reported to Jenna in this time frame, and Jenna snapped, she had had enough. She was going to lead a crusade to disconnect from

Milton, pending his "ethics change," which could only occur through intensive Scientology auditing. The disconnection bomb went off on Milton's "out-ethics."

Over the next four years, I'd be witness to some insane shit. His behavior had no doubt earned a lot of it, but for me at that time, I found the attacks being leveled on him in response to be completely over the top. Students started taking off. Teachers started taking off. Many of these departures were accompanied by Knowledge Reports the size of small novels, laboring page after page to detail his "out-ethics," some of it accurate, some of it completely made-up, much of it in my opinion hysterical and totally overblown. It wasn't just about womanizing and flirtation, it could be the most piss-ant picayune crap. Sample: "Last night in class at the BHP MainStage at 254 S. Robertson Blvd in Beverly Hills, CA, at 8:45pm, in a critique of a scene performed by So-and-So and Whosis, I observed Milton Katselas allude to a point of human behavior that is described by L. Ron Hubbard as 3.5 on the Tone Scale. Milton did not acknowledge Hubbard as the source of this information, and should be handled on this outpoint." No, really. *No, really.* Picture a few more addressing his salty vocabulary. Or his attendance policy in class—he was hostile to student absences for coursework at Celebrity Centre! He quoted Constantin Stanislavsky in his book! (Hubbard once said Stanislavsky was full of shit, and so no good Scientologist could any longer quote him, you see...) It was the fact that he didn't acknowledge L. Ron Hubbard in *Dreams Into Action!* (Enter Stage Left: an eye-rolling project to take thousands of copies of the book that we had purchased from the defunct publisher, and stamp an acknowledgment to Hubbard on one of the blank introductory pages, followed years later by my own project, entering Stage Right, to rip every one of those pages out...) He was engaged in illegal car registration activity! (His Nevada-registered cars were hence all re-registered in California.) Every detail of the way he taught or led his life was now filtered through some jihadist, puritanical prism, and found wanting, found desperately in need of intervention and correction through the miracle of Scientology processing!

I had disengaged from Scientology for a good while by then, but this period of nonstop attacks on Milton sent me reeling. I would spend hours and hours responding to the KRs on Milton's behalf, drafting documents worthy of an appellate court brief combined with as vicious an assault as I could manage on the intellectual capabilities of the originator. One time when I was shooting a film at the Golden Era Productions studio outside Los Angeles, I was pulled aside by some staff person and grilled about the accusations of Milton's various misbehaviors. At Milton's request, I attended a meeting between him and three of his own BHP staff, moderated by a senior Church executive (who would go on to quit the joint and become a noted critic), who were teamed up on this mission to fix his ethics. There was a lot of screaming, all about how he had betrayed their loyalty to him through his actions, about how he was generally an abusive piece of shit, and why couldn't he see they were out for his best interests in trying to get him to change? And in one way I suppose they were doing this out of some concern for the guy, but in another, frankly more prominent way, they were coming off like puritanical screaming maniacs intent on destroying him as much as helping him. This was no loving intervention. Punishment, anger and revenge were in the air, and Milton's energy in the meeting was clearly that of someone defeated and depressed. It was not an energy that suited him, but I know there are many who would probably delight in his finally catching some harsh medicine. For me, though, leaving the meeting afterwards with Milton, I was shaking and furious at their behavior, and Milton actually had to talk me down in the parking lot, because I was so lit by it.

One of his significant antagonists became Grant Cardone, then-boyfriend-and-eventual-husband of Elena Lyons, another beautiful young Scientologist student, with whom Milton had a dalliance of some sort. Cardone is a mucky-muck within the church, a big money guy, a big time donor and renowned Miscavige ass-kisser, and he went nuclear on Milton over the thing with Elena (joining a long line of apoplectic boyfriends and husbands). He wrote a KR that he sent by email, publicly, to 500 people, detailing what he understood to be all of Milton's unethical actions, in salacious detail, and how Milton should be considered in a condition of "Treason" with his fellow Scientologists, all of whom, of course, are pure, ethical, wonderful human beings by definition. The email began:

"It has come to my attention that Milton Katselas continues to go unhandled and it is my intention to stop him finally! The fact that so many of you have left his school and written KR's has not ultimately handled this being, as he continues to go unhandled and will continue to wreak havoc and spread his aberration until his ethics are put in."

You can see in that little intro all the arrogance and presumption that is a consistent trait in the Scientology community. *It has "come to your attention," Grant? Who the fuck are you to have attention worthy of coming to?* He also wrote a letter to Milton, using Milton's frequent refrain, clearly relayed to him by Elena, that the fully aware artist in Los Angeles should "watch out for snipers on the roof." Cardone told Milton in no uncertain terms that he, Grant, was now that sniper, and he was intent on taking down Milton and the BHP.

By 2007, there were barely a few Scientologists left at the school, either on staff or amongst the students. I'm sure many of those who left ended up surprised, perhaps even disappointed, that the roof didn't cave in from their departure, much less that the BHP still thrives all these years later without them. I'm sure all those Scientologists who went after Milton would object to my attitude about it, doth protesting too much their noble, sainted intentions, and saying they were only going after his improvement as a person, that they really cared, and how they were just going to the mat for his sake, in some grotesquely over-the-top version of the "tough love" Milton advocated for as a teacher. I witnessed all this crap, I dealt with all the KRs, I took part in countless meetings, and I only became more and more enraged by it all, and determined to stand by Milton, not because I agreed with everything he said or did, but simply because the guy needed a friend. He needed an ally, someone who wasn't going abandon him in a fit of recrimination, throw rocks from a pristine Scientology Glass House, or judge him with the contempt that was now coming his way from so many quarters.

Phase Five: Now That I Think About it, Go Fuck Yourselves

Between Hurricane Ponzi—largely involving so-called Scientologists, who are supposed to be so great at detecting suppressive people, who are supposed to be a few cuts above normal humanity in terms of *perception* (then how the hell did you all get taken so easily by this sleazy and obvious crook Slatkin?)—and the subsequent Scientology Ethics Jihad against him, by the time Milton died, I could barely stomach Scientology as an organization or the arrogant, puritanical sanctimony demonstrated by so many of its adherents. While Milton was alive, I expressed my point of view on it all privately to friends, and even to Milton himself, without becoming very outspoken in general. Milton considered himself "in" until the end. This was heavily based on his being personal friends with Hubbard—he had a photo behind his desk of the two of them laughing together on Hubbard's ship in the early 70s, and would lament to me that "If Ron were still here, none of this would be happening." I didn't feel there was much point in making any further trouble for him by being outspoken. I worked for him, and as much as I could, tried to protect his interests without antagonizing him or further fraying his tenuous relationship with the church. I dutifully handled his communications, responded on his behalf to the Krazy Reports (as I had quietly renamed them), took whatever meetings were asked of me by church staff, and just lived day-by-day. There was plenty going on that had nothing to do with these fucking people, and I took greater and greater solace in those goings on—namely the still first-rate acting classes that he and I oversaw, classes we even taught together over the last 18 months of his life.

But in 2009, post-Milton, as I became acclimated to the idea that I owned the school and could determine its future as I saw fit, there was a flood of new information coming out about Scientology, through books and blogs written by former church staff members, some of whom I knew personally. I couldn't help devouring this material—some nights I'd be up until 3-4am reading in wide-eyed amazement. My old friend and classmate, Jason Beghe, torched the path with a series of YouTube interviews about his experience, told with a glorious mix of humor, vitriol, and his talent for impersonation. Marc Headley's book *Blown For Good* came out, describing abhorrent activities and punishments being doled out on the base east of Los Angeles, during projects where I had been there at the same time working as an actor. *I can't believe that as I slept comfortably in the guest quarters there, the production crew I had been joking around with all day were doing laps in the mud in the middle of the night…* In 2011, a former high-ranking executive named Marty Rathbun, whose incendiary blog I read religiously, wrote an entry about Grant Cardone and Milton. Marty said that several years back, he had been charged with getting up to speed on Milton, because Miscavige was determined to bring Milton to heel, get him more closely allied with the Miscavige regime. (Rathbun was eventually called off that matter to handle something else, before blowing the joint totally.) But Rathbun told the story of Cardone's 2007 emailed KR on Milton and how this was, in his view, an act of serving Milton's head on a platter to curry favor with Miscavige. Tony Ortega, then a writer with the *Village Voice*, covered this blog post in his own story, and I contacted Tony to give him my take on it, since I had been at ground zero with Milton for all of that. Lawrence Wright, the Pulitzer-winning author, also wrote a long *New Yorker* article on Paul Haggis, which turned into the book *Going Clear*, and then a documentary as well. Wright came to Los Angeles to do research, and interviewed me about the Ethics Jihad started by Jenna Elfman. My interview is in the book, along with a letter I had written to Jenna at the time, which I gave to Wright with permission to reprint.

Participating in these interviews earned me my own "suppressive person declare," which I remember hearing about through a few friends who started disappearing from Facebook. At that time I had a third party plug-in for my browser that told you when you were unfriended, and I'd be a jerk to the Scientologists and write them and say, "Something I said?" One of the cooler ones, who had been on staff back in the day on the cinema crew, wrote back to say she had seen the order on me. Per Hubbard's sainted and inviolable policy, you're supposed to be notified in writing if you're declared, but it was also common knowledge that they had stopped abiding by the notification policy. So I called Susan Watson over at Celebrity Centre, who at various times over the years had been either high level VP or President, and with whom I had a good relationship.

"Hey, Susan, it's Allen over at the BHP."

"Hi, Allen! So great to hear from you! How are you guys!" Perky and as nice as she could be.

"We're good, good, thanks."

"What can I do for you?"

"Well, this might seem an odd question—your tone even with me now makes me wonder about it. But here goes: have I been declared a suppressive person?"

"My God, no. That's completely ridiculous. Where did you hear that?"

"Well, I'm being disconnected from at a relatively furious rate on Facebook, and in real life, and a couple of them have said they have it on good word that I've been declared."

Pause.

"Well I don't know anything about that, Allen. It sounds…I don't know anything about that."

"Would you mind looking it up, and just, you know, if it's true, could you make a last phone call to me to verify it? Because I haven't gotten any notification, and I believe I'm supposed to have—if it's true."

"Of course you are supposed to get a notification."

"So you can look it up?"

"Of course, Allen. I'll do it right now, and call you back immediately."

I never heard from Susan again. I wear it as a badge of honor. The idea that this so-called church deems itself fit to "declare" anybody anything—either good or bad—is a laugh. But it didn't end there. Based on my now being officially a "suppressive person," they went to my third Los Angeles piano teacher, a Scientologist and lovely guy in his 80s named Mario Feninger. They told him he could no longer be in communication with me. It so happens that Mario had recently asked for my assistance, as he was in a tough way financially, and I had gladly responded, and was in the middle of helping sort out his overdue bills and lining up a monthly check I was going to send to help him out. I received an envelope from him in the mail, with my undeposited checks, and a card on which he wrote, "I can no longer communicate with you. Please come back." I called him—he wouldn't answer. I used someone else's cell phone, and then he picked up. He told me he had no intention of disconnecting from me, but that the ethics staff at the "Advanced Organization" insisted he do it, and for him it was simply the only move he could make—his entire circle of acquaintances were Scientologists, and he couldn't sacrifice that. "I'm too old for a fight," he said. I understood it. He had been in at least 50 years by that time, not in the greatest of health, and it was the only choice he could make.

But my seething latent anger at what was done to Milton was ignited by the manipulation of Mario. I put it up on Facebook, and it launched a 100+ comment chain, wherein the few Scientologists I knew who hadn't disconnected from me chimed in to whitewash the entire policy of disconnection, pretending it didn't exist, that it wasn't coerced, that Mario must have made his own decision based on my dastardly deeds. One of them hilariously commented to deny that disconnection policy existed at all, and then promptly disconnected from me later the same day. Another guy implied clearly that I shouldn't talk about it, because the area of disconnection was upsetting to people both inside and out. *Oh yeah?* Well, as I drove around over the next week, the idea came to me: *I'm gonna talk about it. I'm gonna talk about it a lot. This is good material for a play, and I'll call it "Disconnection."* I had by that time written two plays that had been produced, and the most recent, *Years to the Day*, had been nominated for a bunch of awards, and would end up being done in a dozen cities in America and Europe. I started writing the story, and over the next two years it absolutely kicked my ass, as to write a play about Scientology—well, you could spend ten hours on stage trying to get it all in. But over many, many drafts, and many readings, I finally honed in the characters and the story, and we opened in Los Angeles in January 2015, on the MainStage of the BHP headquarters on Robertson Blvd. To my knowledge, it is the first serious play written about this topic. We played for 15 weeks over two separate runs in 2015, to largely sold-out audiences and a lot of nice ink. And so ended a very long, weird trip for me, and for the BHP as well. People asked me why I didn't want to do *Disconnection* at the Skylight Theatre, which has a larger space. I wanted it on the BHP Mainstage because I wanted to send a message: *This is what the BHP is now. We use Milton's technique to teach Acting, Attitude and Administration to professional actors and those who aspire to become one themselves. We don't do anything else. This is where we stand. This isn't your father's Oldsmobile. Scientology can go fuck itself.*

CHAPTER 21

The Call To Teach

Ring-ring, riiiiinnnng. Ring-ring, riiiiinnnng.

A late afternoon phone call from Milton. My adrenaline surged. Something's gone wrong, he's unhappy, he didn't get the stats, the hedge wasn't trimmed properly, MG needs something fixed at her house, why does he only "make $1,000 a month" as a famous teacher, someone fucked up and it's actually my fault…No point in ignoring the call. He'll just call again. And again and again. Then he'll call someone at the office and they'll knock on my apartment door on the second floor of headquarters.

"Hello?"

"Yeaaahhhh."

"Hi, Milton."

"What are you doing tonight?"

"Tonight? I, uh…"

"Good. Get over to the Skylight and teach that class.—is out of town." When a teacher was out, generally the call would go out to one of the other teachers to substitute that night, and that process rarely intersected with me in any way.

"You want me to…Huh?"

"Teach. Teach the class. You know we hold acting classes here, right?"

"Right."

"We're famous for it. Acting classes."

"Right."

"So what's the problem?"

"I just…"

"You just what?"

"I mean, I've never taught a class before."

"So?"

"So, I think the students will be expecting…"

"They'll be expecting someone to come in and teach. Which is what you're going to do."

"Okay."

"Okay. Is that a 'Beverly Hills Playhouse okay'?"

"No."

"You heard of a book I wrote—*Acting Class?*"

"I've heard of it, yes." We had recently finished the first of two full re-writes of that book.

"How long you been studying in these classes?"

"Eleven years."

"Eleven years. Go teach the fucking class. Okay?"

"Sure."

"You still sound dubious."

"I just think they'll want someone older."

Detonation. He'd had enough. *"I was teaching when I was twenty-five fucking years old. Forget what they want. What they want is someone who, at that moment, knows a little more than they do about acting. First job: Wake them the fuck up."*

"Got it. I'll go teach the class."

"Good. Let me know how it goes." *Click.*

I reported to the same little alley-way I entered back in November of 1990, muttering to myself with the same doubts about teaching as I did all those years ago about the idea of taking a class in the first place. A couple of Milton's entourage were there to check me out and report back to him. Awesome. The stage managers called the class into session and I entered nervously, sat in the chair, and said, "Well, look. Either this is a big mistake, in which case it will only last four hours, or you're here for the start of something interesting."

It ended up being the latter. I became the go-to Orientation level substitute for years, and some of those students are friends to this day. During NBA basketball season, I got a lot of experience, because Milton would call Rick Podell, who was supposed to be teaching, and order him over to Milton's house to watch basketball instead. I would get the call to teach in his place. After a while, I would also get the call to sub teach Intermediate level classes, where I really started hitting my stride—the actors there were further along in their training and could really respond to the more challenging directorial feedback I started giving. In 2005, one of the Intermediate level classes had a bit of a meltdown, where the student population plummeted, and I was sent over to figure out what was going on. The vibe was definitely off. The teacher of standing had left as part of the Disconnection Jihad, and the guy who had taken over for her just didn't engender the right enthusiasm. It was strange—I listened to his critiques, and they weren't bad, he was on point with the corrections, but it was just somehow hard to grab onto, slightly out of focus, slightly dull. He was also somewhat lax about the basic class guidelines —showing up on time and paying attention and acting like a pro.

I reported back to Milton my thoughts, and recommended that I simply take the class over. I felt ready, I must have subbed 50 classes by then, and I told him the proof would be easy to see: if the class numbers built back up in a few months, then let me keep the class, and if they continued to fall, take it away from me. I brought in Art Cohan to be my co-teacher, and we traded off weeks for the next two years or so, and built one of the greatest Intermediate class groups we'd ever seen. The numbers shot back up, and the camaraderie and level of work in that class is something we're still proud of all these years later. They produced a half dozen really high-level showcases, and many from that era went on to become stalwart contributing members of the Advanced level. One student actress and director from that class went on to join the teaching staff herself.

Early 2007. Six years after the first call to teach.

Ring-ring, riiiiinnnng. Ring-ring, riiiiiinnng. My landline was still programmed for this identification of Milton's call.

"Hello?"

"Yeaaahhhh."

"Hi, Milton."

"What are you doing tonight?"

"Tonight? I, uh…"

"Good. I'm supposed to teach tonight but I'm not feeling up for it. I want you to do it."

"Oh."

"What's the problem?"

"I, uh…That's the Advanced level."

"So?"

"So I'm not sure—shouldn't we send in someone older?"

"Older than who, man?"

"Older than me."

"Who is this older person?"

"Well, maybe T."

"No. I don't want T."

"Or R."

"I don't want R. Let me ask you something: Who knows the most about my teaching around this joint?"

"That would be you."

"Not me, man. I don't mean that. You don't have to do that. Other than me."

"Well…So-and-so has been here the longest."

"Nice try. The guy who knows the most? I'm talking to him."

"Oh."

"Edited my books. Ran my classes. Runs the business. Directs plays. Teaches for me. How long you been teaching for me?"

"Six years, I think?"

"So shut the fuck up and go teach my class." *Click.*

He and I split the "Milton" teaching nights for the next 18 months until he died, and I haven't stopped teaching those classes since then.

CHAPTER 22

The Piano Recital

Early December, 1994. A weekend morning, about 8am. I'm alone at the Skylight Theatre, and the transport company has just completed an unusual Sunday delivery of a nine-foot Steinway Model D concert grand piano that I have rented to perform what has become my annual winter recital. I have to hang out for a while, however, as the piano tuner isn't set to arrive until 10am. I start playing some of the program, enjoying every note I get to play on this fabulous instrument. These nine-foot grands are something else.

A beam of sunlight crosses the stage, as someone enters the rear door. Huh?

Milton pokes his head in. "What's going on, man?"

"Oh, hi, Milton. I'm just…They just delivered the piano for the recital tonight."

"Oh, yeah?"

"And now I'm waiting for the tuner."

"When's he coming?"

"Ten."

"I see." He ambles over to the seating area, sits down in the second row. "So, play me some of it."

"The recital?"

"No. Chopsticks. Of course, 'the recital.' What's the first piece?"

"Rachmaninoff's Elegie."

"Okay, let's have at it."

I play the piece for him. It's the first time I've performed the piece, but I will go on to record it twice, in 1997 and 2008, and it will even play a part in the opening of my play *Disconnection*, 21 years later in 2015. Milton doesn't respond for a few seconds. It's still relatively early on in our relationship, but I've become used to these pauses, and I've learned enough not to seek to fill them with anything. Eventually: "It's good, man."

"Thanks."

"You like this guy, Rachmaninoff."

"Yeah."

"Schmaltzy."

"Romantic."

"It's schmaltzy. What's it about, this piece?"

"Well, *Elegie* means 'a lament for the dead.'"

"Starting things off with a bang, huh? Lightening everyone's mood?"

"I guess."

"Well, listen, you know about how to play the piano, but I know about music. So don't overdo it. Don't schmaltz on top of schmaltz, you know what I mean? What's that part, that big part, middle of the piece…?" I play the climactic section. "Yeah, that. Just…don't give it all away. Don't give them everything. Particularly at the beginning of your recital. You gotta give us room to feel something, too, right?"

"Sure."

He goes quiet again, looking at the stage. "Is that where you're gonna put the piano?"

"Uh huh."

"Nah. Too close." Milton rises and walks toward me. "Feng shui. Ever heard of it? Placement of objects. Very important." He looks up, down, sideways, assessing the space and the piano's proper position in it. "This thing moves, right?"

The next ten minutes is spent with my moving the piano six inches upstage, then another six inches, and another six. Milton stood in seating section, ordering me to move it another notch upstage, until finally he was satisfied. I took a mark off the rear door and the beams across the ceiling, to remember where it was for later that night, and, as it turned out, for umpteen winter recitals to follow in this space. Milton started for the door, and it looked as if our little improvised session was over.

"You're gonna clear all that shit off the back wall, right?"

The various set pieces used by the classes—wood boxes of various sizes, a couple of tables, a bed frame, chairs, a mattress, door units —they were all stored along the back wall of the theatre. I hadn't given them a thought before. For my first three December recitals, I would just set up the piano in front, turn on some lights and play for people. Very casual. The first year, for Mancini's class, I was so broke I rented a baby grand piano with as many broken keys as the one I first rented at Al's insistence for my apartment. Renting a Steinway 9-footer was my being extravagant, and I hadn't thought of anything else.

"Uh, well usually I just set up the piano and play."

Milton stopped a foot from the side door. "No, man. No way." His attention returned to the stage area. "What's with all these scratch marks on the floor?"

"That's from the stair unit they built for *Dylan*." That year, my recital, which traditionally occurred the second weekend of December, had coincided with a successful, extended run of the play *Dylan*, mounted by the student theatre company of that moment. It had been extended straight through my weekend, but I had enough pull with Milton that I was given the Sunday night for my recital, and the show would be dark that night. This necessitated the special Sunday delivery of the piano that I had arranged. However, the designers for the show had built a huge, heavy stair unit on wheels, and over the course of the run, it had carved scratches and grooves into the stage floor. That unit was the largest single object along the back wall that Milton clearly was indicating as too noisy, visually, for my recital. "They built it here in the space, so you can't roll it out the freight entrance or anything."

"Jesus." Silence. Then: "Get Michael Woody on the phone."

Michael was Milton's assistant. I went into the small office and called him, and Milton spoke with him in hushed tones for a few minutes. Within an hour, Milton dismissed me—there would be people at the theatre to let the tuner in. He asked what I usually did on my performance days, and I think I told him I usually go the movies and generally take it easy, and I'd report back in to the theatre at 6pm. "So go to the movies, take it easy. See you at 6pm."

Nine hours later, 6pm rolled around, and as I approached the rear entrance, I noticed Milton's car, parked where it had been in the morning when I left. I walked into the theatre. Here's what I found: Fifteen people, working. The entire stage was practically empty, but for the Steinway piano, which looked majestic against the clean, exposed red brick of the now-unobstructed back wall of the theatre. The set pieces were all gone. Milton had had the stadium seating unbolted from the floor and moved aside so that the huge rolling stairway for *Dylan* could be maneuvered out the freight entrance into the courtyard, and then the seating was re-bolted to the floor. Everything else had been moved offstage into every available nook and cranny. The floor had been sanded, painted a new coat of black, and polished. The lighting designer for *Dylan* had been rousted from his bed in some outlying Los Angeles hamlet, and brought in to the city, to the Skylight Theatre, to unpatch the whole show, rehang and refocus the stage lights specifically for the Steinway, complete with special light directly above the keyboard to eliminate shadows. A truck had been rented and driven to a nursery, the owner of which had been rousted from his bed, bribed to open his joint so that four trees could be rented. Those trees were now sitting on the stage in a semi-circle around the piano, the potted base of each tree was being painted to match the new floors, and each was lit by its own specially focused instrument above. Milton was shouting orders regarding the lighting cue for the recital, to the no-doubt exhausted and exasperated designer in the booth.

I stood there, slack-jawed, mute, dumbfounded. Milton finally noticed me, raised both his arms up in an exaggerated theatrical pose, and bellowed, "Whaddaya think?!" I couldn't process it. All the work ceased, and the fifteen people, a mixture of staff and student volunteers who had been called that morning to help out, stood quietly, watching my response. I moved haltingly, barely conscious, onto the stage, staring around me, still unbelieving. There was a feeling, deep within, of…*Has my recital been cancelled and replaced by that of a "real" pianist?* "Okay," said Milton, as if everything was normal, "So how do you enter when you come in to play?" I pointed upstage left. "Good, okay, come on in and let's check the lighting." I walked like a zombie from the upstage left entrance to just downstage of the piano. "Bow, man. I want to see the whole thing. Yeah. That's not a good bow. That's a dead man's bow. Can you do it again, like a concert pianist? Better. But stand over there. No, over *there*. Bow again. Lighten the fuck up. Now sit at the piano. Right. Play a few bars of the opening…" I played 20-30 seconds of the opening, and Milton cut me off. "Okay! Good. Alright, then. Have a good show." Without further ado he moved to the exit and out the door.

Milton wasn't a lingerer, and so by the time I'd managed to fire up my stunned neural pathways to chase him out the door, he was in his car pulling out of his space already. I knocked on the driver's window, and he powered it down.

"I don't know what to say, Milton. 'Thank you' seems just completely insufficient. This is…. I don't know…I, uh…"

"You have to demand it for yourself." He powered the window back up, and drove off.

———————————————————

Mid-July, 2012. A weekday evening, about 6:30pm. I am sitting in the courtyard of BHP headquarters on Robertson Blvd. I'm eating some takeout pasta, and I'm exhausted, drained, numb. My mind has somehow gone to thinking vividly of that piano recital all those years ago—eighteen? *Eighteen years.* Milton spent about ten hours of a December Sunday, and probably a few thousand dollars in labor, rentals and bribes, all to teach a 26-year-old me something about being an artist, about being what he called an "artistic killer," someone who gets it done, who kills it, who doesn't fuck around with standards for himself or for others, who takes himself seriously. He spent ten hours and a few thousand to earn in full the seven words he said to me as he drove off. That's some teaching, and to this day one of the nicest things anyone has ever done for me. I wondered if that single gesture wasn't part of how I managed to stay with him for so long.

The actors for the performance that night are walking by to check in, and they are hugging me, congratulating me, "You did it!" The news was out. I had closed escrow that afternoon on my purchase of that very building, and by so doing ensured that the BHP and its headquarters would be united and functioning for years to come. Milton, true to form, had massively screwed up his estate plan, selecting language that placed various parties at war and put at risk the BHP as a business, and its ability to remain as tenant of the headquarters building. My purchase was the final act after what had been four years of unceasing struggle, stress, court proceedings, betrayals, subterfuge, watching old friendships blown to pieces while new ones gathered and solidified in the chaos. MG and I had gone from old friends to opposing litigants in the madness. Yet now it was done. The BHP as a business had been saved in 2010, and now the building purchased in 2012. Back in 2009, a year after Milton died, I had seriously questioned whether either would survive.

During the period of securing this purchase, I had undertaken to direct a production of *The Heidi Chronicles* with a cast of a dozen students, consisting of some of my true favorites from that era. We were in the middle of our one-week run, the first in a series I was calling "Project X," a free-theatre concept, whereby we direct full productions using BHP actors, and give away ten performances for nothing—no money, no reviews, no glory, and we don't even tell the audience what the show is. We just invite them to "Project X" and try to wow them a bit, have a talk-back after each show about what they saw. Milton, back in the day, would spend three months or more to direct 15-20 minutes of a single scene. I figured for the investment of a few months, let's get the whole damned show up! After receiving news that afternoon that escrow had in fact closed, it was if a gigantic boulder had finally been lifted off my shoulders. I went home, took a shower, ran out to pick up some takeout pasta, and arrived back at the theatre…no.

No. Not *the* theatre.

"You have to demand it for yourself." The window on his old Mercedes 6.9 had powered back up, and Milton had driven off.

My theatre. *My* building. Twenty-two years since my first interview, since borrowing a couple hundred bucks from my brother to start class, mumbling to myself in an alley in Los Feliz, that metal door opening only just moments before I would have bolted away from the Skylight Theatre on a chilly November evening in 1990. I downed the rest of my pasta, and my energy returned. I said hello to my students, who were happy to be at the school, at the theatre, to be performing that night for another full house. We made it. We're gonna be here a while. Let's get to work.

PART II

Teaching: The Study And Pursuit of Acting

CHAPTER 23

The BHP Approach

If one is nervy enough to write a book that even partially concerns how-to-act, it might be good to have an essential philosophy at work, a specific technique for which you're advocating. I'm in a trickier position than that, both because this book is more than just how-to-act, and because clearly I was born and raised in an existing ecosystem at the BHP, founded by one of the great teachers in Milton Katselas. When he and I agreed that I would take over the school for him after he died, I promised I wasn't going to do anything radical to change his technique, nor the name of the school, I wasn't going to make it the Allen Barton School of Acting at the BHP. My natural bent (some friends argue it's actually to my detriment) is away from the grandiosity and sycophancy that surrounds acting teachers. I don't have a personal assistant. No one fetches me my lunch. It's not really important to me to have my name attached to a technique or a school, or to be called a "master teacher," as seems *de rigueur* for teachers to advertise themselves as being these days. I'd rather consider myself simply to be of assistance to those students who cross my path, for as long as that relationship is useful and rewarding to both parties. That's plenty for me, it's all I need.

So you have this guy Milton Katselas who was a renowned teacher, with a legendary Greek temperament, who evolved a technique, and a school, the BHP, for delivering it. Then you have this other guy, me, who grew up in that system, learning not just the technique but becoming expert in the very system that delivered it, intimately acquainted with both its message and its messengers, at least since 1990 when he showed up on the scene—and he ends up taking over for Milton years later. One technique, one school, two guys, two styles. So let's define our terms and see "where we're at," as the parlance goes.

What exactly is Milton's technique? It's laid out pretty clearly in his book *Acting Class*, but was factually delivered in an infinity of interpretations by umpteen teachers working on his behalf both before and since my arrival on the scene. Each of those teachers had their own take on Milton's technique, their own points of emphasis, their own points of departure, their own style of communicating. All of them probably felt quite sincerely that they were the best communicators of "pure Milton" teaching.

Factually, there have been many students at BHP over the years—a majority, even—who never saw Milton teach at all, much less with any frequency. Years after his death, Milton as a man exists almost exclusively in the personal memories of those who spent time with him, memories highly subjective and bent by gravitational waves of specific experiences, general nostalgia, romanticism for youthful times of study, resentment, ego, love, anger, you-name-it. Look at the stories I have told about Milton in this book. Who was he, even from the point of view of this single narrator? Many things! Generous. Insufferable. Cruel. Charming. Roguish. Irresponsible. Inspirational. So if the man himself was so all over the spectrum, if the *de facto* communication of his technique over the last 30 years has been, likewise, all over the spectrum, how are we to nail down exactly his technique of acting, and separate this technique from the manner in which it's communicated? Was Milton's technique, and that of the BHP, a matter of how he broke down a scene? Was it how he broke down the actor? Was it represented by his personal temperament? Was it really the format and expectation level of the class? What makes a BHP, anyway?

In his personal teaching style, Milton rarely mentioned his own technique, he almost never quoted his own acting book. What he would talk about, far more often, and with seemingly more pride, usually in group meetings with executives and other teachers, was what he called "the BHP Approach." The BHP Approach is more than just an acting technique. The BHP Approach includes Milton's three-pronged holistic attack on the subjects of Acting, Attitude and career Administration. The BHP Approach is the form the classes take: Master-class-format scene study. Four to six well-rehearsed scenes per class, 10-15 minutes per scene, each earning 30-45 minutes of critique. (Milton would often tell the story of his asking the iconic theatre director and critic Harold Clurman whether he thought a 5-minute critique or a 45-minute critique was better for actors, and Clurman had replied, "The 45-minute critique, because there's a better chance you'll say *something* that I can use.")

The BHP Approach includes the expectation level of the class—that actors treat the class the way they would treat a professional set: show up, be on time, have a good attitude, and bring their best every time out, no excuses. The BHP Approach is about having class executives, comprised of the students, who help their peers become a better group, who help young actors understand and deal with the dynamics of authority, lines of command, procedure and professional collaboration that make up any film, television or theatrical set. The BHP Approach encompasses Milton's directorial style, the way all the teachers use the issue of how to improve the scene in front of them as a launch point for additional discussions of professional attitude or career administration. These various aspects of the BHP Approach, working in concert, are as integral to the overall BHP technique as is any discussion of "Event," "Evaluation," and so on through Milton's checklist. The BHP Approach is a far broader set of guidelines, practices and traditions than is covered in either of Milton's two books, and it's that approach which I'm charged with protecting most of all, as I have observed it for 25+ years to be the sanest and most effective way to help actors move from aspiring to professional.

Over that quarter century, my own particular experiences as a student of Milton's students, then of Milton himself, then as his apprentice, then the guy overseeing the business, and then as a teacher and writer/director in my own right—all this has led quite inevitably to my particular evolution of the BHP Approach. This evolution is mostly a matter of style and emphasis.

First off, I prefer less drama at my drama school. I grew up with a lot of yelling and screaming, then I spent 18 years at the BHP under Milton with a lot of yelling and screaming. I'm kind of done with yelling and screaming. Anger has a role to play in teaching, and I'm not shy about going there, *now and again. Here and there. Not so often, frankly.* Milton himself said the environment he wanted was "safe, but challenging," but I felt the "safe" aspect was sometimes under-delivered. Ultimately, in order to teach actors, they have to *want* to show up for your class. Having extremely temperamental teachers and staff, with Stalinist Stage Managers waiting to grill students upon their arrival about this, that or the other—it just never quite did it for me. I don't want to ask Stage Managers to have meetings with students that I loathed having when I did their job. I prefer a more relaxed, fun environment that nonetheless maintains the "challenging" part: the high standards, the respect for teachers, the no-bullshit attitude about doing the work. If I ever get angry, it's usually because those standards simply aren't being met.

Secondly, Milton, beyond being extremely temperamental, also enjoyed teaching with an intensely psychological approach to freeing the actor's expressivity. He was preternaturally good at diving into an actor's life and finding the traumas and influences that hindered their creativity, their esteem, their expressiveness. And sometimes he would barge in there like a bull in a china shop and break everything in sight. Upon a negative result here—a sobbing, angry or running-for-the-theatre-exit actor, for instance—a meeting at his house would ensue, and often I would be invited to come along. Milton would pour on the charm, a lunch was cooked, and by the end of the meeting, the broken actor would be put back together again. He loved that action. I came to believe he "broke" people with his temper in part so he could fix them again afterward. He was certainly skilled at both sides of that equation.

But I always thought this part of Milton's personal teaching style— the roaming around the personal psychology of the actor, had the danger of being misunderstood and confused with what he wanted the *actor* to do in relation to their work on a role. Because while Milton would freely use his unique powers of perception and his obdurate will to extract the maximum expressivity and esteem he could from each student, his analysis of any particular *scene* was always much more down-to-earth and story-based. It was much more about the writing, the basic situation of the story ("What's going on here?"), and how to bring it to life in a true, logical, interesting and revealing way.

So if Milton was 50/50 on psychology of the actor vs. story-based analysis, then I probably tend to a 5/95 balance. I have a very audience-focused approach. My emphasis is almost entirely on the story, and how we as actors, writers and directors can best communicate that story to the audience. I believe that the only customer that matters for all these skills we're developing at the BHP is the audience. Any personal benefit or sense of reward to the artists involved in that task is ancillary. We have a job to do at BHP, let's focus on it: Our job is to make you good at *your* job. If you, the actor, are good at your job, and you administrate your skills, you have a better shot of being paid. It needn't be any fancier than that.

Finally, I want the BHP Approach to be one that is constantly factoring in *context.* Acting training shouldn't be myopic. In an increasingly fractious world, the big picture of how best to go about study, knowing what skills actors are really developing, en-suring the professional administration of those skills, conforming all of that to a fickle business and an ever-evolving personal life— this can all mistakenly get lost sometimes in a thicket of minutiae about acting technique. Storytelling has its rules and conventions, and actors have a very specific function in that process. There's plenty to talk about there, but then there's this: getting into a po-sition even to *be* hired to fulfill that function requires stamina and a skill-set all its own before the acting even comes into play. Fully 95% or more of an actor's life is spent *outside* the words "action" and "cut." The BHP Approach, in full, aims to contextualize that journey, to look not at just the minutiae of this moment or that, or why the character chose to use chopsticks over a fork this evening. The BHP Approach, applied correctly and over time, teaches the actor *when* to worry about the chopsticks or the fork, how to look at the writing and what it's doing, how to study, how to act, how to administrate, and how to live life as an actor so you hear the blessed "Action!" or "Places!" more often.

The essays that follow are organized into those four groups: On Acting, On Study, On Administration, and On Life as an Actor. I hope they are of assistance in the wild and wondrous journey from aspiring to professional actor, a journey which for many is equal parts oasis and insanity.

ON ACTING

CHAPTER 24

Proficiency: Who Needs It?

I'll go ahead and say it: Acting is a profession more tolerant of lack of ability than perhaps any other. You can actually make a fair sum of money in acting without knowing much about how to act, and I take no satisfaction in making that statement. It's frankly embarrassing. But there *is* such a thing as proficiency, and in the end, proficiency will win. If you're serious, if you want to last more than a year or two in show business, if you have any sense of professional ethics, then proficiency is what you should be pursuing first and foremost.

Yet these days, more and more, serious study can be devalued as something outdated and unnecessary, and "competence" measured not by your demonstrated ability, but by whether you have listed on your resume some in-vogue piece of micro-training that is seen as potentially linked to being hired. Or you might get a certain job purely because of how you look, and after that you are judged competent because, well, someone hired you already for that job. The jobs keep coming without your ever really having known why or how.

Part of the Big Frustration with pursuing an acting career no doubt comes from this rather tenuous relationship between *competence* and *employment*. The writer starts the ball rolling with a script, and actors are among the last hired to complete the team in charge of getting this story to the public. There are a million stories, of infinite quality, across an increasingly crowded spectrum of content delivery. Many of those stories simply don't require "high achievement acting" to do their job or make a lot of money. But in any case, the lead character who is in every scene?

Actor. The guy who pops his head in with one line? Actor. The background players? Actors. The film that just won 15 Oscars? Full of actors. That daytime soap? Full of actors. That sketch comedy show? Actors. All considered to be professional, they're all being paid *something*, but the range of actual competence is staggering. The number of actors who are being paid *something* to act in *something* every day far exceeds the numbers in other professional art forms, or in sports. The entire NFL is fewer than 2,000 players. The entire NBA is fewer than 500 players. You gotta be good— clearly, demonstrably, seriously good. Now, how many actors do you think are being used across the entire spectrum of storytelling and content delivery—just domestically? It has to be at least many, many thousands, every day.

It's hard to get your head around it, because in just about any other field of endeavor, a proven level of competence would seem clearly to be a necessary prerequisite for getting paid, and usually that competence is easily identified through a known, highly visible technique: *Hey! Look at that violinist! She must have spent a bazillion hours of practice to get that good. Hey! Look at that athlete! Imagine how much dedication and training it takes to be that good.* Medicine, technology, cooking, the various building trades—could anyone make an argument to the contrary? I don't think so. Joining a union in some other skill usually requires a certain number of years, with measured hours on the job in various capacities. In acting? You can join SAG-AFTRA by being a background player, and the single union now covers actors, radio deejays, and TV meteorologists. The union has *zero* proficiency requirements, and the notion of acting proficiency itself is highly subjective. With acting, the better the technique, often the more invisible it is, and you just see a "person" in a story.

In the near term (under 5 years chasing acting professionally), it can *appear* that actual competence has little role to play in your career. It just seems too much a lottery, and that some lucky new person who's been in town three weeks gets a great audition or books a swell job or signs with that perceived awesome agent/manager, while you, perhaps trained and responsible and caring and artistic and dutifully having adhered to the latest diet regimen—you are unfairly left behind, unrewarded for hard work, talent and sacrifice.

Hence one can see a hell of a lot of randomness in the actions of actors in the early chapters of this strange novel—constant changing of teachers, approaches, philosophies, desperate grabs at weird projects, too many bad plays, too many bad comedy skits, a sudden veering toward improv workshops, *no*, sitcom workshops, *no*, on-camera workshops, *no*, such-and-such a motivational speaker, *no*, a new Significant Other, *no*, back to the old Significant Other, *no*, New York, *no*, Los Angeles, *no*, writing, *no*, new agent, *no*, new manager…On and on it goes. Actors can veer from one major decision to another along the steep, jagged slopes of morale and inspiration that mark the early part of the journey. There's always a nice little high you get from *making a decision*, implementing some sort of change, but around the bend awaits the same old discouragement when this change didn't yield the desired result: regular acting work, a feeling you're breaking through at last.

But as you move past five years in the profession, I've observed that the business does become more and more a meritocracy. Yes—there's always politics, celebrity, vapidity, nepotism and money at work (as they are in all industries), but overall there is a meritocratic response. If you look at actors you admire who have been at it for 20 years or more—they really do know how to act, and how to comport themselves in professional situations. Even the character types who aren't celebrities but work all the time—they know what they're doing. You rarely see a total no-talent boob who ends up "making it" over the long haul. In the end, I believe talent, or frankly more importantly, professional competence, wins.

Certainly for Type-A super-achievers, who are used to being recognized as such in more conventional environments like job-jobs and fixed-size organizations where their competence shines quickly and is rewarded, the morass of The Biz and its seeming non-responsiveness to their intelligence, responsibility, and work ethic is particularly infuriating.

But proficiency will win. In the end, it will win. It's a proficiency with acting on a technical level, but also with managing your own morale, and building a career, managing that. A lot of success is just built on *being there*, day after day, being good at the little things day after day, having people walk away from working with you glad for the experience, day after day. A few years in the business will bring that much more certainty about the various skills, what to do, how to do it, who can help, how you can get them to help—*perspective*. Some actors have an innate maturity that lends itself better to older parts, and their 20's may just be a long training period as they wait for their look and their casting to match up with the music inside. Others need to break out of bad 20-something romances, or get off the parental dole, or develop a stronger work ethic, or knock off the (insert non-optimum life situation here)—all of this in addition to developing their skills as actors.

Don't indulge the manic panic. You've set upon a course as a performing artist, and while it can feel as if career certainty has gone out the window, the wheel slowly turns and you get better, wiser, more connected to the business—and the business will respond. Life can be unfair, the world unjust—for sure. But try not to make too many major veering decisions on those early jagged slopes, thinking that those micro-level moves will have a major effect on the slow turning wheel of your career. The house-of-mirrors freak show that no doubt seems to describe your thoughts, feelings, confidence and psychology on any given day frankly matters very little. Persistence, diligent work on your skills, supplemented by increasing and steady career administration— that's what will fuel the wheel's rotation, and lead you ultimately to proficiency, professional competence, and measurable results over time.

CHAPTER 25

Acting Is A Gang Bang

Affecting the audience is the very point of telling a story in the first place.

None of this is about you. It's not about your connection with your scene partner. It's not about your connection to the story. It's not about your liking or disliking the story, nor pontificating upon that like or dislike. It's not about how you feel you're doing as an actor. *It's about what you are doing to ensure the story affects the audience.* They're the customer for this story. You're part of the chef's team, they're the diners. This would seem obvious, but many actors would probably tell you that if the communication is "honest" between them, or if they are "connected" (often per some completely subjective standard), then that's all that's necessary. *Wrong.* A supposed "connection" between two actors on stage, or any reaction felt by the actors that cannot be perceived by the audience, is a tree falling in the woods. No one can hear it, no one can see it, so even if it happened, no one cares. Whether it's on stage or on film, this matter of impinging on the audience needs to be understood. Actors, directors, writers and designers are all collaborating on a story *so as to affect the audience.*

Anyone who ever watched Milton direct a scene can attest to his sitting in the back row, often with lit cigar in hand, yelling, "WHAT?!" As in, "What did you just say? I can't hear you." But it wasn't necessarily just about volume. It was as much "I'm not getting what you're doing or what you're after." It was about intent. It was about passion. It was his one-word *cri de coeur* for actors to cut to the heart of the moment at hand, and of the story overall. He would admonish that "the play happens out here," in the audience, where he was sitting.

The communication between you and your scene partner is not a direct line between you. The words of the script leave your mouth, circle out to the audience, specifically for the benefit of *their* understanding and reaction, and then come back around to your partner. That's the actual "line" of communication, that's the actual pathway, whether in live theatre or in film or television. Your job is quite specifically to ensure the audience understands what is happening, and hopefully cares about it. The basic job of any story is to ensure the audience understands it, cares about it, wants to know what happens next. Now sometimes the script sucks, in which case the love child of Marlon Brando and Meryl Streep couldn't make the audience understand or care about the story. But as Milton would often say, "The writer is a genius until proven otherwise." The actors must do *their* job, which is to pierce the audience with what the story is doing to the characters. That's what I think Milton meant with his constant cries of *"WHAT?!"*

If you finish a performance and think you sucked, that nothing happened to you, that you didn't "feel it," and you go out to the lobby and a tearful audience member gushes to you that you were brilliant and you moved them and made them contemplate their life or what-have-you, you know who's right? The audience member. The customer was happy. That's what counts. No one gives a shit if the cook is happy, or the waiters are, or the salespeople in a store—the entire enterprise exists to affect the customer, make the customer happy. Acting ain't just about you, kid—we're watching, and we have to be involved.

CHAPTER 26

Script Analysis That Actually Helps

I find that the script analysis many actors do isn't worth crap, because this analysis mostly exists to satisfy stale theoretical notions of what's going on, without yielding a change in the emotional experience of the audience, which is where the experience matters. So you ask an actor about a scene, and either they'll just offer up the plot ("Well, I just found out I lost my job, and then I come home, and she's here, and she's just like, completely unsympathetic..."), or they'll talk about some invented "choice" that has no particular relevance to the plot:

ALLEN: So, you get fired, you come home, you're expecting what from her?

ACTOR: Well, I chose I don't really want to come home. I chose that I really want to go to Alaska.

ALLEN: Why?

ACTOR: As a response to being fired. Like he just wants to leave everything.

ALLEN: Is there anything about him going to Alaska in the script?

ACTOR: No, I just thought, I know when I've been fired sometimes I just want to skip town.

ALLEN: But how am I supposed to know this character wants to go to Alaska, if there's nothing in the script about it, and you in fact are here, in this scene, coming back to your apartment, and not going to Alaska?

ACTOR: At first I chose it was because he's always wanted to visit states in alphabetical order.

ALLEN: That'a a long trip from Alabama. And still has nothing to do with…

ACTOR: But then I chose it was because he likes grizzly bears.

Meaningless. It's all pure theory, fantasyland, totally academic, a distinction without a difference, turn in your papers at the end of class. Look, either the writer put into the script that the character responds to being fired by wanting to go to Alaska—or not. The writer provided a reason for that trip—or not. Your making a "choice" about that is simply not relevant.

Almost the entirety of "character biography" work falls under the same fallacious distinction-without-a-difference analysis. The details of "character biography" stay in the actor's head as an intellectual understanding, but don't often enough emerge as a perceivable trait that helps the audience experience the story. *I chose that his father abandoned him as a child. I chose that she is a political centrist. I chose that he likes abstract expressionism. No, that's wrong, I'm changing it. I'm choosing that he likes Pop Art.* I'm talking here of "choices" that are not addressed by the writer in the script in any way. Almost every time I hear an actor begin a sentence about their character with, "Well, I chose that blah-blah," it ends up being an explanation of something that was not perceivable in the scene. It was just something the actor *thought* about the character, but never entered the *playing* of the character. Regardless of whether these biography choices are valid from a purely theoretical standpoint, regardless of whether they'll get you an "A" on a term paper about the character, the fact remains: *a choice is only as good (or bad) for the acting as it can be perceived by the audience.* To that end, I offer two items of script analysis that I think will actually help you act the story correctly:

1. EARN THE LINE

Go through the script and highlight everything said *about* your character, whether it's a trait or a state of mind. Most writers will give actors abundant clues about how to play your role, if you know simply to look. It's not difficult, and yet it's missed with startling frequency. Here's an example from one of the most frequently performed acting class scenes, *Barefoot in the Park*: "What are you so angry about, Paul?" Ta-da! If you, the actor playing Paul, have not demonstrated anger prior to that moment, that line then goes unearned, and that precious belief between audience and play begins to diminish. Then later he says to her, "What fight? We're just yelling a little bit." Ta-da! You both need to have been yelling prior to that line. Still later on, Paul says to Corey: "You belong in a nursery school!" Ding! Corey needs to have the emotional life of a 4-year-old. If you, the actress, have played Corey with an adult form of bitchy contempt up until that moment, then this line will ring hollow and unearned. Corey has to have the sweet, reckless, impetuous freedom of a young child. Throughout the script, and in much of Simon's work, there are these abundant clues as to character and emotional life.

It's been many years since I pursued acting as a career, having moved into directing, playwriting, teaching and running the BHP. But every so often I get up there on stage, and most recently that was as Marc in the play *Art* by Yasmina Reza. Marc is an interesting guy, and he cracks me up. But let's look at the clues given by Reza as to how Marc comes off. The following is said to and about him:

There was no warmth in the way he responded…just a vile preten- tious laugh, a real know-it-all laugh.

This attitude, you better watch that, you're getting bitter. (To which Marc replies with my favorite line, "Good. The older I get the more offensive I hope to become.")

You're behaving very strangely.

You're acting really sinister tonight.

At last you've said something remotely human.

Some deep insecurity must lie behind (Marc's) insane aggression.

Pretentious, know-it-all, bitter, strange, sinister, remotely hu- man, insanely aggressive—these are all some damned descriptive terms. All of them must be earned by the performance. Then the challenge is to reveal *in addition* an inner life that demonstrates his "deep insecurity." There is no particular genius required to read the script and glean from it the clues therein about your character.

2. BOMBS AWAY/THE PIVOT

Now, go through the script again and highlight any occasion on which your character either delivers or receives information that is important, surprising, and/or emotional. Look as well for any action taken by a character that precipitates a crisis, or at least a marked change in the dynamics of the scene. (The making or rejection of a romantic pass is a frequent example of this.) In a decent play, the very existence of the scene is tied to the delivery of such news or action, so it's gotta be there somewhere. I often call these moments the "bombs" —if a bomb went off near you, you'd be shocked, you'd freeze, it would take a moment before you continue. When you act those moments, simply add 1-5 seconds of time right there, particularly if you are receiving that news.

I often ask actors where the "pivot" of the scene is. When exactly does the scene become…*something else?* It's usually linked to these bombs going off. Before the bomb, it was about X, but after, something has happened. It's different. It's not about X any more, that's for sure. Actors have to understand this pivot, because your performance should be geared to making it clear. If you take some time when the bomb goes off, it will usually be beneficial to understand that you should drive some energy toward that bomb, or that pivot, so the time you take stands out in relief. A very common scene structure is that characters are talking about whatever, yada-yada, and then the bomb hits. The yada-yada section should cook a bit, have some energy, so that when you take the time for the bomb, it dramatically changes the rhythm of the scene. So you generally don't want to drag and take too much time leading up to a bomb going off.

Let's look at this in relation to Act 1 of the play, *Rabbit Hole*, which is a clinic in scene structure and bombs going off. **Scene 1:** When Izzy reveals she's pregnant. Before that: yada-yada, the story about Izzy punching a woman at the bar, this guy Auggie, something weird there, Becca knows she's full of shit, lying about something, and then…BOOM: "Auggie told her I was pregnant." **Scene 2:** Becca's rejection of Howie's pass at her. Ouch. Before that: yada-yada, they're talking about Izzie, Howie's trying to talk her off the ledge about that, and about her friend not calling her, some funny stuff about the birthday gift, he's giving her a back rub, and then…BOOM: She rejects him, goes to clean the room upstairs instead. Pivot. An action (her rejecting him) has precipitated a crisis. Now the scene is something else. And the bombs start to drop: Becca says she wants to sell the house, and then two huge ones: Becca says of Danny, "He's everywhere!"— the maximum expression of her grief so far, and then: Howie brings up the idea of having another child. **Scene 3:** When it's revealed that Howie and his mother-in-law have been talking behind Becca's back. Before that: yada-yada, a long, humorous exchange driven by Nat, her whole theory of the Kennedy family tragedies, the gift exchange and then…BOOM: "Howie says you're not going to group anymore." Now the scene is something else. The party goes to complete shit as the recriminations fly. **Scene 4:** An early, huge, bomb here, the only yada-yada is confusion about what is playing on the VCR, then BOOM: "That was Danny's tape. You recorded over Danny's tape." And the bombs keep going off to close off Act 1. BOOM: Howie thinks the accident with the tape was on some level intentional. They're now seriously going at each other, building to BOOM: Howie's terrifying explosion, screaming that she needs to "stop erasing" Danny. Then a quieter, but devastating revelation: Howie clearly alludes to possible divorce.

Or in the popular play, *Proof* —the big scene between the sisters, four whoppers in that scene. But first: Yada-yada, Claire is hung over, some banter there about the party, the dress, etc. Then, four explosions, each larger than the last…BOOM: Claire wants Catherine to move to New York not for a visit, but permanently. BOOM: Claire has in fact already sold the house, and clearly has been working on the sale for months. BOOM: Claire thinks Catherine could be as crazy as their father. BOOM: Claire in fact has considered professional care housing for Catherine once she moves to New York…Most of the time I see the scene, those moments are simply not being addressed with the building astonishment, shock and betrayal, each step of which requires time for the actor to experience. (Or, to put it more accurately— *each step of which requires time for the actor to instruct the audience to experience.*)

To properly address all of a play's important moments, the ones I often think get missed, would probably add 3-5 minutes to the average total runtime, but right now it's a crucial 3-5 minutes that are missing. Because without the proper emphasis on those important bits of news, all information seems the same, of the same importance (or lack of importance), and the communication between the play and the audience gets messed up. The audience can't grab the import of certain moments in the script because the actors are blowing right through them. My musical instincts come into play—I'm always sensing we need some rubato (bending the flow of the piece at certain times), or even a full-out *rest*. In music, the composer lays it out with extreme precision— the notes are *here* and the rests are *there*, with highly specific indications for phrasing, accents, ornamentation, staccato, legato… But in dramatic writing, even if the author were to indicate after the crucial line, *"Catherine, in shock, can't speak for three seconds"*— it's far more open to interpretation.

So. Mark the important pieces of information, the big reveals, and take some time in your performance to respond. Stanislavski referred to "reflective delay" as a technique calling the actor's attention to the time needed for a character to process information, and Milton incorporated that into his own Checklist for Takeoff. That bit of time, often a matter of a split second to five seconds, allows the audience to hear the news, respond to it themselves, and then direct their attention to you and your response. That bit of time, particularly if the dialogue has been flowing up until that moment, is a clue to the audience: *Hey! Pay attention, something just happened!* As a director, I'll often yell out, "THREE, TWO, ONE…Okay, go ahead." after one of those lines, to force my sense of reflective delay upon the actor receiving the information. But I'm definitely yelling out, "THREE, TWO, ONE…Okay go ahead—" a lot more often than I am, "LET'S MOVE IT!"

Knowing your writer is important here. Even in a fast-paced Sorkin script, it's a matter of finding the moment where you can take some time to absorb something important. For instance, in *A Few Good Men*, the scene where Kaffee comes in drunk: When he reveals that Markinson is dead—BOOM. That's a moment. When, after a page of back-and-forth, Galloway suggests they should subpoena Jessup and put him on the stand —BOOM. That's a moment. Galloway leaves, and Weinberg and Kaffee have a conversation about seeking the approval of fathers, where Weinberg convinces our hero he's better a lawyer than he gives himself credit for —this whole section can be a touch more relaxed and "natural" than what we may think Sorkin allows in general. And of course, in the final climactic scene, BOOM: "You're God-damned right I did." That's a moment. That's *the* moment. That's so big a bomb going off, it resolves the entire story. A ton of energy is driving towards that bomb, with Kaffee and Jessup matching wits to escalate their confrontation step by step.

Ideally, a good director is in charge of all this, but here's the bad news: *you only get a director once you book the job.* To book the job, you may have to do much of this yourself, on your own analysis, so that you kill it in the audition. Life is short. Prep time is limited. So free yourself from all thoughts regarding character biography details that aren't provided by the script. Free yourself from thoughts about stuff have nothing to do with how the audience will perceive your character on a behavioral, emotional level. Again: The only items of interest about your character are *those that can be perceived by the audience.* Take all the time you're wasting on useless academic thoughts, and simply add that to your performance when the "bombs" of important information go off, and you'll be doing script analysis that finally pays dividends.

CHAPTER 27

Feelings Don't Matter

They just don't. There is the job you do, and then there are your feelings about your job—and only the former is of any consequence or import. Now as an actor your job has to do with manipulating your own feelings in service of a story, so this no doubt gets tricky…

Image #1: You've got a leaky faucet. You call the plumber. The plumber comes over and he either fixes the faucet or he doesn't. You generally don't give a crap how the plumber may feel about his own work, you may or may not be aware of the full range of his "talent" as a plumber, or whether he thinks this plumbing career will really pan out for him. All you want is for him to fix the faucet. He may have been engaged in suicidal thoughts the entire time, but if he mentions them he becomes really annoying. If he shows up when he said he would, stops the leak, and charges a reasonable fee—you're all set.

Image #2: A pianist is someone who uses hard-earned technique to play varying combinations of 88 different keys and 3 pedals in an infinity of patterns and dynamics, so scripted by a composer, and interpreted by the pianist, to bring a specific piece of music to life for the audience.

So with these two images in mind, let's look at the three pillars of the BHP training: Acting, Attitude & Administration.

ACTING: Your feelings don't matter. I know. *I know…* How is this possible? Because you're a plumber. Or, if you prefer (and I do)—a pianist. Your "piano" is the emotional instrument *within* you, expressed through the physical instrument that *is* you. You manipulate your feelings just as a pianist does a keyboard. You can play that emotional instrument at an extremely high level without needing to feel "connected," or "in," or "inspired," or whatever actors like to say about their own work. (Some would say it may well be better that you do it this way. It is possible that the more dispassionate you can be about playing that instrument brilliantly—the better off you may be in acting.)

When we listen to a recording of Horowitz at the piano, we have no clue about what his feelings were at that moment. We don't know if he felt "connected." Maybe he vomited with insecurity ten seconds before playing the first note. We don't know. All we know as we listen is that he's executing the hell out the piece. He may well have felt like shit about it, but who cares? Your favorite brilliant actors—we have no clue what they're feeling or thinking at the moment they act. Nor does what they *say* about that process on talk shows mean what they say is true. Actors mythologize their own process all the time. "I really just tried to get in touch with this guy's pain. It's my pain. It's all our pain." *And the talk show host nods sagely, the audience oohs and aahs in admiration.* It sure sounds great. But it's simply unknowable. There are very happy actors who play their instrument well, don't torture themselves, and can make us cry in any given moment, and there are very sad, depressed actors who constantly torture themselves for "art" and yet can't make us feel a thing. And vice versa. There simply is no connection between your feelings and the quality of work—other than a connection romanticized by actors regarding "process."

There is no correct thought or feeling you need to have about acting. You can cry without feeling sad, you can yell without being angry. You can manufacture tears and anger, compellingly authentic, suitable for the scene, believable by the audience— all the while thinking you suck as an actor. Conversely, you can aim directly for putting yourself through what the character goes through, to experience literally what the character is experiencing—and you can feel you nailed that and everyone may respond accordingly—that's nice, too. Whatever gets the job done. (Cue the possibly apocryphal but no doubt entertaining story about Hoffman v. Olivier in *Marathon Man*.)

My point is only that one process is not intrinsically better than the other. You're like the pianist—you play the instrument you've got, and you study to improve your ability to play that instrument. All that *passion* and *feeling* about the process of acting may well fuck you up. Or, to switch metaphors—as an actor you are using your emotional instrument to channel water (the dialogue or emotions of the script) in the direction it needs to go for the story. Your feelings about that process are as important as a plumber's in arranging pipes beneath your sink.

Technique is that which you use to play the instrument. Actor A, contemplating a moment of grief in the script: she thinks of a sad moment in her life and then her instrument responds, her breathing gets weird, her eyes tear up and the audience experiences sadness from her. Actor B, confronting the same moment of grief in the script: she needs to use a physical trick (onion, etc.) to make her eyes tear up. Some may say Actor A is "personal" while Actor B is "fake"—I disagree. They just have different means of playing the emotional keyboard. (And, by the way, both actors may use elements of either technique depending on the day, the moment, the specific situation at hand.) If both actors (and more importantly, the director) are going after the result of fooling the audience utterly, so they sit out there in complete belief about this moment in the script—we'll be fine. It's the *audience's* belief that matters, it's the audience's perception of whether the work seems personal that matters. That's the only measure. It's about whether the audience believes you are sad. *It's emphatically not about whether you make yourself sad.* We're all liars here, it's just about how good a liar you are. What we're trying to do in acting class is develop your ability to lie effectively under various forms of professional duress.

Acting is a skill. It has technique—the vast majority of people walking the earth behave awkwardly and self-consciously on stage or in front of a camera, and sound wooden when asked to say lines written by other people. You don't. You like to perform, and you are using technique to fool the audience into temporarily believing what they know damned well is *not* real. They don't want it to be real. Horror films make billions each year. Snuff films are a horrific crime. Famous love scenes are famous love scenes, but porn is just porn. Trust me, the audience knows it isn't real, they don't want it to be real. They want the *ride*. Theatre and film are no different from Star Tours or Space Mountain: *We know it's a ride.* We want the ride to be a good one. And safe. That's all. It's nothing more than that. Your technique as an actor is that of taking the audience on the ride. Now, improve your technique so you can play the damned piano brilliantly and stop kvetching about your feelings.

ATTITUDE: Your feelings don't matter. I know. *I know...* But for those who've read Milton's book, you'll notice that the introduction to the "Attitude" section does not mention the word *feel* or *feeling*. Not once. The main point of his teachings on Attitude was that Attitude is a choice. When you come up against an actor with a "bad attitude"— you make that judgment not by being inside his or her head and listening to thoughts and feelings. You make that judgment based on behavior! The actor *outwardly demonstrates* a moody, hostile or argumentative demeanor. It's there for everyone to see. We've all known cheerful actors who "feel great!" but who are also chronically late, or fucking high, or seriously incompetent. Or the actor who is smiling and cheerful ("feels great!") and then takes apart the director and the other actors through vicious gossip in the commissary. Similarly, you can "feel like shit," "have no confidence," "feel uninspired"— and still show up on time and behave in a cooperative fashion, smile a bit, do your job, play your instrument in a compelling fashion that tells the damned story, and be known as a terrific actor with a good attitude. Like the plumber mentioned above. I don't give a shit how he feels—I want him to show up on time and fix the problem. If he does those things, I'm his fan. So you do *your* job. Attitude has behaviors attached—choose the right ones. Feelings are utterly unknowable by others except through their undisciplined outward demonstration in behavior.

ADMINISTRATION: Your feelings don't matter. In my position as teacher at the Advanced level at the BHP, I see many very talented people, swell personalities, mostly good attitudes, and generally (as with actors across the board) a problematic deficit of solid, consistent Administration. But as consistent with our theme, Administration is, by definition, a collection of behaviors, not a collection of feelings. Milton wrote a book focusing on career administration and called it *Dreams **Into** Action* —not *Dreams **About** Action*. Administration consists of those actions you take to move your career in the direction you would like. Done. You don't need to feel good about taking those actions any more than you need to feel good about going to the gym a few times a week. Often we're dragging our asses there only to feel good after the workout, right? Enough said.

So please stop the madness. In my opinion the world is becoming weaker and weaker the more one's personal feelings are emphasized—or at least to the extent this emphasis invades the workplace. The theatre is your workplace. Your class is your workplace. Now, no one has a perfect record here. Milton was a master teacher, one of the best to come down the pike. His temper was also legendary, and his wild mood swings could really dictate the tone of an entire day for better or worse. Sometimes you feel a certain way and, dammit, the world is going to know about it. Sometimes in a professional circumstance those insecurities or minor depressions or hostilities become all-too-visible to others. So be it —this is not about perfection. But let's stop targeting "feeling good" as a goal, or basing our acting, attitude or administration on some prerequisite of "feeling good" about any of those three elements. As far as your professional life as an actor goes, feelings are an internal house of mirrors that have nothing to do with anything.

CHAPTER 28

Name That Tone

When Milton and I reworked the *Acting Class* book in 2008, we flirted with the idea of moving "Who's The Author?" to the top of his famous Actors' Checklist for Takeoff. The reason? The proper understanding of the traditional first item on the list, the Event—*what's going on here?*—is so strongly affected by the author's unique sensibility. A marital fight in a Sorkin script is a different animal from a marital fight in one by O'Neill, which is different again from that fight written by Tennessee.

Another aspect of my recurring actor-as-plumber metaphor: you've got to know whose story you're in, and how that awareness may help you figure the choices that will help the author out. Picture asking a plumber to fix the leak on your kitchen sink and you return later to find he's built a small, beautifully artistic waterfall cascading into your basin. I'm sure you'd be, well…*What the hell?* Right? It's not that the guy wasn't very talented to be able to build a waterfall in your sink, but it just has nothing to do with what you needed or wanted from him, and it really interferes with doing the dishes.

So for those occasions where you've watched a comedic treatment of *Schindler's List*, or a plodding, emotional, pause-ridden scene from *Sports Night*…These are usually not an issue of the actors' inability to create a realistic circumstance, nor lack of courage in making a choice, but rather that of their improper analysis of the tone of the script, leading to choices that did not fit the story.

Anyway, having been on the "other side of the table" in plenty of casting sessions, I can say that the most common feeling I have is not so much whether the choices were well executed or not, or showed talent or not…but *are they right for this author and this kind of story?* Actors are building waterfalls when I need a drip-free faucet. They're drip-dripping when I want Niagara in my office. Talent and ability aren't really the issue—when someone comes in who has no talent or ability, that's…whatever that is. You roll your eyes and move on quickly because there's no time to really contemplate it, nor joy in doing so. I'm not writing for people of no talent or ability, but rather for those who hopefully possess *both*, so as to learn something about channeling *both* in the right directions at the right time for success.

And the proper assessment of the tone of the script is vital. That tone is established through the uniqueness of a specific writer. In TV, the creator and executive producers all establish the tone of the show out of the gate. So TV shows have a tone that is a reflection of the writer who created it, in combination with what the network may want or specialize in—maybe the tone is established by committee on network television, but it's still identifiable. Sometimes you have a certain writer's very unique voice—Sorkin and Milch come to mind, and if you know those writers you can see how the acting can probably be a bit broader in the choices with Milch than with the generally fast-paced intellectual horsepower of Sorkin. And then you've got the vast canvas of film, which, as the old saw goes—is written three times: on paper, in camera, and in the editing room. The director has far more power to determine the look and style of the entire film than on television, and many more tools at his or her disposal for telling the story. But of course there's gigantic variety in film, from intense compact visual styles with naturalistic acting, to the dry-humor mockumentary (tediously overused), to films like Tim Burton's, and the wildness and imagination that an actor like Depp brings to that work. And even within a single film— we've all observed that the heroic character tends to be more stoic, while the Black Hats get to twirl the mustache—Bale vs. Ledger in *Batman—Dark Knight* comes to mind as one of many vivid examples of this.

So can the same actor read beautifully today for *Law and Order: Super Unbelievably Psychopathic Bad Guys Unit,* and then book Sorkin's latest the following week, and next month be in consideration for a play at a good Equity theatre? I say yes, absolutely— but he/she has to identify the tone of the script, has to know the voice of that writer and where the acting fits into that voice. You need to know which parts get afforded permission for bigger choices (e.g., bad guys generally get to make bigger choices). There simply isn't one kind of acting that serves all masters, and I believe a professional actor in the contemporary marketplace, where there are a zillion distribution channels and voices and concepts and styles all happening at the same time, needs to be savvy about the proper placement of the acting in an overall tone set by the writer. And while this is not meant to diminish actors' traditional emphasis on an honest and truthful examination of the given circumstance—what the character is going through, physical work, etc.—we need to ensure that *in addition* to that work, there is a proper awareness of the writer's voice, the tone of the script, and what kind of acting best serves that particular story.

So how does one know when to build waterfalls and when to tighten an unseen bolt under the sink? Experience. Many scenes in a good class. Many auditions under your belt. Research—in this case meaning you should watch at least one episode of everything on TV, as well as being well-versed in different storytellers at work—whether that's in theatre, film or television—and their particular styles. (YouTube can be a useful resource here—just about everything that ever existed in theatre, film or TV has a piece of its existence memorialized on the site.) As Milton used to emphasize, in his own unique vernacular, "You all can't go get fucked by movies any more." Meaning: You can't simply be a civilian, looking to be entertained. You have to look, analyze, you have to see what's going on, who's making what choices and why? Sometimes simply removing the civilian uniform can shed a lot of light on these matters.

CHAPTER 29

On Being Personal, Part 1: Overview

The concept of "being personal" in one's acting work is universal, and universally misunderstood. Milton's definition of *personal* as it relates to acting: "being affected by and allowing yourself to experience specifically what the character is going through on an emotional level." He spoke about actors "crawling their way" into the experience, and that it's the actors personal feelings and responses that are needed to fulfill work at a high level. This hunt for *personal work* goes to that traditional first question all actors ask themselves: "What do I know about this experience? How did I deal with it in my life?" The Event. Item number one. Milton's first question: "What's going on here?" The idea that the actor on some level experiences what the character is experiencing is probably one of the most revered by those who feel they are going for *serious acting*. This quest can lead to journeys that are fruitful and very rewarding, but also ones fraught with danger, or even completely mistaken, fallacious in logic and intent.

I have no problem with the general idea that the actor needs to be "personal" in his or her work, and I would laud the general intention to "go for it" and "crawl into the experience," etc. One can only admire the work ethic of our best "full immersion" character actors. But there is a trap in so much generalized talk about being personal: Can we *really* tell if an actor is *personally* involved in what he or she is portraying? If actors *say* they are involved personally, we tend to believe them. But I think frankly that actors lie about their process all the time, they weave a narrative designed for a specific response from teachers, classmates, their fellow actors. And sometimes, this awareness of "personal work" comes from our *knowing* the actors specifically as friends. We might look at certain work and recognize aspects of the person we know outside class, outside that performance —and this can help us determine that they were "personal" in their performance.

But the fact is we're not training you to act for your friends. We're not training you to say things in interviews that will make everyone nod in affirmation and agreement. We're training you to make the audience believe in the story. There is simply no other result desired from good acting. Make us believe. Make us care. Draw us into the experience of this story, so that when the lights go up at the end, we've been on a fantastic ride, a ride suitable for the nature of this story. Public relations people know this back and front: half the Hollywood romances in history were partly cooked up to help sell the story of the movie those actors were in!

So with that in mind, I would offer this revision to the generalized notion of being personal: work that is considered "personal" is that which *seems to the audience* as if it is truly happening to the actor, and thus *appears to be* incredibly honest. The fact is you can lie your ass off and think about your overdue taxes as you perform, and still make us think you're being devastatingly personal and honest. In fact, that may happen far more often than we might want to believe. Actors tend to look at their favorite performances and reverse engineer an acting approach that matches their desires. *Look at Famous Actor's performance. My God! How does she do it? Look how personal she is! How invested!* But is she? We don't know. Maybe that was a take where she felt she phoned it in from miles away. Maybe she never went for that "personal" stuff, and is a technician at heart. Maybe it's different for different roles, different for varying scenes within the same role. The fact is we just don't know.

The bottom line is that your work is personal if the audience believes it is.

CHAPTER 30

On Being Personal, Part 2: The Fallacy

As I mentioned above, the journey to personal work can be "fruitful and very rewarding, but also fraught with danger, or even completely mistaken, fallacious in logic and intent." Let's take a look at the fallacious version of this pursuit.

It goes like this: "The character is written to be X, but I have a vision. I have a concept. I want this story to be about what I want it to be about. So I will choose that the character is *not* X. He's in fact Y. I'm going to Y the shit out of this role, and this is A-OK, because you know what? I'm making it my own.'" Sorry. You didn't just make your work personal, you didn't "make it your own." You just misused those concepts to fuck up the character and the story.

The fallacy is that personal work means "I can make any personal choice that suits me in the pursuit of the role." This mistaken analysis is a byproduct of that good, traditional first question in acting: "What do I know about this situation? What is my truth about it?" I'm not trying to knock that traditional question, but I find there to be a major pitfall with singular "what is my personal truth?" analysis: *Sometimes your own truth about a given situation is simply not appropriate to the story before you.*

In this business, the concept of being personal, "making it your own," or "putting your stamp on it" is celebrated almost without question. You'll hear actors justify a bad choice often by a sentence starting with, "Well, I chose…" It's their choice, you see. Solipsism. "It's right because I chose it." The notion of singular artistic vision is romanticized, seen as heroic, and begins to warp the actor's sensibility away from doing the simple job that will most often get them hired: *fulfill the needs of this particular story.* And when that story gets messed up as a result, I'm the jerk who wants to reply, *You chose that…what? You chose that you wanted to fuck up the story?*

As a result, you'll have a simple love story, and some student director or actor, acting in the name of "being personal" or "having a concept" will kill off the love in the name of some vision of hatred and contempt. Or, conversely, the scene in question will be a humdinger of a confrontation, one that we've been waiting for since the curtain went up, and the actors back off of it because they personally don't like confrontation, and would rather "find the love" instead. It's all okay, you see, because it's their *vision* of it. It's their *concept.* It's *personal.*

And if that "personal" choice is linked to some kind of trauma or victimization in the actor's past, look out! The actor will make an incorrect choice, but justify it by saying his father beat the crap out of him when he was a child, and then the whole class keens and cries because this actor's journey through trauma was moving or what-have-you. I'm then the *serious asshole* who says, "Yeah, sorry about your dad beating you up, but the story is fucked up if you make the choice you made based on that."

In my class there was once a disturbing/hilarious example of this warped kind of analysis, when an actor in class did the classic *Marty,* but played the guy as an angry, wounded animal, resentful for his loneliness and alienation, who ended up assaulting poor Clara when he brought her home from their night out! The resulting critique became downright hilarious, as the light dawned on the actor how epically wrong this choice was for the scene, and we decided to rename his particular version *Rape/Marty.* And to this day, I refer to the famous *Rape/Marty* scene as a the ultimate example where actors make "personal" choices that just utterly destroy the story. Personal work is work that serves the story *and* seems so "real" that the audience believes the actor must be revealing their actual life on stage. If, however, you inform your performance with something from your personal life to the detriment of the story? That's not "being personal," it's just wrong.

CHAPTER **31**

On Being Personal, Part 3: Dialectic

I was once asked to write an essay about "Being Personal," for a book that was to be a collection of essays on the topic from people in all walks of life. The book never came together, but I think there's still some value here.

I wrote it in form of an acting class critique, as a dedication and paying homage to Milton, who based much of his book *Acting Class* on actual transcribed conversations with actors. Here goes:

On Being Personal

A scene in an acting class concludes. The audience applauds, the two actors sit for their critique, and Allen points to one of them:

ALLEN: So, what do you want say?

STUDENT: Well, I guess I wanted to be personal with it, you know...

ALLEN: "Personal with it." Good. Now. What does that mean, exactly?

STUDENT: Well, I mean...Just to have the specifics, you know? The situation. I really wanted to have the breakup.

ALLEN: You mean you wanted to "have" that specific event. You wanted to feel here on the stage the way you might feel in life when your girlfriend breaks up with you.

STUDENT: Right.

ALLEN: Uh huh. And did you have that feeling?

STUDENT: No.

ALLEN: That hit in the gut? I always felt it in my stomach when I got dumped.

STUDENT: Me, too. No. I thought about it, but no, I didn't have any feeling at that moment.

ALLEN: I see. And being personal? What does that mean?

STUDENT: Uh. Hmph. It means being personal, I guess. I don't know how to put words to it.

ALLEN: I know. Everyone says they want to be personal. In every acting class on the planet, there are actors sitting down and telling the teacher they wanted to be personal. And by just saying it, I guess a lot of them get approving nods from teachers. I mean—how can you quarrel with an actor who says they want to be personal? It would be bad form.

STUDENT: I'm not sure where we're going.

ALLEN: Here's where I have to say, "I'm fine with the concept of being personal. You can't argue with that desire." Okay? I've said it. But what does it mean? What does it really mean?

STUDENT: Well, I think it's about spotting those aspects of the character that you understand, that you can identify with.

ALLEN: Identify with how?

STUDENT: Well, if the character is like, "I grew up in Boston" and I myself grew up in Boston, then you know…

ALLEN: You can identify with that? Boston?

STUDENT: Right.

ALLEN: The smell of autumn—the frustration of the Red Sox, that kind of thing. You're too young to remember that Red Sox fans were frustrated for decades.

STUDENT: I know. My father told me not to get spoiled—he thought he was going to die without ever seeing them win…

ALLEN: I'm with him. They won in 2004 and I said to myself, "I can get hit by a truck now. Anytime. No problem."

STUDENT: You're a Red Sox fan?

ALLEN: I'm from Boston.

STUDENT: Oh!

ALLEN: So—there's a character biography thing you're hitting. The character is from Boston, you're from Boston, so that makes it personal for you?

STUDENT: Yeah. I didn't know you were from Boston.

ALLEN: Surprises every day. Did you just identify with me a bit more? A little surge in the biochemistry of student-and-teacher, right?

STUDENT: Sure, of course.

ALLEN: Didn't have to think about it. It was just there. *Boston.* And the connection sparks. But here's the thing: I could have lied to you, right? I might be from Bozeman for all you know. Knowing you're from Boston, I could have lied so as to create an affinity between us, to facilitate the communication.

STUDENT: You could have.

ALLEN: And acting is a lie, right? We're making this shit up. Right?

STUDENT: Yeah, I guess.

ALLEN: Damned right. When I said I'm from Boston and you felt your chemistry change just the slightest—that was both personal, and possibly based on a lie. So if the character you're playing is from Cleveland and you're from Boston, what do you do?

STUDENT: Well…

ALLEN: Can't be personal with it?

STUDENT: Well—I mean, that would be kind of dumb.

ALLEN: Why?

STUDENT: Because that would mean I can only be personal when I'm…When I'm….

ALLEN: When you share biographical information with the character?

STUDENT: Right.

ALLEN: And that's dumb?

STUDENT: Sounds it.

ALLEN: Good! It is dumb. Biographical similarities have zero to do with being able to act a character "personally." Or impersonally. They can help. Or not. Zero relationship.

STUDENT: Okay, good. I'm still worried you're going to kill me.

ALLEN: Kill you?

STUDENT: Well, the scene. I'm worried the scene sucked.

ALLEN: How could it suck? You said you wanted to be personal. You wanted it, and you thought about it, so how could the scene suck if your intentions are so good?

STUDENT: Because…well. The ball didn't go in the hoop.

ALLEN: Okay. Moving to basketball—Celtics are historically much more used to winning. So no matter what you *think* about a ball going in the hoop, or what you *feel* about a ball going in the hoop, how much you *visualize* a ball going in the hoop, no matter how personal or impersonal you think you're being as you shoot the ball —it either goes in the hoop or not, right?

STUDENT: Yeah.

ALLEN: So in acting, what is it to say the ball went in the hoop?

STUDENT: Well, I guess that is the question.

ALLEN: Yup. That is the question. Here goes: I would say the ball in the hoop is that the story is told well—the audience believes in, cares about, and is moved by the story. The director is the stand-in for the audience along the way. So if the director is good, he or she is a reliable barometer for what the audience will experience. And of course you have different audiences. Different people within a single audience. So it ends up being a consensus thing, that you've put the ball in the hoop. But fact is they want to care, to be moved by the story. Your job is to do your best to ensure the audience has that experience.

STUDENT: Sounds…I don't know. Inorganic when you say it like that. Like a recipe.

ALLEN: It is a recipe. The greatest chefs in the world use recipes. And most storytelling follows a recipe. There's no shame in that. But I think actors romanticize this process. They think if they were really a good actor, they'd just…*commune with the gods of acting.* Like some sort of religious experience. Beyond analysis. And if you have an impure thought, well then you have *sinned.* An impure thought like, "I hate my life as an actor" or "I hate the camera person" or whatever. Anything other than *the thoughts of the character.* Because there are whole approaches to training that say if you're having an *impure thought,* then supposedly you're "out" as opposed to "in," and you're not being "personal." But that's the same as saying that the basketball going in the hoop only counts when the player is "personal" at the time he shoots. Ridiculous, right? So with basketball there's an observable phenomenon that everyone can agree on. How do you take the same idea and apply it to acting?

STUDENT: I don't know.

ALLEN: Exactly. We don't know. This personal thing. No one knows. No one has it. It's not the formula to Coca Cola, locked in a safe somewhere, objective, works every time, tastes the same everywhere in the world. No one has the first fucking clue. But the rules of storytelling, these can largely be thought of as recipes that work more times than not. And those recipes are not locked in a vault. They can be seen, studied, copied, mastered. So I happen to think actors should worry more about what is knowable based on the story, rather than what isn't knowable about whether they're trying to be personal or not personal or in or out or connected or disconnected, all that shit.

STUDENT: So is "being personal" just a bunch of crap?

ALLEN: It's not crap, not at all. I think any serious person in the arts would advocate for being personal in your work—but the question is *what does that really mean?* For me, I believe being personal is a sense of your work coming off as honest. That the work originates from within you as an honest effort to tell this particular story well. And maybe I'm splitting hairs, but there's the literalness of "being personal in your work" and then there's what's necessary for storytelling: "the *apparency* of being personal in your work." Is "apparency" even a word?

CLASS MEMBER: I don't think so.

ALLEN: No? It is now. For tonight it's a word. I'm crazy like that. And since we out in the audience haven't the first fucking clue about whether you're actually being personal or not, and there's no test for it, all we have left is the apparency. So yeah, of course, we're on a search for the truth in our work. Truth is subjective in art —but if you're looking for a real experience in some way, telling that story honestly, that's the closest we can get to our analogous basketball hoop…The two points count when the story communicates. when it *lands*. BUT. BUT…that communication may or may not be personal for you on any given night. So I guess I'm saying it's not so much about whether there is personal work going on, but is there the *apparency* of personal work going on.

STUDENT: I think I'm getting you…

ALLEN: I mean, I've never met them, I don't pretend to know the inner workings of their brains—but I'd bet if you ask Meryl Streep or Daniel Day Lewis or whomever you admire to dissect their thoughts at the moment of acting—they can't tell you. I don't think they're analyzing their work in the slightest. That's my bet. They're prepared, they're researched, they've figured out physically or voice-wise what they want to do, but then they let go. And I would bet a smart director lets them go. The director might say—*more here, less here, quieter here, louder, let's try it such-and-such a way*—I don't know. A discussion, for sure—about the story, about what's happening in the scene, about behavior. But I don't think there are on-set conversations about the actors being *personal*. I think those are conversations that occur only in acting classes. And the danger there is that we teachers introvert the actor, and mistakenly develop in them some inner voice that yells at them while they act: *You impersonal piece of shit. This is the part where the breakup happens, you'd better get emotional on this line and it needs to be personal—get personal, man, you're so fucking impersonal right now, you suck so fucking bad…*

Class laughs.

ALLEN: It's like that Garfield cartoon I remember once: Jon asks Garfield if when he walks, he alternates legs or moves the left legs together and then the right legs together. There's a box where Garfield just looks down at his legs and then in the last box he thinks, "I'll never walk again."

Class laughs.

ALLEN: So truly, I'm not putting it down—the *concept* of being personal. It sounds as if I am, but I'm just…I'm trying to make a logical point here. I'm only putting it down as a robotic thing that actors always say and that teachers always acknowledge. If a teacher says to you after a scene that this work is "really personal," I'm just the asshole pointing out they have no idea if it's personal or not, but certainly it must have had the *apparency* of being personal. You can think you suck as an actor, even at the moment of performing, and still tell the story well. Conversely, your "being personal" may be experienced by you, but not by the audience. Or you'll have those occasions where you're certain that you and the audience have gone on some transcendent ride together, and the director visits that night— and he or she is unhappy, and gives you two pages of notes about how you fucked it up. So in the end you have to do it for the Fat Lady.

Silence.

ALLEN: Total silence. No one in here knows the reference, right?

STUDENT IN AUDIENCE: "It's not over until the fat lady sings."

ALLEN: No, that's different. *You have to do it for the Fat Lady.* Nothing. Crickets. Jesus. SALINGER! *Frannie & Zooey!* Anyone ever read it?

A couple hands go up.

ALLEN: Dear God. Okay. Zooey is a young actor, and he's telling a story about when he was a kid, and they were a showbiz family of sorts, and I forget—one of them doesn't want to go on, maybe it was Zooey—he doesn't want to be looked at as a freak or doesn't want to tie his shoes for the show they're doing or whatever, and the older brother at that time tells him to do it for the Fat Lady. And Zooey then tells his sister, years later, who's having a religious experience of sorts, that the Fat Lady is Jesus Christ. And trust me I'm not advocating for religion, I've been there, no thank you. What I'm trying to say is that if you're acting for a review, or for money, or for me to say "nice scene," or for some authority to come in and say, "Now THAT was personal," you're doomed. Act for the Fat Lady. You define the Fat Lady, you make her whomever you want. But for me, the Fat Lady represents a sincere desire to serve the story, to get it right, to fool the audience into believing it for an evening. With that desire, that mindset, I think that whatever there is in acting that can be looked at as a basketball—it will go in the hoop. And it if doesn't make the grade by the measure of you…Well, just shoot the ball again. Clear? Or at least clearer?

STUDENT: Yeah. So…

ALLEN: Yes?

STUDENT: So are you from Boston or not?

ALLEN: Between Buckner's error and 2004, I was a broken man.

CHAPTER 32

A Prism Doesn't Think

An actor is a prism. The writing is the light.

Each writer, being utterly unique, will create a different variation of light.

Each actor, being utterly unique, will refract light in his or her own distinct way, before even thinking of making a choice about the matter.

A director's job is to look at the light, figure out which prism does the best job refracting that particular light, and manipulate a bunch of prisms during rehearsal or shooting so in combination they create a light show…like that. No…Like *that*.

So one thing you can do is ensure you, the prism, are clear, not cracked, not sharp to hold, that you're easy to move this way and that, and that the light shines through you in a nice vivid way. Meaning: say the damned lines correctly and in order, and of course imbue them with reality and emotions appropriate to the situation of the story and the tone of the script, and style of the writer. Once you do that, the nature of your instrument—including age, voice, look, body, ethnicity, etc.—will either contribute to your being right for the part or not. So the part of that equation you really control is the "imbue them with the reality and emotions appropriate to the story point and tone of the script and style of the writer."

Now: Picture the prism with a brain. And the brain generates all these damned thoughts about light, about what the prism should do with light, it argues about the color of the light, it offers up a bunch of doubt about whether the prism should be a prism, it wonders if it should refract light at all, and it's decided it will give it another six months of refracting light before going to grad school to become coal. Perhaps the prism comes to the grand light show of The Biz with occlusions and cracks, and just as soon as their acting teacher, sorry —*prism repairman*—has got it shiny and new, the prism, of its own accord, jumps into acid during a party at a friend's house, falls down on the asphalt, drags its ass home, only to wake up a few hours later looking next to them in bed at the hammer they picked up at a party. Then they complain about how their agent sucks. *Yeah, that's why you're not getting some light to refract.*

Obviously each actor should be able freely to pass light through the prism—anger, humor, irony, love, exasperation, overall dynamic range, etc. Occlusions present themselves as an inability to present vividly some of that light. The light gets stuck in the prism. Will the proper thought get it out? Perhaps, but I am known for being highly dubious that there is a blessed correct thought the actor may think that will really change much about their acting. Sometimes the answer is simply to stop thinking about it. And since thoughts are unknowable outside your head anyway, the entire black hole comprised of discussions about thinking the right thought have very little value to me. Picture a prism in your hand, and you're moving it this way and that, you're checking out the light on the wall. If that hunk of glass is thinking something while you do that…it's pretty damned unimportant.

For most commercially-tilted film and network television, I'd say the prism should shut the hell up and be a prism. The writers have created light—it has a quality, a color, a certain style to it. When it runs through a certain kind of prism, the effect is exactly what they want and what advertisers will pay to make commercials for. There simply isn't much the prism is going to contribute to that equation by manipulating its innards in some effort to do a double-special super-personal omni-sexual refraction that will just blow these producers away. It's pretty much the light, the prism, and that's that. I'm not seeing very much "character" work on network television—the people you see in those roles are pretty much exactly as they appear when they are a guest on late night talk shows. The most productive work your brain can do here is to ensure you're one of the prisms that gets called in on a regular basis, so you get a chance to refract a lot of different light for a lot of different people.

The frustrating part of being a prism with a brain is that by having a brain you're constantly pulled in the direction of using said brain to monitor refraction, modify refraction, doubt refraction, and it's possible you have now forgotten you already have all sorts of qualities that are going to refract light if you'd simply let yourself do it. Actors tend constantly to monitor refraction and change it, occluding it entirely sometimes, rather than ensuring the prism is in good condition and being seen by a lot of people. Milton would sometimes say, "Acting is actually easy, the difficulty is in seeing how easy it can be."

Are there circumstances where prisms need to think about light? Of course. The point I'm making with this metaphor is that I believe your average prism is thinking *too much* about how to refract, and often to no useful effect whatsoever. If you have on your hands a delicious bit of theatre writing, or its television cousin known as the badass cable series, or a terrific independent movie, where the stories, characters, and scripts are far more audacious—here the work can certainly benefit from a sharp intellect and bolder character work, so you can decide to cancel out all "red" from the light and man, do you suddenly pop in the role.

There are some special prisms out there for sure—Streep, Hoffman, Blanchett, Day Lewis, Depp, Oldman, and umpteen others who can seemingly refract light in an entirely different way for each role. And as a teacher you every so often come across some of those special hunks of glass, and you do your level best to develop that talent as fully as possible. But looking at the entire spectrum of light being created for all content across the acting universe, there's a lot of work to be had by a simple, clear, healthy, vibrant prism. Or, if you'll forgive the radical shift in metaphors…You don't need Vladimir Horowitz to play "Chopsticks."

Then there's this one: you might have on your hands a prism with a particular occlusion that's perfect for a certain light, and if that light is really popular, you can have an occluded prism that is in some friggin' demand. That can be pretty infuriating if you're the really special kind, to see that occluded prism booking jobs right and left while you sit alone and splash gorgeous light across your one-bedroom in the Valley.

Tricky thing, this calibration of light and prism. The point here is to try to get actors to separate the light, the prism, the people who are picking prisms for various reasons, and try to focus their attention on what will be useful for them over the long haul.

CHAPTER 33

Hold The Grenade

One of the most common story-telling conventions is that of giving a lead character a previous trauma that occurred before the story begins. The question of how to deal with this trauma as the actor can be vexing. Authors will try to "help" you by offering statements on this matter, and usually they will caution not to play too much emotion regarding the trauma. The writer is certainly well-intentioned, because if you have a play where some inexperienced actor cries in every scene because someone died just before the play begins, you'll probably have a pretty bad night in the theatre. The danger of these warnings, however, is that of an over-correction by the actor: they act as if nothing at all out of the ordinary occurred. Scar tissue all the way.

ALLEN: Hey, according to the story, your child died right before this play begins. And yet you're acting like…this is supposed to be the worst thing in the world, and you're looking relatively sanguine.

STUDENT: Well, the playwright has a note in the beginning about too much emotion. So I made the choice to play the cover, she presents a front to the world to cover her pain.

That's all well and good, it's logical, and you can find plenty of people in "real life" who mask their troubles with a brave, happy face. I would argue, however, that a play *exists* to reveal that pain, not to hide it. The play *exists* to demonstrate the conflict between the character's outer life (hide the pain) and inner life (ouch). The play *exists* for actors to pick up a metaphorical grenade, pull the pin, and blow it up right on stage. Your job as the actor is to hold that grenade and let it blow up. Reveal both those sides in vivid fashion. It's a balancing act between two mistakes— that of crying all the time and that of revealing nothing. But I would say the more common mistake in the student actor is the latter—showing nothing—or at least showing far too little. To me, the better an actor becomes, the more lacerating they can be in revealing the emotions caused by the trauma, while at the same time maintaining a dignity, humor and a certain class at other times. This is a very difficult balancing act, but no different from a really good musician who can blow your mind with how rich and deep their sound can be a certain times, while revealing such poised quietude at others. It's the mark of a high-caliber actor. Making mistakes in one direction or another along the way is common.

The mistaken analysis is to make it a binary: either cry, or be stoic. I would encourage you to reveal the emotional cost of that trauma when you can. Don't save it so much. The more valuable skill to develop is to get in there and reveal—once you get used to that, control will be another phase of your development. But the tendency to avoid revealing the trauma, to play always a stoic front, has the *technical* downside that the student actor will play to this low-affect "strength" too often and never develop emotional range, and the *storytelling* downside that the audience gains insufficient access to that emotion.

Speaking of that emotion, tears are not your only tool! Reveal that wound through taking too much time to respond to certain communication. Reveal it through the 1,000-yard stare. Reveal it through weird anger responses—getting angry at the wrong time over seemingly small provocations. There are many more ways to manifest grief than just crying, and the use of all those colors is again the mark of a fine actor.

CHAPTER 34

The Do-Less Conundrum

Ask an actor for the most frequent adjustment they hear when going in for your average film or television audition (but particularly the latter), and there's a good chance you'll hear that the casting person told them, "Do less." Some thoughts on this:

1. They said *do* less, not *be* less. I think after a while, this cascade of "do less" feedback leads actors to be afraid of choices, afraid of evaluation, afraid of their shadow. But don't actually become less of who you are. It may simply be a matter of learning to do less with that evaluation you've already got. That's why I sometimes try to use the word *placement*—like in tennis. You want the ball to go right there in the corner, but that doesn't mean you have zero intention, just standing inert on the tennis court for fear of overhitting it. There's still energy, focus, intention— all of it…but in the service of a particular shot, or this particular story.

2. Coffee-shop naturalism rules the day. I'm not advocating for it, and it's probably not the kind of acting which stirred our youthful dreams of art and performance. But for the most part that's what's happening on television, particularly in the drama category. Procedurals dominate—and acting isn't what moves procedurals, it's, well…the procedure. At around 45 minutes into every episode of *House* (one of my old favorites), the B-storyline would feed Dr. House an idea that led him to solve the A-story medical mystery. That doesn't mean Hugh Laurie didn't kick the shit out of it—but you generally are looking at a lead performance that can be

fun to watch, but these days is often still pretty restrained in the acting. Surround the lead with a gang of other generally less vivid characters (except for one who's always a bit more "out there," some kooky desk assistant or nurse) and add in a plot structure that's rigid as a rock. All the *CSI* and *Criminal Minds* and *Law and Order* franchises operate the same way—and it's not the acting that is particularly special about any of it. (Serials offer more opportunity for interesting acting choices, they give the actors far more latitude than you find in procedurals.) So this fits in with my essay on "Name That Tone"—you have to know the tone of the show, the style of the acting, and place your acting and the choices accordingly with the project. I would say most actors who have ended up seeing the episode of the show they were up for probably looked at the performance as cast and muttered, "That's *it*? That's all they wanted?"

3. There's a lot going on other than you and your performance. For TV, you're walking into a situation where you've got a show-runner and/or writer-producer whose job it is to maintain the world of the story, the characters, the overall tone, in addition to all the logistics of budget of a big production. Then you have a gaggle of writers working on each script, they're managing a bunch of characters who show up each week as leads and supporting leads, and then you have the actors in those roles and all those personalities and egos, and then different directors for each episode. They have 100+ people at work on a series every week in and out, and then there's you. You feel perhaps as if you're on the outside looking in, but you've got this opportunity to go in to read for your scene or your guest star or what-have-you. We have to ensure that despite the fact that this audition was one of three you had this month, or this quarter, or this year—you don't corrupt your instrument and psychology so that you feel you need to burst upon the scene with this particular sucker and damnit, *they're finally gonna see you for the talent that you truly are.* I have an inkling that actors sometimes do about five auditions' worth of acting in a single audition, and so the choices get perhaps unintentionally amplified given the overall picture of what's happening in

the lives of those doing the casting, not to mention the story
and what's required for it.

4. Actors are unaware of what energy they bring into a room
   just as themselves. Take an empty room with a chair in it.
   Got it? Now someone walks in and sits down in the chair.
   The room is already different. The actor needs to be aware of
   this, or at least aware enough that they don't blithely go past
   the change in energy that has already occurred and double-
   down on it with a big choice. The result can be that it seems
   "too big for TV." If Ethel Merman comes in the room, that's
   a presence. Now if she doubles down on it with a huge
   choice—she may not get that part on *CSI: Boise.* Not these
   days. Some actors have a strong physicality, some bring a
   shyness, some bring a sharp wit—I won't pretend to be the
   arbiter on what quality you're bringing, nor do I mean to
   introvert everyone into deep analysis of how they change an
   empty room. What I do want is to call attention to the fact
   that, particularly for the naturalistic style of most current
   television, simply being in the room and knowing the story,
   the tone, and being truthful to that—that's oftentimes as
   much as you need. What's needed to tell the story correctly
   will rarely require all the talent you have.

5. Don't resent the correction. They're not wrong for saying,
   "Do Less," even if to you the note seems frustrating. They
   may actually want a little less. Maybe they're just repeating
   what the Casting Fairy told them to instruct actors. Maybe
   they're checking that you can be compliant with a request.
   Or perhaps, *mirabile dictu,* they in fact know more than you
   about the style of the show, what the director that week likes
   or dislikes, or what the writer-producer wants for the style
   they're after. So—no chip on the shoulder, no resentment,
   no subconscious urge to wring their necks while launching
   into a five-paragraph soliloquy of intense emotional revelation. Just easy-going compliance. That easy-going nature is
   in and of itself a highly attractive element in casting a role,
   because they'll get from you that you're going to be okay in
   the middle of a stressful environment.

6. Lighten up. You simply cannot take any of this too seriously, nor at all personally. There are a number of "overall type" factors that may keep you from the part despite even the most brilliant acting —they want the role taller, shorter, greener, pinker, deeper voice, more innocent look, a touch older, a bit frailer, a bit less like the lead actor, not quite as funny as the funny supporting actor we've got…It's so subjective and while I do believe that any actor is capable of changing any preconception about what the role should be—each actor for their own sanity has to have the long view in mind and not allow the maddening "do less" aesthetic of some film and dramatic television affect their morale one way or the other.

CHAPTER 35

Why Comedy Scenes Go Awry

Two reasons, generally:

1. Lack of energy. Comedy is often a dramatization of two or more colliding points of view. The verb *collide* is key there. It's not two points of view that meet for a relaxed latte at Starbucks. It's not two points of view sensitively recognizing each other's essential humanity. It's a collision. Sparks fly through application of force. Now that collision isn't necessarily violent, it doesn't mean that the energy I'm talking about means screaming and sweat pouring down the brow and broken furniture all over the place. (Although some comedies…they get that crazy, yes.) It just means there is a sharpness to it, an edge, there is electricity coursing through it—I often tell actors that the scene must be "plugged in." When it falls flat you feel as if the thing was simply never turned on. All the questions of "Evaluation" from Milton's checklist are particularly relevant to comedy. That's why the ol' saying goes, *Dying is easy, comedy is hard.* But if you look at those who do it well, you'll almost always see actors who understand the energy underneath that fuels the collision in points of view.

2. Insufficient understanding of how the writing generates humor, and/or what makes this specific writer tick. This is a matter of experience and work ethic far more than it is of native intelligence or official education. An actor who does twenty comedy scenes in a few months' time will be better at it than someone wading into those waters for the first time.

Ditto for dealing with different writers. Sorkin is different from Durang who's different from Simon who's different from Shanley who's different from Ephron and on it goes. The understanding of a specific writer's voice and rhythms, when not instinctually present, can be developed through old fashioned hard work. Shanley, specifically, provides a very rich, sweet, humorous tapestry in his work, and his plays are excellent training ground.

So, are there some actors who understand these elements better than others, who perhaps are more skilled at presenting these elements in the proper dosages to get the almighty laugh? Absolutely. Did they develop that acumen through a lot of hard work, reading, participating in a ton of comedic theatre or the like? Quite probably. Did they emerge from the womb gifted in comedy? Unlikely. Did they grow up in a family surrounded by others who understood these rhythms, and hence picked it up through years of that kind of experience? Yup. Lots of ways to skin a cat, to get this comedic sense in your acting. But I think too many actors rely on the generalities of "I get it" or "I don't get it" to assess their abilities with comedic material as a whole, or this week's three-page comedic audition. The fact is ability here can be developed, and the material itself understood through application of work and sought-out understanding.

CHAPTER 36

Naturalism, Honesty And Heightened Reality

I once had an interesting chat with an actor in class who was questioning whether my taste and his taste were compatible for further training. At issue was the topic of "naturalism," for which my from-the-hip definition would be, "that style of acting where the unadorned presence of the actor, delivering the lines of the script in a 'real' way, is all that is required to tell the story."

I perhaps too often decry naturalism, not because it isn't useful or in demand, but because it's boring. I find the acting in most network television to be boring, and the style these days is marked by excessive naturalism. That being said, I've written plenty about how actors need to know what project they're reading for, and if the show is marked by a naturalistic style, they'd better serve it up and give themselves a real shot for a paycheck.

Prior to our conversation, I'd seen this actor do scenes from Guirgis' *Motherfucker With The Hat* and Mamet's *Race*. I don't believe either of those writers deals in naturalism as a style, and in both, I felt this actor's naturalistic tendency was inhibiting the full expression of the writing. So I redirected both scenes as part of my critique, complete with line-readings, because I'm *that* guy—the jerk who'll give line-readings from here to Timbuktu if that's what it takes. The actor was not pleased—hence our conversation.

He felt "naturalism" was more closely related to "honesty." To be natural was to be honest, to be real, and that was the start point of all good acting. So he hears "natural" and thinks "honest," and I say "natural" and mean "boring." So…You can see why he was wondering whether to continue!

I enjoy conversations like this, actually, because I figure there are others who think just as this guy thought, but he happened to be forthright enough to come and speak to me about it. So to be clear: We both want the work to be honest, to represent real people in real situations, so the audience believes what is happening in the story. To me that's a good expression of the ultimate simplicity of acting's purpose: "To make the audience believe the story." That is a very agreeable start point for me in judging acting—*do I believe what's going on here?* And yeah, simple naturalistic acting, if that's what the writing and the story require, is often good enough to make me believe. Job done.

I just happen also to think we go to the movies and to the theatre for something a touch beyond that which we see every day at a coffee shop. And it's not just the stories that will take us there, but some vivid acting—this is particularly true in theatre, which as a form is auditory, versus television/film, which is a visual medium. So in theatre I believe we really have to *hear* the play, and each has its own music, its own rhythm. Playwrights are often much freer to express themselves at length, and in order to bring the music to life, something beyond simple reality is necessary. And, further, I believe that actors who can use good writing to expand their expression will be better suited and more valuable even to those naturalistic styles and shows, because every so often, even in TV/Film where actors are afraid of being "too big," you need a little *ka-pow*, and a little rhythm, and some more expressive moves.

So in class when I decry "naturalism," it's only that for most advanced level actors, to sit there and be "real" is not so much a chore, and I don't want to be the guy who collects tuition to validate what they can already do. I think a class should also serve to expand those boundaries, and encourage actors to look at writing that allows, even *demands*, that expansion. For the beginning actor, getting them to be natural on stage, and able to bring to life a simple conversation without artifice—this is very important. So this essay is somewhat directed toward the more advanced actor in class. For many of these actors, the job of getting work on a naturalistic network show is more a matter of administrative discipline and getting a significant number of auditions than it is one of acting *ability*. Terrific careers can happen on the usage of 30% of your talent, but I think actors need to be in the gym, working out 100% of the talent in order for even that 30% to shine the way they want.

CHAPTER 37

Ferrari At A Red Light

In Los Angeles in particular, which tends perhaps more than other cities to a relentlessly naturalistic acting style, the concept of acting with high evaluation is fraught with anxiety. *What if they say I'm too big?! What if I'm told to "do less"?!*

And look, I'm a big believer that a professional actor doesn't act in one style. A professional actor is equipped to assess the material and know where to place his or her shot. Not every shot in tennis is a smashing forehand. Not every script or character demands high evaluation. If you're going up for a network procedural, you should serve up the acting style that is most likely to get you hired for that gig.

Both a Ferrari and a Yugo can go from 0-40 MPH. On any day walking around Beverly Hills, you'll see a dozen or more cars that cost over $150,000, going from red light to red light in first gear. A junker goes from red light to red light, too, but it doesn't catch our eye. Why doesn't it catch our eye? Beyond the eye-candy factor, I believe it's a sense of potential. *See that Ferrari? That sucker can do 200 MPH.* (I sure hope most of these people who drop that cash have access to a track where they can open the throttle on those cars, because otherwise what's the point?)

I think the really good actors always project that sense of potentially hitting 200 MPH, even when they're going from red light to red light in first gear on some network guest star or what-have-you. The best way to develop and have confidence in that potential is to take a class, where you can open up the throttle on material that supports it. I've observed, however, that too many actors are simply coasting around town, taking classes that ask them to putter about from red light to red light, and as a result they show up for auditions and drive 0-40 MPH, but like a junker and not a Ferrari.

There's the fun of knowing you can do anything as an actor, while *choosing* to withhold the open throttle—that can create a very interesting dynamic. People turn their heads. But then there's simply being afraid of choices. Junker. People walk past without another look.

CHAPTER 38

On Innocence And Guilt

Play innocent. It will almost always be the right choice. There are three possible denouements for an innocent-or-guilty story: the character ends up demonstrably innocent; the character ends up demonstrably guilty; or it will be ambiguous, with no definitive answer, a circumstantial case where known facts generally point to guilt, but the character protests innocence, confusion, or "can't remember" all the way. No matter which it is, playing innocent is the way you have to go. If the character is proven innocent, well then *of course* you played it that way, it's what's true per the story! If he's proven guilty, *of course* you played innocent. Why act guilty, when it's not going to help at all your cause of getting away with it? It would ruin the surprise when we find out the character is in fact guilty—we generally have to feel at that moment like, "Aw, man! I liked him! I believed him!" If it's ambiguous, then it's up to the audience to fight about it on the way out of the theatre, and your portrayal should still likely tilt towards, yes, innocence.

(The only exception to all this would be somewhat dishonestly constructed "red-herring" stories, popular on television procedurals: In the first 10 minutes of the episode, facts clearly point to someone with all the motive and kind of a guilty demeanor, and then with ten minutes left in the episode we find out—*shocker!*—it was actually the sweet-as-sugar person who was dismissed early as clearly innocent. In this case, the red-herring character should come off kind of guilty. But it's clearly just a trope for this specific story trick. Unfortunately, the sides you'll get for the audition rarely tell you whether you're the bad guy or the red herring.)

Let's apply this to John Patrick Shanley's play, *Doubt*, a great example of the ambiguous guilt story. I've met many an actor who seems to think they need to answer for themselves whether Brendan did it or not, did he molest the boy or is he innocent? And the answers are all over the map, individual to each actor. Some actors dig into the sins they have in their own life, trying to hook them up to the character.

But instead of coming at Brendan with "Did he or didn't he?", how about my favorite question for actors: "What does *Doubt* require of me?" Well —it sounds obvious as hell, but it requires...*doubt*. Where? In the audience. The last line of the play is Aloysius': "I have such doubt." The audience needs to leave asking whether he did it or not, and why, if Aloysius in fact had any doubt about her relentless campaign against Brendan, was she so determined to nail him? That's the argument we need them to have in the lobby on the way out. As the actor playing Brendan, you can go on stage for a couple hours thinking you did it, you can think you didn't do it, you can spend the play wondering whether you left the iron on or whether you fed the cat. It doesn't matter. Your thoughts about the character do not impinge on the audience or affect their experience. No matter what thought you have before performing or while performing, the bottom line is that the words of the characters and the action of the play have been designed by Shanley to result in *doubt*.

Aloysius says you did it. You say you didn't. The actor's thoughts have no role to play here. The script requires you to play innocence. She thinks you're guilty, you say you're innocent, and the play doesn't give us any solid information one way or the other, other than that interesting back-and-forth between them about their own sins and how they have dealt with them. Brendan says, "There are some things I can't say." It sure is an interesting line, but it simply does not point conclusively either to guilt or innocence. I think if you play any form of guilty, I don't know how the play stands up in the end. We have to like this guy. He's the lead of the play. He's selling a friendlier, more approachable form of Catholicism. The audience has to invest their belief in him and his innocence. If your performance telegraphs guilt from the beginning, it's going to be a very long night. Hell, even if at the end there was a *deus ex machina* device where someone had a videotape of Brendan molesting that boy, you would still play innocence all the way through until that moment, and perhaps even past it. Even if he was a monster, about which Shanley is purposefully ambiguous, how many of those monsters have we seen on television, the real guys, when they're busted—they're either denying it, or they act completely justified in their choices, almost proud of them! So. The script requires you play conviction and passion and innocence. Think whatever you want during prep, in rehearsal, during a performance—it doesn't matter in the slightest. It's all about what you *play.* And aside from red-herring cop procedurals, playing innocence will serve you most of the time.

CHAPTER 39

Victim Vs. Fighter

When playing a character beset by loss, difficulty, physical injury, crime, betrayal, corruption, poverty, addiction, abuse, grief, etc. (and let's face it, characters exist pretty much solely to be beset by *something* on that list), don't be just a "wictim," as Milton humorously used to pronounce it. Audiences will tolerate stories about victims of a shit life comprising any or all of the above, but would prefer a healthy dose of the fighter. Avoid for longer than about twenty seconds the choice to capitulate to circumstance, to sit in some metaphorical corner and cry softly. You're allowed a moment of that. Everyone just died? Okay—sit in the corner and cry. But not for long. After that you'd better demonstrate the desire and need to fight for survival, whether that's emotional or physical (or both). Balance grief with righteous anger. Balance the craving for a drug with knowing somehow you must fight for freedom from that need. Balance the pain of injustice, the frustration of dealing with an uncaring bureaucracy, with the steely determination to prevail. You might even find some desperate humor in the character's predicament.

Nobody likes a wictim, everyone loves a fighter. It's not what happens to you that counts, it's how you deal with what happens you. Design your performance with that in mind and you'll heighten the storytelling, and the audience's rooting factor for your character.

CHAPTER 40

Sexuality Neurosis

One of the biggest acting class cliches are actors who say they are "working on their sexuality." The fact that 90% of those working this "note" are females, so assigned from a male teacher, well, that's just part of the cliche.

(Disclaimer: I'm from Boston, we have Puritanical roots, and I've often joked in class that we New Englanders don't talk about sex even when we're engaged in it. I can barely say the word "sexuality" without wanting to barf. So I fully admit that the following is based in a big fat eye roll about sexuality in stage and film, or at least conversation about it. It just kind of bores me as a topic.)

So, disclaimer disclaimed, let me say that I think actors (and possibly teachers) of all genders and orientation are too worked up in general about sexuality, and this leads to all sorts of fairly useless introversion and introspection and analysis about why one's sexuality might be "blocked," and then crazy exercises about how to "unblock" your sexuality—it all just kind of creeps me out, frankly. As a teacher I don't consider this my business, and it seems very indulgent and possibly damaging.

First question: Does anyone actually believe about themselves that they're so damned sexy? I say no. I can think of a few who would, in some trying-too-hard "positive self-image" manner, *say* they feel that way. But I have found that people will on occasion voice the very opinion of themselves that they don't actually believe. Right? Or, they have a narcissism disorder. Or they are empirically incorrect (couldn't resist). No, I would say very few walk around thinking themselves sexy. That person over *there* is sexy. And that one over *there*. If someone finds *us* sexy, it's gratifying but they're wrong. We unsexy mortals who actually walk the earth, rather than hover over it in a gravitation-reversing sexy energy field, might have a shot at it if we finally go through at long last with that P90XYZ/Pilates/Cleanse/Crossfit (PPCC Super Bod Package—only four installments of $199.99), after which we can peek askance in the mirror and wonder anew.

Next question: Okay, we're evolved enough to know that physical godliness is cool for health but probably not necessary as a component in sexual appeal, and maybe it's that whole "confidence" thing that is covered in chick mags and on the Oprah Winfrey Network. That way we can carry a few more pounds than we should and still qualify as sexy. Well, let me ask: Who is it who is walking around actually feeling so bloody confident about themselves? As in—on a regular basis? *No one.* If anyone does, they're probably employing some desperate mantra like Brenda in *Four Dogs and a Bone*. Everyone doubts. All the time. Maybe there are blessed moments—like when those NBA players get into a rhythm and hit six three-pointers in a row. But I would bet there's not a solitary second of those streaks where the player is saying to himself, "I'm really confident right now." They certainly aren't thinking, "I'm in touch with my sexuality, too." I think they're in a zone and aren't thinking at all. Perhaps a certain technical point about follow-through or hitting a certain spot on the floor to take the shot. Confidence is as confidence does. I would bet on an individual basis that confidence is actually believed in far less than we think by those who seem to exhibit it so effortlessly.

So here's my point at last. Sexuality in story telling is technical. It is a script point—brought to life by actors who relate to each other in a believable way. It has no more or less significance than the assumption of an accent or physical trait. Sexuality as a story point is not impacted by nudity, by simulated sex acts, and most importantly we don't need belief, confidence, awareness of your sexuality—none of it. We need you to behave in a certain way with the other actor so the audience believes there is an attraction, if that indeed is the story point. Going further—we can stage a love-making scene so it's believable. Done. There is simply zero psychology necessary for the job. You don't have to like yourself. You don't have to be in touch with your sexuality, or not in touch with it. You don't even have to like the other person. (Remember the stories about the supposed antagonism between Debra Winger and Richard Gere in *An Officer and a Gentleman*?)

No one bloody cares about your sexuality—its makeup, its components, its practices. No one wants to know your orientation, I don't think anyone should be aware of any of it, unless they're actually involved with you. (Those that do advertise their orientation do so at their own risk of having to surmount the age old showbiz obstacle—can a known gay actor play straight and vice versa? Is it a useful, evolved conversation embracing tolerance and blind justice? Probably not. Is it a real one that occurs in the world every day and affects casting? Absolutely—see the essay on *Diversity Distress*.)

I recall a scene where the sexual chemistry between the characters was an important element in the story. But the actress was sitting on a bench and her legs were locked together so tight and she seemed uncomfortable and wouldn't move and it was a classic *Where's Your Sexuality?* moment. And then it came to me—she's worried about her short skirt. The stage is elevated, and she's worried we can see up her skirt. So here was my fancy psychological critique about her sexuality: Get a different skirt. Or stage it differently so you aren't risking that embarrassment. Done.

I think sexuality has little or no place in a discussion about acting. People think that the *schwing* factor that brings two people together in the real world has to be actually present to tell a story about sex, so they worry about whether they have enough *schwing*, are they in touch with their *schwing*, they should have done those *schwing* exercises…And it's just total crap. I've directed plenty of plays, and stories being stories, they involved attraction and sex and relationships and all that, and not once did I say the word sexuality or have a discussion with actors about it. There were only discussions about how believably to stage a story point to communicate the relationship effectively, in accordance with the tone of the script. Chemistries between actors were either there or not, but it didn't matter. Casting for love stories is crucial, and yeah they want to see if there's chemistry. But I'd bet a lot of money that never was there an audition or test for casting a love story that involved a discussion about individual sexuality.

So lighten up, and please hereby free yourself of the sexuality neurosis.

CHAPTER 41

Script, Uh, Discipline

My rapidly advancing age has perhaps made me downright persnickety, but for some reason my ear has become more sensitive to the increasing lack of discipline with, you know, uh, saying the words of the script, uh, and, like, only the words of the script. Right? Huh?

This kind of sloppiness is a bad habit, and particularly so with theatre scripts, which tend towards greater density of words and potential power of expression, all of which get fucked up by what my purist classical music-listening ears pick up as an increasing cacophony of contemporary verbal pollution. One hopes the writer has done a good job arranging just the right words in just the right order to bring a circumstance to life in an interesting, enlightening way. (Read Stoppard on the art of writing in Act II, Scene 1 of *The Real Thing*—brilliance I shall not try to emulate here.) If he or she has failed, let them fail without your additions to the equation. Then the teacher can make a clean call on it, by advising you work on better writing or somehow helping it along in some way that will benefit your training via the scene in question.

(There are related topics here—the translation used for foreign language scripts, different adaptations, different edits, combining film scenes to create a better stage scene for class purposes, the free-fire zone of rehearsals that allow exploration through improvisation, paraphrasing, etc. I'm not talking about all that. This post is really targeting the moment of performance, and the concept of largely reflexive, often unconscious verbal pollution.)

So, cutting to the chase, stop with the following:

1. Adding "…right?" to the ends of sentences.

2. Adding "…huh?" as an intensifier to the ends of questions.

3. Adding "like…/uh…/um…" in the middle of sentences.

4. Saying a character name more often than is indicated in the script.

5. Adding "fuck/shit," etc, where they are not so indicated.

6. Relying too much on the "I'm so dang real right now I don't know what I'm going to say and so the line will kind of emerge from me in this brutally honest, way—like I don't know the line." This kind of reflexively "authentic" line reading, which is based on a good idea…I mean, one of the basic questions of acting is how do I make the line appear out of nowhere, as if from spontaneous response to the situation, even though everyone involved knows exactly what everyone is going to say and do? How does an actor "not-know" the script that has been so well rehearsed? Acting 101 stuff there, but I would offer that while this is an excellent question, eternally so, the answer is NOT: "…To be…uh…Or…uh…Not to be. Right? Huh?" *Actor pauses as if to find the next words*…"Whether 'tis nobler…in the fucking mind…"

Shakespeare gets so much reverence and fear from actors, that one wouldn't dare mess with his writing this way. But I do often wish that contemporary writers were treated similarly.

When the writing is good, it will benefit from clear, expressive, unornamented delivery by the actor, who by their natural or hard-won talent will bring to life the reality and emotions of the situation, and in the proper style. If the writing is not good, why the fuck, uh, are you…uh…like…fucking working on it, right? Huh? Okay? Pick better stuff!

I will now desist, and go out to yell at the kids on the street that that crazy rock 'n roll music will ruin their morals.

CHAPTER **42**

Manic Behavior

Somewhere out there, somewhere magical, where everything is *just so*, there lies the sweet spot regarding the issue of actor behavior in a scene. My definition of this sweet spot: "Physical action enough to lend logic to the premise of the story, its location, the specifics of the characters and the scene, without veering unnecessarily towards excessive wandering, tinkering, dusting, wandering, vegetable-peeling, makeup-applying, wandering, trash-disposing, stuffed-animal cuddling, coffee-stirring, drink-making mania."

Behavior should serve to give a patina of observable logic to something that should already be true (but is in fact often false): *the communication*. So unfortunately I'm too often witness to scenes where the communication is unclear, or wrongly evaluated, or inappropriate to the style of the piece, but boy oh boy oh boy, *Look at that set! Look at the stuff! Look at the actors move over there. And then over there. And then back again. And then sit, but then to rise again. Look at the actor walking backwards!*

You could have a set designed to the nth degree, with furniture and glassware and rugs and doors and baubles galore, but if the communication sucks between the actors, no set will save us from the misery. Conversely, if the communication between the actors is honest, vivid, passionate, and clearly conveys the story to the audience, then very few will much care about the set and where you walked during the scene.

Too often I am seeing actors wandering around their sets without a purpose other than to get an "A" in behavior. The emphasis here is *without a purpose*. Are you moving because there is a task to execute? Is the task logical to the premise, setting, and events of this scene? Fine. Or are you moving because you're panicked that you haven't moved in a while? If the script says you need to get the other character a drink, then have at it—go pour a drink, bring it back. But lately I feel a simple task like pouring a drink becomes…*walk to the bar, muse over which glass to use, polish it with your sleeve, look at your sleeve, have a moment ("I made the choice that my first girlfriend gave me this shirt and it makes me think of her"), pause to choose which bottle of booze, open it meticulously, pour, sniff, pour again, wipe up a drop that spilled, start walking back, reverse course, pick up napkin, bring napkin with glass across stage…*

So behavior can be your friend or your enemy—if it's imped-ing the flow of the script, it's the latter. That's why when I come in to help out on a scene in the rehearsal process, or even during a critique, I'll often just have the actors sit in chairs several feet apart and read the damned scene without all the behavior. When I direct a show, we'll spend weeks sitting in chairs reading it aloud before I block a single move. If the story doesn't come alive in chairs, it ain't gonna happen anywhere else. *Romeo and Juliet* should be passionate, funny, wild and tragic in two chairs, or else all the vine-climbing in the world will just be a waste of time.

Now this may all seem to be sacrilegious, as "Behavior" comes early on Milton's famous Checklist For Takeoff, and anyone who ever was directed by him knows that you often had so many tasks to execute that you didn't have time to think about acting, which was often quite beneficial to the proceedings at hand. But the behavior was linked to a logic, and it *assisted* the event without *becoming* the event. And yes, behavior can be linked to imagina-tion. You want to set *Romeo and Juliet* in a surreal underwater universe? Go for it. Behave away—in accordance with the logic of that underwater concept. That's not what I'm talking about. What I'm talking about is some crazy bi-polar deal—the aim-less wandering without a purpose, and its evil twin: excessive OCD-like, task-oriented behavior that ends up distracting from the scene, its event and the flow of the language.

So fear not, this isn't some revisionist anti-behavior departure from the norm, and we still bow our heads before Mr. Kazan and his dictum that the job of the actor is to turn "psychology into behavior." I would just advise nailing the communication *before* you obsess about behavior. *Great communication is in fact the best behavior.*

And then there's this little inconvenient fact: It is very unlikely that behavior will be a part of your getting the job. Getting jobs will involve sitting in a chair, or standing on a mark, talking to a reader or talking to a camera, and summoning the event of the scene, its evaluation, the style of the piece, and doing it clearly and consistently over many auditions. Behavior will not be a part of getting the job, and yet in proper measure is part of fulfilling the job.

CHAPTER 43

POV

One of the best ways for an actor to sell a story well is to identify the essential point of view of the character, and hold strong. Storytelling is generally fueled by conflict, and that conflict is often represented by different characters having strong points of view that collide via whatever plot the writer had come up with.

A mistake commonly made by actors in this regard is to *lessen* the strength of their character's point of view. Why? Firstly, because they never identified the point of view in the first place. Secondly, there is some misguided notion that it's advantageous to dilute that point of view with "other colors," because it's seen as better to be, well, colorful in this regard. I think it quite possible in these "I want to bring more colors" cases that the actor on a personal level simply doesn't *like* the POV of the character, doesn't agree with it, and (sub)consciously works against it. In my experience this is particularly prevalent the more a role is considered unlikeable, unapologetic, unreasonable, or espousing of the "wrong" view politically.

Point of view, understood, clearly delineated, and delivered without apology, is as important in my opinion as action, behavior, and psychology in presenting a character that really serves its purpose in the story, and in a way the audience can grab on to.

CHAPTER 44

Film Vs. Theatre

There's a *thing* in the drama world about acting for film versus acting for stage. It's loaded with judgment and snobbery in both directions, regarding who has the real chops, who expresses more, the relative pay scales, etc. There are whole classes about film acting technique, etc. Milton wrote in his book about his utter lack of concern for the "difference" between film and stage acting. To me it's a matter of mathematics on two variables:

1. **Number of scenes.** A movie can have 40-60 scenes in it, while a play generally has fewer than ten, and sometimes each act is a single scene. Sometimes the entire play is a single scene. So a movie can burn a few dozen scenes to tell a story, and a play generally cannot. Per that math, there is generally more happening per scene in a play than in a film, and thus more an actor must reveal about the story per scene. A scene in a movie could be something as banal as the character leaving her house, getting in the car and driving off. Film scenes can exist purely to advance the plot incrementally, leading to one "blow-away" moment where various story elements combine for a single climactic scene or sequence. Those early incremental scenes don't show up in the play version. If a scene exists in play at all, it is specifically to put the characters through something, and usually from the get-go. In a play there is simply more work for the actor—they have to track and experience a far higher number of emotional-elements-per-scene.

2. **Number of story-telling elements at work.** To be reductive, let's say a play has these five elements: writing, acting, directing, lighting, sound design. Those are the tools the team is going to use to communicate this story to the audience. In a film you have those five, but then we can add five more: camera movement, lenses, framing, special effects/CGI, and music. Even in this simplified analysis, a film has twice the number of storytelling tools at work, and that's before we attempt to rate the relative importance of any of them. For instance, in a actor closeup with some impactful music underneath, the lens, framing and scoring could be doing 80% of the storytelling work, and the actor's face, in closeup, could do something incredibly simple to do the final 20%. In a play, none of those other elements is available, and I would argue that the writing and actors alone comprise 75% of the storytelling power to begin with.

The specifics can be argued, or the percentages, or I should have included this or that, or excluded the other in favor or something else. That's not the point. I would stand by the basic math that since a play has fewer scenes per story, more acting per scene, and that acting is a much higher percentage of the story-telling power than in a film with its minimum ten elements, this makes for a lot of the perceived difference in film and stage acting.

In terms of training, working on plays is the way to go. The story per scene is much higher, the percentage importance of the acting is higher, and the actor through this work hopefully grows to understand what it's like to control the story for ten uninterrupted minutes or more, which will almost never happen in film or television. Anecdotally, I think the list of stage-trained actors who successfully translated that work into film and television is about one billion times the number of largely film/television-trained actors who successfully kick ass on stage.

CHAPTER 45

Character—How Much Is Necessary?

The lights go down at Carnegie Hall, and a hush comes over the crowd. The lights rise slightly onstage, empty but for a nine-foot concert Steinway grand piano. The side door opens, and the pianist emerges. He is wearing pink pants, each shoe has its own different color, he walks with a pronounced but clearly artificial limp, is assisted by his use of a clearly unnecessary cane, and he has a squawking parrot on his shoulder. The pianist bows, sits on the bench, and begins to play. Now: Where is the audience's attention? On the music and his interpretation? No. They're probably whispering to each other, or throwing amazed glances around about this very bizarre performer. *Is that a parrot on his shoulder?* No one's attention is on the music. How could it be? It's absurd. Who is this guy? What's his fucking deal?

This is how I often feel about "character work" being done by student actors. It's too often indulgent, excessive, and occurs at the fatal expense of language and clarity. The first job of any story is to involve the audience—we have to understand what's going on and care about it. If those two items are in place, we'll probably want to know what happens next, and if we want to know what happens next, you're on your way to a decent story.

The actor's job is to help with that process, not to obliterate it with arbitrary and often masturbatory *choices.* I'd almost love to eliminate the word "choice" from the actor's repertoire and replace it with "obligation." These obligations are dictated by the given requirements of the story. If the story says your character has a physical injury, you are obligated to nail that. And you should be getting to that work early so you can fully realize it. If the story says your character is from specific region or city associated with a certain accent, ditto. If the story says your character is "the uptight one," opposite another character who's more of a slob, then you're obligated to nail those "uptight" aspects, and certainly there can be a lot of creativity involved in fulfilling those aspects.

Any of the great character actors you would want to name—they aren't doing those amazing choices randomly. I would argue the great character actors are specifically needed for certain roles where the story obligates the actor to achieve some out-there technical feats. *My Left Foot* comes to mind, *Midnight Cowboy* comes to mind, *Richard III* comes to mind, but there are a million other examples. The level of identifiable "character work" should rise only with the demands the story makes to fulfill that character. Too often attempts at "character work" are either arbitrary and unnecessary to sell the story to the audience, or may well be necessary, but exist completely out of proportion to the equally necessary work of language and clarity. The cart is before the horse. Let's get the sequencing right: Clarity, understanding, the essential point of view, delivered cleanly and unapologetically. Then: Character traits as necessary, obligated clearly per the story. Then: Character choices fueled by your imagination and pure artistic interpretation.

CHAPTER 46

We Planned Energy For Later

Does the following sound familiar?

A couple actors have performed a scene. It was rather dull. It's a known script. Or unknown. It was supposed to be funny, or not. Perhaps a couple of weak mercy-laughs emerged from the audience during the performance, but other than that just a weird silence.

Clearly the evaluation was off. The sucker just didn't have a pulse. Why? As the actors begin speaking of the scene - sometimes knowing it failed, sometimes unsure, the teacher might ask Milton's favorite question on acting: "What's going on here?"

STUDENT: "Well, my character is trying to assess this guy's motives…"

TEACHER: "Uh huh. Assess them how?"

And after a back-and-forth or two, you get a variation of this:

STUDENT: "Well, you know—this is just the first part of the scene. Later on there's a big fight between them."

And there you have it. The "We Planned Energy For Later" excuse.

Now don't misunderstand: As Milton said, Evaluating the scene properly doesn't mean screaming and throwing chairs all over the place. Energy doesn't mean unceasing volume or violence. But that *potential* should be there, as it is there in our lives. And when you "plan to have energy later" or think, "But the fight happens later," or "But the confrontation happens later in the script" or any of these variations… I think it was Uta Hagen who said, "If it's in the end, it's in the beginning." The "big fight" may occur later in the scene, or later in the story, but its elements are present now, and throughout. Ditto for big romance—even if the characters fall in love later, then the chemistry has to exist *now*.

So this leads to two pieces of advice:

1. Choose for your scenes those where there is a dynamic of conflict or major development for the characters. A good script should have this in place already, but we know good scripts are rare. Most good actors can sit in chairs and talk comfortably if that's what all the scene requires. But there's rarely a good teaching moment in validating that you're good at "being natural." If it's a film script, don't pick early scenes in the story that are often setting up plot elements that are more deeply explored later in the script —instead, do those later scenes. They will give you more to chew on as an actor. (Plays introduce conflict sooner and more potently, usually in Scene 1.

2. If it's in the end, it's in the beginning. Don't get trapped by planning the "big moment" for later in the scene, playing against that moment so strongly beforehand that you find out everyone has checked out on your performance before you got there. Or the teacher has stopped the scene. Or, there are those times you're saving for the big moment and when the big moment arrives—you don't have the goods. So the whole scene has now fallen flat. Always have a sense of how you are affected by what happens in the scene, how you affect others—throughout. Not just at the "big moment." In your actual life, you can get up in the morning, put the coffee on, make toast, get dressed and leave and that's all that's happened. In a script—that scene would likely be cut. In a script, a good story, something is always happening. A story is a version of life that has been crafted and sculpted to be interesting and keep the audience wanting to know what will happen in the next moment. There's an energy and potential for acting excitement that is present throughout— you can't plan it for later.

CHAPTER 47

Don't Make Me Angry

Some on-the-fly definitions for use by actors:

Contempt = I hope you freaking die soon, and that it hurts along the way.

Anger = You're pissing me off so badly right now, I could seriously break shit. Doesn't mean I don't love you, but…*shit.*

Exasperation = I adore you but you're making me nuts. Ralph Kramden , with a clenched fist: "To the moon, Alice!"

One of the most frequent errors I see actors make—with regard to relationship stories in particular—is to play contempt and anger when what is really called for is highly-evaluated exasperation. Some really funny scenes, and some very charming relationships, have been made very unfunny and very uncharming by young, usually male actors playing a full-on anger, throwing furniture around the stage, or even grabbing their scene partners, cocking their fists like Sonny Corleone with his dander up. The error on the women's side tends less to physical anger, but is still present in disastrously misplaced eye-rolling disdain, bitchy petulance, or the brutal cold-shoulder. *Barefoot in the Park* in particular has died many thousands of terrible deaths from actors playing Paul or Corey with coldness, anger and contempt. *Motherfucker With The Hat*—ditto. Everyone in that quartet actually loves one another, but you wouldn't know it from the way I've often seen it played. *HurlyBurly*—the fight about the restaurant? That's funny, people. It's one of the most famous relationship fights there is, and it's humorous. It's not about Eddie getting ready to beat the crap out Darlene. It's not some emotional tragedy about her abortion from years ago. Now…*Closer?* That's contempt. It's British, so it still has some wit to it, but...Not funny-funny. And no, I don't think any of them truly love each other. I would consider *Closer* and *Motherfucker With The Hat* to be the opposite ends of the spectrum of messy quartet relationships.

Perhaps the most difficult writer to nail is Edward Albee—a true master of brutal humor between men and women. He can be insanely funny while writing the most devastating dialogue—it's a very difficult line, because exasperation won't work, and yet the high-octane marital anger can be truly hilarious when played well. Or Martin McDonagh, who manages to write hyper-evaluated contempt and violence and paint it all with incredible humor.

Now, how should an actor figure out which of these colors to play in response to conflict in a love story? Well, the know-it-all-teacher answer is that you should perform a hundred scenes in a good class, and I bet you'll learn. But from an analytical POV, you can ask some questions: are we supposed to care about the people involved? Are we supposed to root for the success of the relationship? Let's face it: at the end of the day, do these people love each other? Is this a comedy, or does it at least have comedic tendencies? If these are all answerable with a "Yes," then chances are the right move is for you to layer in a healthy dose of I-love-you-but-you're-driving-me-nuts exasperation. If we ever thought that Ralph Kramden was going to sock Alice in the face, there would have been no "Honeymooners," no Jackie Gleason as comedic star, no nuthin'. The charm of it was that we knew with all our hearts that he loved her to death, that in a million years he wouldn't harm her. And that's in the casting as well—James Caan would probably have made for a really shitty Ralph Kramden, and vice versa with Gleason playing Sonny Corleone.

The dramatic space where *anger* is most appropriate is when it's righteous. Generally the material is probably tilted further away from comedy. Then: is the anger motivated by a pursuit of justice? A defense of the innocent? A false accusation? Confronting an act of betrayal? An indictment of the corrupt? All of that can exist within a romantic relationship. If it's there, well, then pound your desk and let it fly. Hello, betrayal scene in *Fences*.

But there are a million-and-one love stories that are built on the they-love-each-other-but-drive-each-other-nuts-in-an-exasperated-way formula. A huge chunk of the love-story spectrum is taken up by it, with varying degrees of love vs. exasperation. At the far end of the spectrum, and relatively rare, are the stories built on behold-the-toxic-true-utter-contempt-for-each-other. Those darker, Albee-esque stories are out there, and if you play a true contempt/anger moment with the levity of exasperation, you'll fuck that story up just the way you fuck up the sweeter ones with contempt/anger. And there's an entire spectrum of colors in between— Albee tests the limits of love with his brutal dialogue, Simon writes some devastating dramatic scenes in amongst his clever lines and infinite charm, and McDonagh manages to write torture scenes that have us laughing our asses off. How does the professional actor know what to play? Ask the right questions, and do a couple hundred scenes where you make the mistakes in one direction or another, and you'll get the hang of it. Some actors are simply better suited to different qualities as required by the story, and that's why casting is important as well.

My unofficial from-the-hip estimate: About 65% of relationship stories require exasperation as an important, if not predominant, color for conflict, 25% need full-on righteous anger, and 10% are actually about true contempt.

ON STUDY

CHAPTER **48**

Training Pixelation

Actor training in Los Angeles over the last fifteen years has been pixelated more and more into a dozen subcategories of "skills," inclusive of improv, audition technique, comedy technique, camera technique, commercial camera technique, camera audition slate-your-name improv sit-com technique, how-to-shoot-your-demo-reel classes, how-to-market-yourself-on-social-media seminars, on and on and on. The price tag for some of these items can be $500 or more, and I would submit to you that the most certain result of any of these "educational opportunities" is that whoever is delivering it gets their $500 or more, per student. And then once you've spent your $500, say, on some workshop, they'll come to you with the next level. And the next after that. And then there's a weekend intensive by so-and-so, and you don't want to miss the weekend intensive with so-and-so, because so-and-so is *so brilliant.*

I'm not saying these workshops don't impart any knowledge, nor that there is zero utility in them. There is greater-than-zero utility. How much greater than zero? That's tougher to answer. But here's the lie that has been sold to a million actors hitting the ground in Los Angeles: X Workshop = Paid Work. And that, I tell you, is a big fat ol' LIE. What they're really selling is the *perception* that X Workshop = Paid Work. They're selling a *feeling* the aspiring actor will have, after the workshop, that they are acquiring skills that will matter in an audition, and lead to paid work. These pixelated micro-skills will not matter. They won't get you the job. Frankly, a micro-skill trained actor often sticks out like a sore thumb at auditions for being significantly incompetent at the basics of using acting to tell the story right.

And now, there are these completely artificial casting and representation fences that have been constructed: *You won't be seen unless you've done Level Q of Workshop X.* It's absolute bullshit. It's just an arbitrary fence, designed to keep people out because with electronic submissions and the like, offices have become overwhelmed. So now they are intimating that you won't get in without meeting this *completely arbitrary* standard, a standard that has *no actual causative relationship* to being competent or getting paid work. I'm sure several people who recently completed Level Q of Workshop X booked some decent jobs. You know what? So did several people, thousands of them, more than that, who did *not* complete Level Q of Workshop X. If they created an arbitrary fence that the only actors to be seen were those who had done at least 50 scenes in any of the five most established no-bullshit acting classes in town, well…Then they'd have a fence that was worth something. (I know—I'm the guy running one of those schools. But I'm telling you, that fence would be worth something. And I have to think that the actors know this on some level. Deep down, they know that training that doesn't cost them some blood, sweat and tears probably won't add up to much in terms of real skill. It's almost as if there is an industry-wide trance, each group desperately hoping that what another group says about this "fun" workshop-level training comes true, and that acting is for some reason the one performing arts skill on planet earth that doesn't actually require tough, hard practice over a number of years. In any case, I can practically guarantee that people who've done those 50 scenes in a decent class are in general better at acting than those who did Level Q of Workshop X, and who had so much *fun* doing it!)

My unofficial estimate is that at most 20% of the actors in town are really playing the game at a certain level, a SAG level, where they have, annually, at least 50 meaningful auditions for a reputable project, and are booking some of those gigs. You want to be playing that game. The 20% game. What gets you there? *None* of these pixelated micro skills that are taught in ubiquitous little 1-to-10 week sessions. What gets you there is *holistic acting competence:* knowing the story-telling process from all angles, knowing tone and style, understanding writers and writing, knowing the design of the scene you're performing, diligent professional behavior—all of this developed over a number of years. If you want to name your friend who is an exception to that, go ahead, but I don't know how that serves you. They're the exception.

Beware anyone who says they have the "magic pill" for your career via a fixed-length paid workshop. Try to dial back the noise generated by all the panicky "you shoulds" of the ever-evolving workshop world. Beware all these artificial fences, anyone who says they won't consider you unless you have such-and-such a workshop on your resume. I believe the serious people in this business, the 20% group, who have paid their dues and know what's what in the land of storytelling—they wouldn't put up arbitrary fences, and they know better than to think Level Q of Workshop X means anything, really. The sum of all these paid micro-skills workshops is less than their parts by far, and I wouldn't rate the parts highly. The greater skill—that which will earn you acting work on an ongoing basis—is a skill developed over time, dedicated generally to a single, more holistic approach.

CHAPTER 49

The Batting Cage

An aspiring baseball player approaches home plate, ready for batting practice. His teammate pitches the ball, and the player swings his bat. It's a hit. Or a fly-out. Or a foul ball. Or a strike. Immediately, he turns to his batting coach, and asks, "How am I doing as a baseball player? What are my chances? Do you think I'm ready for the big leagues? When do you think I should start trying out for teams? What do you think my real problem is as a baseball player, and what path should I be on to fix that? Do you see me more as a power hitter or utility guy?"

This is what it is sometimes like to teach actors. There is the misplaced expectation that a single scene in class and its critique will yield significant answers as to what the future will hold, and exactly how to get there. The context for scenework in class is out of whack, and because of a simple math problem: To swing a baseball bat takes a fraction of a second—but to do a scene in an acting class? You have to find a class in which to enroll, pay for it, actually show up, get a scene partner, agree on a scene, rehearse…Even simplifying the analysis, eliminating the part that gets you into a class in the first place (after all, the baseball player had to buy a bat and find some people with whom to practice as well, yes?)…Let's say it takes at least 10 hours to get a decent scene ready for class, and compare that to the fraction of a second to swing a bat. How many swings will our itinerant baseball player make in 10 hours of practice? How many scales for the musician? How many times through a difficult sequence for a dancer? That simple math problem, that it takes an actor more hours to swing their "bat" than with perhaps any other art form, can lead actors to treat each scene with an out-of-context level of importance. Sometimes a scene comes along that is a watershed moment for one or more of the actors involved, or where the realization of the scene is something you'd have gladly paid money to see in a theatre. These breakthrough moments are a blast for sure. And then sometimes as a teacher I'm just gonna say, "Looks good. Swing it again." There are plenty of scenes that have average writing and the actors do a good job of it, good enough a job that I could see them competing for these parts were this script being cast. Good. Nice work. Swing it again. Keep swinging. Always. And again after always.

I will tell new students that it's important to get five scenes out of the way fairly quickly, because it requires at least that many just to get the vibe of what the teacher will be honing in on with you. Next step: get to 20 scenes, and now you're going to know a lot more about this class, the environment, your peers, ongoing collaboration, and that's on top of the acting notes you'll be getting along the way and the application of this technique. Next: Show me an actor who's done 100 scenes, and I'm going to show you someone who knows a lot about how to act. But it takes time. It takes 3-5 years to get there, and for some reason if you tell a young actor in LA they're going to study for at least 3-5 years to become competent, if not perhaps 5-10 years to be a true ass-kicker, they'll get a little wobbly and their eyes will roll up to the back of their head. But while the math is wildly different on hours-per-swing, the fact is that a good class should get you functioning well as an actor in 3-5 diligent years. Athletes and other performing artists, operating at far higher "reps" per hour of practice, spend a hell of a lot longer than 3-5 years to be professional. So stop yer' bitching! Any less than that, it's a crap shoot. Doesn't mean you don't know how to act, nor that you will or will not book work without at least 3-5 years of training. But I don't know how you can look at approaching a profession with the immense variety of skills that an actor must possess, and think that no training, or an 8-week workshop in this or that, scattered here and there, will serve your ultimate goal of being a professional who works for years and years.

Get thyself to the batting cage, and swing it.

CHAPTER 50

Acting Class Porn

Acting training has the danger of allying more closely with religion than science, with therapy more than technical instruction. This is a natural outgrowth of the subjective nature of acting skill, and the fact that the instrument and the instrumentalist are intertwined into one entity. Milton spoke of "work on oneself" as integral to overall progress as an actor, but he clearly delineated that work: body, voice, the ability to open up emotionally. That's the instrument. You need a first-rate instrument to make first-rate music. To me this is different from when acting classes veer towards "spirituality" and, as students have sometimes called it: "Chair-apy," and its inherently psychological emphasis.

I've come to conclude that acting study can dangerously over-emphasize actors' individual psychology, as if the closer the actor hones to "personal truth," the truthier the performance will be, and the more likely it is the audience will believe it, the more likely it is the actor will be hired. To me, this is like saying the best magicians *actually think* they are extracting quarters from a child's left ear, and if a magician *actually thinks* that, then he or she is a "more truthful" magician. It's bullshit. Make me believe the coin magically appeared, and I'll think you're talented. Tell me you *actually think* you made a coin appear, and I'll think you're fucking crazy.

I think there's a huge difference between the actor trying in literal fashion to be personal and true, and the actor's true art of *coming off* as if they are being personal and true. It's technical. It's the art of a magician, the practiced sleight of hand, the effortless, artful distraction. The teacher's job is to identify the true art, which is not the method you use to dredge up various emotions, it's the *skillful application of those emotions to the specific story and its requirements, so it seems real and is compelling to the audience.*

Actors aren't hired to excavate their psychology, nor to make appropriate "substitutions" between a character and a real person in that actor's life. Those are *possible* technical approaches to the real job: They're hired simply to get the damned story right, so it affects and entertains the audience. They're doing a bit of magic, the audience is served, and no one needs to believe it's *true for the actor.* But it's a very popular approach to encourage just this kind of psychological approach to acting in the name of "truth." Or for the teacher to use an actor's weakness in a certain role to speculate that it's because of a similar weakness in the actor—a deficit of empathy, for instance, that needs counseling to rectify properly. The constant discussion of personal truth and its myriad spinoffs (character biography, personal tendency and trauma, substitution for real people and actual events, etc.) is actually more likely to be detrimental to a successful end result of a good story, well told, and I've come to believe that these discussions mostly serve as what I call "acting class porn" for teachers and students to get off on together.

acting class porn, *n.,* the often well-intentioned pursuit by teachers of supposed personal psychological gain in their students, a gain represented generally by highly personal "realizations," sometimes accompanied by a flood of tears, all as a requisite for better acting.

And hey, watching porn is popular for a reason. It titillates. It grabs the eyeballs. At that moment, maybe it's better than alternative activities. Teachers can feel good thinking they've helped a student in that highly personal way, and students can be grateful for that help. None of that is necessarily bad. I just don't think that stuff gets you any closer to good acting. Talking about acting is a delicate matter. I've seen classes at the BHP and elsewhere, where there are entire laudatory conversations, tears, acting class porn, "breakthroughs" on the psychological front— all concerning a total shit piece of scene work. Every syllable of the discussion was subjective reality. The truth of these personal "gains," or of a certain personal "connection" to the work, is often believed heart and soul, yet factually is utterly unknowable. It's a story like any other. So let's make make the stories of what you learn in class good stories. Sane stories. Stories that help you with that audition tomorrow. I've never been much into porn, it just doesn't do it for me in the slightest. The scripts for porn films are total crap.

CHAPTER 51

Coffee Shop Naturalism And The Avant-garde

Training an actor is a very dicey proposition: An actor is both the instrument and the musician, and you need a minimum of two actors working together to really assess either one's ability. As the teacher, one has an infinite combination of potential issues to address with the instrument, the musician, and then the material and/or the actor's approach to it. On the actor's side, just getting to the moment of critique is more challenging than any other art form. As a pianist, I have two pianos staring at me in my living room, and one of them is digital and can be used late at night without disturbing anyone—it's me versus the piano, it can happen any of the 24 hours in a day, and the practice and the progress on any piece can happen quickly and intensively with my work alone. With scene study training, you need to get at least one other actor in order to do any work at all, you have to rehearse, and at the BHP we expect you to bring in a finished product, something you've sweated over and thought about.

It's best if all that effort went into material that helped us make you better, right? So follows is a list of the kind of scenes I feel are counter-productive, and a final note about The Grand Exception that gets you a pass on any of it:

Coffee Shop Naturalism: Two people sit in a coffee shop (or its outdoors variant, on a park bench), chatting. Nothing much happens, little is revealed—some story history or character biography, perhaps. Or maybe a weak romantic pass is made and deflected. No one gets particularly upset. No one gets particularly happy. One of the characters leaves, aaaaaaannnnnd *scene.* Just avoid all this stuff— if you're at the level of work where you can believably listen and have a conversation, then these scenes do little to challenge you, and the material will often fray when you try to apply bigger choices to it. (Included in this genre is the famous DeNiro-Pacino scene from *Heat*. Zero happens in that scene—its purpose in life was to get those two actors acting together for the first time in history. I've seen it performed a dozen times in class and it never works.)

Avant-garde/Dreamworld: Study requires material that has rules, logic, discernible conversation, a sense that these characters inhabit a known world here on earth. So I'm not knocking avant-garde work and experimental theatre, etc.—but it just doesn't make good training material. Ditto for its first cousin, the dream sequence. No good. I once went to a "piano recital" where the pianist had hung beer bottles from the strings with varying levels of liquid in each bottle, and he hit a felt mallet against the side of the piano while holding down certain keys, and there was some weird sonority that resonated through the beer bottles. Okay. I just don't know what that had to do with a piano, and there was little pianistic skill involved—it was mostly a compositional exercise. If I brought this piece to my teacher for a piano lesson, I'd be dismissed with a grunt in about three seconds.

Science Fiction/Action/Fantasy: I love *The Matrix* as much as the next guy, but it's no good for training. This Sci-Fi/Action/Fantasy combo has produced some massively popular entertainment, and it's not as if there isn't any good acting in some of these movies, but generally the world inhabited by these characters is one that needs huge production value, and it's tough to extract scenes that have any meaning or excitement outside the context of the *experience*.

Persona-Driven Glib Comedy: There's great cinema entertainment available in this genre, but they are generally highly reliant on the persona of a known comedic actor, rather than real acting. Some of these comedians are actually really talented actors (Steve Carrell comes to mind), but the persona driven glib comedy is generally incredibly stupid from a script standpoint, and absurd from a logic standpoint—and neither problem matters because it's about the comedic persona coping through all the madness. Not good for training.

Smoldering Chemistry Film Scenes: The ultimate example of this is the pick-up scene from *Body Heat*. Never works. It always comes off as a very flat conversation about chimes. A lot of smoldering chemistry film scenes are just coffee shop naturalism that is followed by a sex scene. The pickup scene in *Fatal Attraction* is another. They are greatly assisted in the originals by the presence of movie stars shot in closeup, sound design and scoring. Without all that, and in a class setting, we're watching two actors doing coffee shop naturalism and thinking to ourselves about William Hurt throwing that chair through the window, or Douglas and Close in the elevator. Avoid, unless by Grand Exception below.

High Concept Scripts: Amongst the most popular here are works by Charlie Kaufman and Christopher Nolan: *Adaptation, Eternal Sunshine of the Spotless Mind, Being John Malkovich, Memento, Inception, etc.* As screenwriters go these guys are hugely imaginative, but I've never seen their work translate well to a scene study training environment. It's possible—but a tough job for sure.

If you're thinking, *Well, what's left after what you listed above?*, then I would submit that you're operating from too narrow a frame of reference. It's easy to note that all of the above are most prevalent in film scripts rather than stage plays, and a snob could easily just ban screenplays from acting training and they would have a point. But we're in the 21st Century, the BHP is headquartered in LA, and many people enter acting with small and large screen aspirations and these dreams were often sparked in a movie theatre. There are countless terrific, actable screenplays that have real meat on their bones, so bring 'em on. There are countless terrific, actable stage plays which, by their very theatrical DNA, avoid many of the pitfalls above.

And here is the Grand Exception that gets you a pass even on all of the above. (It's an "exception" in terms of getting past my considerations on the material, but is certainly a "rule" of good acting in general):

Imagination. With some imagination, and its siblings creativity, passion, interest and originality, you can bring any scene to life in a vibrant, exciting way. Years ago some students brought in Tolkien's *The Hobbit,* and killed it. They were fantastic, they had lighting design, sound design, they completely committed to the characters of this fantasy world, and we were all captivated by it. The only time I saw *Body Heat* work was when one of our teachers teamed up with a choreographer to create a very different and vastly more expressive experience from that depicted in the movie—and the actors responded beautifully. I've seen exciting and original adaptations of James Bond scenes, coffee shop naturalism scenes that have taken off and moved people, smoldering chemistry scenes that have burned hot. I witnessed Milton himself assign such scenes as *Airplane!* and *101 Dalmations* to actors (generally so they would stop taking themselves so seriously), and they were hugely entertaining. But all of them involved a heavy dose of imagination, a boldness and originality that acts in direct opposition to the idea of acting training as a rote form of non-artistic dictation, what I call "movie-matching": *transcribe the film scene and act it essentially the same way those stars did.* No way. If we can derive from this discussion at least the idea that actors should stop taking dictation, and that their imaginations are a huge and often untapped force, then that alone would be worth it to me.

CHAPTER 52

The Forest And The Trees

The forest is the *story*, and communicating it to the audience in a way that makes them give a shit, that makes them care about these characters and what happens to them. The trees are just about every other consideration. You're not going to get hired for your scintillating props. Nor the details of the groceries, the color of your shoes. You're going to be hired for nailing the story and how this character fits into that story.

But man oh man, can actors obsess about the trees. Teachers, too. I see teachers obsessing about trees—they are not immune to my point here. I think a good test for the worth of a "note" by a teacher is: "Will this note help the actor's understanding of story and character in a way that helps them get a job? Maybe not this job, or this role, because let's pray they're not going to remake *Streetcar*...But one like it? Does this note help the actor begin to ask the right questions for themselves, so they solve these issues on their own, and to their hiring advantage?"

It's certainly good to train actors to have an eye for detail, who can engage the Props and Costume departments in professional conversation, but in order to have a conversation with Props or Costumes, they need to have booked the job! What's required for that? There can be a shit-ton of acting class time spent on intoned, authoritative blather about trees, the bark on the trees, the ants on the bark...*The way you buckled your belt is wrong. The shade of pink on your shoes is wrong. Are you sure this guy would really eat a ham sandwich here? I think roast beef. Were you being truly personal in that one moment? I think not. The flowers on the shelf over there—not the flowers this girl would pick. You say your character is from the Bronx,*

but your accent is pure 120th Street. The items you took out of that
Ralphs grocery store bag - they're actually not sold at Ralphs. This is
acting instruction reduced to simple nit-picking. At the audition,
actors aren't bringing props, they're not dressing too literally
in character, they don't have time to "think the thoughts of the
character." They simply have to nail the story and the character,
summon the energy of that moment in the script while standing
on a mark, holding the script in hand, hoping they don't suck,
contemplating negatively their entire existence as an actor, yet
still reading brilliantly opposite someone who probably shouldn't
ever be permitted to read lines out loud again, or doing all this
into a computer for a web-dition. And that's just for the acting
part of an acting career. That's not even factoring in the daily ins
and outs of Administration or Attitude.

Now, the danger for your cuddly author is that he is misunderstood, and that it's assumed he has gone insane and come
out against…*details!* My God, man, the greatest artists of all time
have gone apeshit over the details! After all, they say *God is in the*
details! (Oddly, the idiom also works 180 degrees opposite: *The*
Devil is in the details.) Now apparently no matter how you say it,
the idiom is meant to encourage paying attention to the details,
but maybe for the purposes of this essay, "God is in the Details"
means you have a proper *balance* of attention to the forest and the
trees: the forest is lush and green and each tree a wonder unto
itself; whereas "The Devil is in the Details" means that the forest
is ignored, it's burning up, the smoke is choking us, the entire
ecosystem is dying a fast and painful death, but you're sitting
there looking at ants on the bark of a single tree, doubting the
color of your shoes, trying to think the thoughts of the character,
or running around fucking up the prep for your scene to worry
about placement of a beer bottle in the background, or making
sure there are 12 extras in your simple restaurant scene (as if we
won't believe it's a restaurant until you have 12 extras acting up a
storm and stealing your scene from you).

So fear not. I'm not coming out against the details. But I
want the Godly version. I'm coming out against *imbalance.* I have
a preference for less clutter—both physically in the set design,
and in the mind of the actor, which I would gently opine is full
of useless clutter about acting. But that's my preference, and I
don't need it to be others'. The bottom line is whether the story

sells us, involves us. Details have their function here, of course. For my play *Disconnection*, I needed the lead actor to play piano realistically at the beginning of the play. But get this: I needed the body and arm movements to be accurate to the piece they were "playing," and yet the piano itself was a total fake, just symbolically shaped wood meant to suggest a piano. So why are the details of the playing important, but not so much the physical piano? Well, if the actor's arms and body were completely out of sync with the music, then we risked the audience's awareness going to that discordant image, we'd risk their attention going away from the music and its flow. Right at the top of the play we'd have risked interfering with the delicate process of building the audience's belief, their empathy, their care for the story, and and I felt the music had an important role to play there. The piano itself? That was just furniture to serve a greater goal.

So, if a seemingly small detail goes to the heart of audience belief, then sure, pay attention to it. Don't pull a carton of Twinkies out of a Whole Foods bag. Don't do something so careless as to be blatantly discordant, and thus draw the audience's attention to your *lack* of attention. But at the same time, stay away from OCD-level obsession on to details that have no real impact, stay away from heavy-handed literalness. I find that audiences will believe any rule you want to set up, including non-literal set design, as long as it's consistent. If your restaurant consists of just a single table with your two leads, and some background noise playing low over the speakers—guess what? The audience will know they're in a restaurant. Even with one table. They'll get it. Really. And the other patrons are simply not important, what they're eating isn't important, their utensils are not important. The Budweiser sign you plugged in—it isn't important. I don't believe any more strongly that I'm in a bar because you hung that fucking sign.

Details for actors are particularly important if they are *human*, if they are *emotional*, if they relate directly to the story and how the audience will receive that story on an emotional level. Do that consistently and you'll book work. And when you book work, the job will come with a director, a props person, and various designers who will sweat beautiful, endless drops of sweat over the details. Let those professionals do their work. You do yours: Go for the clarity of language, the emotional arc, the structure of this scene, bring the emotions of the story to life, make us give a shit. Actors' obsessive attention to strictly non-acting details that are best addressed by a director can sometimes become overwhelmingly irritating, particularly when it dwarfs proper attention to clarity of the story and its human and emotional elements. That's your job. Teachers should be helping you with that job. Let's all focus on God's work there.

CHAPTER **53**

Black Sheep

Like any teacher, as the years go by I have an ever-increasing collection of students who just disappeared at some point, having gone AWOL from class. I remember chasing down one young man at some point, and as it turned out, since he took off, he had taken 3-4 other classes around town to see what else was out there. We finally grabbed a coffee, and he told me that in all of these other classes, he heard a strong chord of dishonesty, in that the teachers seemed unwilling to say what he thought was the truth for many of the students: *Get the fuck out of this business, you suck, it ain't for you, you'll never make it.* His answer as to the "reason" for this supposed dishonesty was that financial concerns kept us teachers from booting the untalented from the room. The budgetary need to "keep the numbers up" corrupted all teachers, and so collectively we feed years of false encouragement to those clearly destined for failure in the biz. He even offered me a deal: When he made the $100 million that he intended to make, he would give the BHP $10 million under the condition we only enroll actors in class who were up to his kind of snuff. This would include a policy to kick students out if they had an insufficient number of auditions a month, etc. *Wow!* I took a pass on his offer.

An acting school doesn't exist to render judgments on talent, it exists to develop whatever talent is there in any student. It's not as if you power up the television to find only really talented actors who are working. There are plenty of working actors who frankly may not be that gifted, but through some confluence of hard work, some ability, some "luck", have been given the opportunity to work regularly. I don't judge those actors negatively, nor, conversely, would I necessarily revere a really talented actor who never breaks through on the career Administration, never books meaningful professional work. This whole discussion was why Milton devised an approach where we talk about Attitude and Administration as being critical to the long-term success of any actor. I believe part of what a school provides is an oasis from the negativity and seeming hopeless odds of the entertainment industry. I can say enthusiastically that I believe a good class can provide continuity, a place where, for a few hours of each week, creativity and storytelling rule the day. Sometimes the class is the only place where that creative spirit gets its exercise during the time a career is being built up, or is experiencing a trough.

I question the idea that "success" as an actor can only be defined as "acting is the only thing you do in your life, producing the only income you'll ever need to maintain your life." That certainly is the best case scenario, but to say you love the arts enough to pursue them professionally not only means an absorbing dedication to your abilities and your career administration, but also to designing a life that can handle the boom-and-bust nature of an artistic existence.

Realistically, there is zero percent chance that everyone in any acting class will be a star. Zero. There is zero percent chance that everyone in any acting class will even make $100K a year from acting. *However…* I truly believe there is a 100% chance that all students in an acting class can have a fulfilling life in the arts. The variables are infinite, the income streams may have to be multiple, from both artistic and non-artistic endeavors, there will be years of drought and years of plenty. But that love of acting and storytelling can be maintained, can be given a voice, there can be significant projects each year where the artist is able to thrive. I believe the student who wants a life in the arts more than ever has to have the entrepreneurial instinct, the ability to put other talents to work for money, or at least the willingness to work a longterm job-job for rent money. There are many professional actors who have long and fulfilling careers, who also supplement their income from other sources.

Milton would every so often tell a story about his early days of teaching, and that a well-known actor had called him to inquire about studying. The actor asked him, "Well, who's in the class?" Milton got ornery, and responded, "I'm teaching the class. That's all you need to know." This was my feeling as well about my student's complaint that there were some in the class who weren't in it as seriously as he was. It shouldn't be his concern, at least not on an individual level. If the class as a whole represents a certain standard, if the overall approach is one that assists in your making progress in both craft and career, then hang out and reap the benefit. If the student next to you doesn't meet your expectations, that's not your problem. I've seen plenty of those students, the ones thought of as the black sheep, go on to kick the snobby superior asses of the supposed ass-kickers. So you just worry about your own work, and whether the class is helping you with that work.

On Rehearsal

There are a million ways to rehearse, and ultimately you have to find the way that works for you on a consistent basis. But it's constantly variable because you're always working with someone new who may have a process different from yours. Here's my very simple advice, and this is not meant to be offered as *the* way, it's not something written on a stone tablet. It's just *a* way, but it works for me and has for many years as a director: set up a couple chairs about fifteen feet apart. (It's fifteen feet so you can't mumble to each other.) Act the script aloud, off the page, at least 25 times or until you're solidly off-book (whichever is more). "Solidly off-book" means you could deliver this script perfectly under any circumstance: in a monsoon, hanging upside down from a trapeze, half-drunk, while people throw rocks at you. *Nothing is more freeing than total certainty with the lines.* Knowing your lines backwards and forwards will help your acting, not hinder it. I don't care about those stories of Brando getting his lines off of post-its affixed around the set, it's bullshit. You're not competing with Brando. You're trying to build a career as an actor. Slightly— or more than slightly—not knowing your lines does not make them "organic," it just makes you unprofessional. Know your fucking lines. Study them outside the rehearsal setting. There is simply no excuse here.

Note that I wrote, "*Act* the script aloud." Just because you're in a chair, reading from the script, doesn't mean you're not giving it your all. You still act it out full-on, with appropriate levels of emotion or anger or what-have-you. It's not like you're in some stale, casual "reading mode." Only after you hit 25 and off-book, should you start putting it on its feet. This way, whatever behavior needs to be implemented to sell the story is being put on top of acting and communication that is already rock-solid. I have found that working with this sequence helps get the horse and cart in the proper order, and everything proceeds much more smoothly, with a more consistent result.

CHAPTER 55

The Professional Scene Partner

One of the most frequent complaints about the study of acting, across all schools and all approaches, concerns the issue of scene partners. Fill in the following sentence:

"My damned scene partner just—!"

There is an infinity of options to fill in that blank, right? Right. So having heard just about all I would ever *not* want to hear concerning scene partners, I thought I might offer some ideas on what I *would* love to hear about in a scene partner:

The Professional Scene Partner…

- Has decisively agreed to participate in the scene. Don't do scenes without a sense of passion or real interest. Doesn't mean you have to like your partner—that's a bonus. Much of your career may be spent working with people you may not like personally. What it does mean is you have a sense of purpose about the scene and ability to work together toward the common goal of killing the sucker.

- Is not late. Period.

- Is not high. Or drunk. Period.

- Does not cancel because of apocryphal "last minute auditions." Real auditions—well, okay, but the proportion of *real* last-minute auditions to the number of *fabricated* "last-minute auditions" is a very small number.

- Has his or her lines down cold ASAP.

- Has read the entire script and/or seen the entire film ASAP.

- Endeavors to read other scripts by the same author. No one would realistically expect knowledge of every other script by the author, every time out. But if you read this and think, "You know, I've never read other scripts by the author as part of my specific work on a scene," you should make more effort to do so. If you are unable to answer "who wrote this script?", you should be summarily executed.

- Does not use rehearsal to make romantic advances. Make romantic advances after the scene has been performed.

- Does not "improvise" violence or sexuality in the scene without agreement up front.

- Allows multiple points of view and willingly investigates them. If there is a disagreement about any aspect of the scene, a very effective solution goes like this: *today let's do it with your ideas, tomorrow let's do it with mine.*

- Does not string a partner along for weeks before pulling out of the scene. If you're going to cancel, then cancel fast and let that person move on with their life.

- Does not direct the other person, nor allows himself/herself to be directed. Except by willing cooperation.

- Does not come into rehearsal with a bad attitude relating to events of his or her personal or professional life. Leave your crap outside.

- Does not "wonder why this scene was assigned." If you don't know— ask the teacher, not your scene partner.

- Has showered recently.

In summation, the professional scene partner shows up on time, alert, energetic, with a good cooperative attitude, knows the lines, knows the script, knows the author, doesn't flake, doesn't cancel, doesn't make passes, has heard of the term "breath mint," and works with the same professionalism and passion s/he would (presumably) bring to a big money job.

CHAPTER 56

Stay Classy

Some items of etiquette to maintain for solid relations with a good teacher/class, should you be fortunate enough to find one:

- Follow the guidelines of the class to the T. I assume for most classes, this would include being the hell on time for *everything*.

- Don't lie, including those of the supposedly innocuous white category. The little ones are actually very corrosive, and teachers know more often than you think when you're doing it. Get honest. The use of white lies to evade confronting a situation is a corrupting, soul-sucking, esteem-lowering habit.

- Don't make excuses for lack of preparation in your scene work. This whole business is built on being great on short notice. In Milton's day, when actors presented work with the irritating proviso that they only had a week or whatever, he'd reply, "I could build a yacht in a week." Time and quality are not in a monogamous relationship. Of course the ideal is that you have sufficient rehearsal and prep time, but lack thereof is no excuse for not killing it anyway.

- Don't blow up the class with your personal drama. This would include the fallout from torrid affairs with your classmates, but I know I'm whistling past the graveyard on this one. If you need to have your affair, do so with some discretion and tact. The best affairs begin and end with hardly anyone knowing or caring. Advertising your shiny, new, acting-class relationship via in-theatre PDA is seriously tedious.

- Return communication from the teacher in a timely manner. Within an hour is nice. Certainly within the day. Pretend we're your agent. (This happens to be my personal all-time make-my-dang-head-explode issue with students.)

- Say please, thank you, etc. All the stuff you hopefully learned at four years old.

- Never mention the financial relationship between student and teacher (See "I'm Paying You.")

- Treat everyone who works for the school or teacher the same as you would treat the teacher. Coming up at BHP, I remember all the Milton acolytes who would treat me and others who worked for Milton like total crap, like the household help of some bygone era, and then suck up to The Man in the most barf-inducing way. Don't be that person.

I humbly submit that a good teacher whom you trust is a rare gem. If you're lucky you'll have five of them your whole life, inclusive of different areas of study. You want to treat those relationships well, tend to them a bit better than you might others. Communicate more, and more carefully, and perhaps forgive more, and a bit more easily. It might well be worth it to you over the long haul.

CHAPTER 57

I'm Paying You

Annually, there are always several instances where a student, unhappy with the direction of a critique, or with a policy, or with something that didn't go their way, will reduce their side of the argument to this very odd justification: "I'm paying you." As in, "I'm paying you, so tell me what I want to hear." There's a variant: the teacher addresses a less-than-ideal attitude or deportment, and the student counters that this attitude is justified or tolerable in an environment where they are paying tuition, but will be *of course* be different when they're being paid to act. As in, "When I get paid, I'll behave better, I'll accept slings and arrows with infinite charm and aplomb."

The argument is as insulting as it is untrue. It's 100% unadulterated bullshit. Those who think they can look like shit, dress like shit, act like shit, mope around, indulge their petulance, their hostility, their "how dare you talk to me this way" haughtiness, but yet think that when money is on the line—a real audition, a meeting, a blessed gig— they will suddenly snap to and become professional, are kidding themselves. I have never observed evidence of this amazing ability. Over the years, I've observed countless students in various non-class professional situations, and you know what? The ones who can tend toward being a hostile pain in the ass in class have the exact same tendency on set. And the ones who are a pleasure to deal with? They're a pleasure on set. So we teachers all beg you to wake up. Be a professional. All the time. Don't kid yourself that you'll be a professional *when you're being paid*. The fact is this: *With that attitude, you simply won't get to the point of being paid—or at least nowhere near as often as you would like.*

You're a student, not a customer in a store. An acting class isn't a place where "the customer is always right." And yes, teachers have their foibles and flaws, of course, but the very premise of a class is that it exists for the teacher to improve you, not for you to improve the teacher. The premise of the entire relationship is that you're in the school to learn, and generally teachers have the discretion on what exactly the lesson is, and how it might be delivered. So stay away from telling the teacher how exactly you prefer to be spoken to. Or how some issue needs to go your way because *you pay tuition*. Performing arts instruction isn't a dialectic, it's not a court case. You do the work, teachers tell you what to do to make it better. That's it. When you're paying for professional communication—particularly in a context of any kind of training—it is a rookie and/or tasteless move to call attention to the direction of the payments. I remember Milton getting into it with a student during a critique, and at some point she said, "Look, I'm paying you, here," and he replied, "Not any more you're not." And that was the end of the student's tenure at BHP.

CHAPTER 58

"The Bed Always Wins"

It wasn't long working with Milton before I heard him say it, and hear him say it I did a thousand times after that. Up near the top of the list of reasons why actors leave a class, or even the business as a whole, is "the bed." The relationship. The boyfriend girlfriend husband wife stupid hookup unreciprocated obsession cupid-arrowed relationship. The need to serve it handle it hide within it envelop oneself in it, to repair it fracture it anew nay blow it to smithereens and then humpty-dumpty that shit back together again.

A poor acting class doesn't have a chance against The Bed. Nonetheless, I have experienced and/or observed at least a billion times the following types of Significant Other (SgO) trouble signs, and offer them up with a caution flag (no doubt in vain):

- An actor-actor couple is difficult. So my early and easiest advice is to find what I only-half-jokingly call "a civilian." Most actor-actor couples I've known have ended up as actor-somethingelse couples, and that's if they survived even remotely long enough for someone to make that adjustment. (To those who have made it down the long road, I bow down in your general direction.)

- Don't get serious with anyone prior to your career having some momentum, which I would loosely define as "booking somewhat regular paid work," in combination with your paying your own bills through your own efforts across the board. It takes a lot of focus and work to get there, and along the way you'll meet many who are "supportive" of this effort, sometimes with seemingly wonderful financial assistance, while at the same time, behind the veil *(What? A veil? In Los Angeles?)* wishing you would stop so as to better serve whatever their ideal image of their SgO is. If you're dependent on this person financially, that will slow down your ability to recognize the situation.

- Anyone in your own acting class. Particularly if you like that class. Because there's virtually a 100% chance at least one of you is leaving.

- Anyone whose presence causes sudden or gradual contretemps with your circle of trusted friends, even if the new SgO seems bright and happy about them all. How many times have I seen some bright, new, attractive, talented little penny show up as the new SgO of someone in a group, everyone is entranced, and before long the group is completely at odds with each other? Check the penny, people.

- Anyone who seems actively to disdain your circle of trusted friends (or teachers!), or after whose arrival you find yourself withdrawing from this circle.

- Any guy who's reflexively suspicious/jealous of your male friends, any woman who's reflexively suspicious/jealous of your female friends.

- Anyone you met on a social media application designed primarily for stupid meaningless hookups.

- Anyone who drinks heavily or uses drugs. How many times have I seen huge investment in a relationship get blown sky high by addiction issues? And so many times, it turns out the SgO was drinking or doing drugs *on the first date.* One of my early girlfriends, I remember showing up at her apartment for a second date, and she was clearly a little fuzzy. She gets migraines, no big deal, she explained. *Okay! So sorry gee-wiz, no problem!* She has "medicinal absorption problems," and has to take several fiorinal per headache —could we stop on the way to dinner to refill the prescription? *Okay! Gosh, never heard of that. No problem! Hey, what—you don't believe in banks? Why do you have piles of cash all over the place?* She is a broker for pre-Columbian art, and doesn't trust banks, tells a story that would have you, Dear Reader, pulling your money out of your bank. *Hey why were there police at your door as I walked up?* There have been break-ins in the building, they were just canvassing…But I was so naive, so excited that she was into me, I deluded myself into believing that this clearly significant narcotic addiction (and likely side career in the distribution of same or worse), and the ongoing chaos it created, was something else entirely, because, well, *no one just lies to your face about, or hides completely, major aspects of their existence, do they?* And I know that so many people smoke pot—this was before the legalization of it, and now it's practically a grocery item, but I tell you, it's doing nothing for you. And at some point, you'll probably see that for yourself, want to stop, and if you're with a pothead, that's gonna be a moment.

Almost the entire list of caution flags would apply to anyone of course, not just actors, but because actors are involved in pursuing a particularly dicey, unknowable, and unpredictable path to success, I think the drama of The Bed costs them more per episode than those who are pursuing more standard careers.

CHAPTER 59

Instruction Ad Absurdum

"What scene should I be working on?"

"When you say 'write a thank-you note', do you mean on paper? Or a card? What kind of card? And what do I say? Just…'thank you'?"

"If my handwriting is bad, should I still write a note? Should I type it?"

"Should I email them? Or call? Or like a private message on Facebook? And when? On Monday? Thursday? Not on the weekends. But maybe…Do you think?"

"What scene should I be working on?"

"When you say 'it's probably best that I do X,' do you mean that's the only way, or can I do Y instead?"

"You said to read that chapter in the book—where is that chapter?"

"So-and-so and I want to do a scene. Which scene should we work on?"

"When you said to let you know about how it went, how do you want to know and what do you really mean? Like, an essay? A sentence? Can I text you?"

"I couldn't find the article you referenced. How would I find that?"

"I can't think of any scenes to work on. What do you think?"

"When you said I should nail the costume, do you mean like…What do you mean? Should I rent it? Where?"

"How do you think I should…?"

"When do you think I should…?"

"Where do you think I should...?"

"I was going to, you know...But I didn't know if they would...You know?"

"I'm wondering if my very existence is offensive to someone. Should I... you know?"

"I'm trying to think of scenes to work on, but can't come up with anything. Do you have any ideas?"

There would seem to be a trend lately that people are waiting for ceaseless instruction, endless permission, a completely con-textified sequence of steps to take, lest any step they take on their own is a wrong one. There's too much fear about making a move without specific instruction on how to make it, when to make it, with whom, where, should they at all? Could they be disliked as a result? Would it be offensive? Eeeek! A mouse!

To quote John Gielgud's iconic butler in *Arthur*, "Please stop that." We're training you to be professionals in your career, who can assess a situation, take action, take initiative, find the person to talk to, use Google, consult a table of contents or index, make a phone call, handle a situation, hell—even write a cohesive sentence or two.

It's not like I'm against answering a question—teachers are there to answer questions for sure. I take a healthy break between scenes in class so as to facilitate conversation amongst students, and to give time for them to ask me questions as I indulge a cigarette substitute outside. But neither are teachers there to make themselves your lord and master, your oracle, the person-who-must-be-checked-with, the-person-whose-approval-is-so-necessary. Ideally a teacher helps you to be self-sufficient, training you to ask and be able to answer on your own, in a way that will lead to success. There is a disturbing level of passivity and frailty behind the endless sequence of questions that arise from the simplest instruction. For instance, on my basic tenet that actors should follow up all professional work (including auditions) with a thank-you note, I swear to you I have fielded 1,000 questions over the last five years. Then there are the numbing, soul-crushing questions about where to find particular references from Milton's books or my writing—stuff that an index and/or about thirty seconds of active curiosity will answer.

As for "What scene should I do?"...I must say I've grown to loathe the question. I've played piano for over 40 years, and plenty of those were under direct weekly instruction from a variety of teachers, and I don't think I ever asked a single time, "What piece should I play?" If you'd like to avoid my ire, the better question goes something like this: "I've read a bunch of plays, watched a bunch of films, I have a list of ten options for scenes I'd like to work on—can I send that list to you and then you tell me what you think?"

CHAPTER 60

On Technology And Training

There's a fabulous documentary on the topic of making Steinway pianos —*Note by Note: The Making of Steinway L1037*. It follows the creation of a single nine-foot concert Steinway at the company's U.S. factory in Queens, New York. To see the breadth of knowledge, passed down through an old-school apprenticeship system, carried out by largely blue-collar New York workers of every imaginable stripe and ethnicity, applied to the assembly of these sophisticated pianos, the selection of which you then see carried out by a diametrically opposite economic/social stratum of world-class musicians—it's something else. Highly enjoyable, and not just for pianists. And as always with documentaries—*great acting.*

Anyway—it made me think of what we do at the BHP in training actors. Steinways are made by hand. There have certainly been some technological developments in the last 100 years that may help out, but it's startling how little of it you see in the documentary. You see a lot of elbow grease, and a lot of guys with tool kits that are decades old, with instruments bizarrely fashioned to some arcane, specific purpose related to piano assembly, but mostly you see raw expertise and exacting standards. Technology has very little to do with it.

Back in 2004, there was a teacher who recommended that the BHP install cameras in the theatres, record every scene on multi-cam digital video, etc., Milton and I had the same reaction: *Nope.* Let's set aside the prohibitive technical logistics, the myriad ways it would get fucked up every night, and the staffing requirements—Milton said to me in ironic response, "I think they had cameras back when I started as well…Yeah, there were movies back then. Yeah…" He continued without irony: "But even though it was still largely a movie business, I didn't see any cameras in Lee's class, or in Stella's, or in Uta's…I don't remember anyone talking about cameras or 'film acting' or any of that, and if I recall they turned out some pretty good actors."

And Milton writes in his book regarding the concept of "film acting:" *I don't see any difference. I don't buy into this whole film-acting, stage-acting dichotomy. Obviously when you're in a closeup on film, and the lens is 18 inches off your face, you can't move a lot, because you'll slide out of focus. Maybe a choice that works for a thousand-seat theatre won't work for a closeup, but that doesn't mean the acting is fundamentally different. The work is the same. The emotions are the same. The story is the same…Acting is acting…And I think the whole "film acting" thing, when it's thought of as a completely different way of acting—that can be confusing, in the sense that it can scare the actor, make him possibly refute the basic truths of his work that he knows, and even limit him from making the bold choice.*

Over the years, there has certainly been a revolution in digital video technology and its instantaneous planet-wide mass distribution. But, regardless of what many may say, I don't feel there is any corresponding revolution to be had in the field of acting training. Technology simply has zero to do with artistic training. And if you need any further proof, doesn't *Rocky IV* provide it conclusively? I mean, there's the big Russian dude having his training regimen and the strength of his jab measured by computers, and meanwhile Rocky is hauling tree trunks through the snow. So there you have it. Done.

I think actors are made the old-fashioned way: With in-person communication. It's hard enough, acting training, without adding the element of video technology—whether that's to look at yourself on camera, or whether that's to have a friggin' Skype acting class, or to let the world in, via a webcam, on what should be a private and safe space for actors to work. I've said no to all of it. And I know, *I know*, everyone says it's valuable to see yourself on screen, to realize you have an eye tick or that you tend to "do too much in closeup," and all that. Perhaps it's better to have a Skype acting class than a cancelled one—but there's something about it that just rubs me wrong. With regard to acting well on camera, until the DV revolution, these nuances of film work were learned primarily through professional experience, and I haven't seen any dramatic increase in acting ability since then—either in classes or in the industry at large.

The bottom line is there is simply ZERO correlation between actors taking all these video workshops and being better actors, ZERO correlation to any higher rate of booking jobs.

If anyone really had this mythic secret that would yield a measurably higher booking percentage—well we'd all be out of business and that teacher could clean up.

No. The best way of getting the job, any job, increasing numbers of jobs, higher quality jobs—hard diligent work on both acting and career over time. And even then, Showbiz, she is a fickle lady. Look at the cover of an entertainment magazine from five years ago and see how fast it can all go. *What ever happened to ___?* So I prefer consistent communication. The BHP is a scene-study outfit, that's how Milton set it up, and that's how we'll remain. We make Steinways. How you choose to use the instrument we build, whether it collects dust in the corner or is played every day—that's up to you. Setting up a camera to record it doesn't change how the instrument plays.

Even in our audition workshops, the big emphasis is on knowing the story, making choices that tell the story well, presenting yourself professionally, etc. We spend 85% of the workshop on those elements, and then at the end—yeah, many auditions now occur on camera, or even via internet, so we include that just to ensure the actors are comfortable with the mechanics of that stuff. But it's not intended as a means of analyzing or critiquing one's own work as a whole.

I do think it's important for actors to be knowledgable about the technical aspects of how a film gets made—going out and making short films, realizing what sucks, what doesn't, what you care about as a writer, etc. But I believe that's different from the idea of looking at yourself on screen and using video as a heavy part of your acting training. There's a reason many directors don't allow their actors to view dailies—it's because the actor often (always?) has a subjective and often insecure filter through which they look at themselves. That's why I think it's best to keep cameras out of it, just do the work in a good class, do it consistently, over time, on a stage, and have a trusted teacher give you input that moves you forward.

CHAPTER 61

Holiday Hiati

They're coming. The holidays. Visible on the horizon right after Labor Day. Now personally, this is my favorite time of year—the sun gets lower in the sky, the temperature falls (in a Los Angeles context - brrr - 60 degrees!), my fond memories of New England autumns stir, and I'm sort of a jacket guy, so I get to wear those jackets and sweaters. For twenty years, I would do a piano recital each Christmas, so the changing light outside has its own associations with intense practice at the keyboard.

But I probably speak on behalf of all administrators and teachers of acting schools in Los Angeles, (or for that matter, private artistic workshops everywhere) that the Holidays can spell impending disaster for the psychological health and artistic commitment of our students. It's as if the entire last 8 weeks of each year is written off under the mass justification: "It's the holidays."

He has to take off for a few weeks—it's the holidays.

There are no scenes on the books—it's the holidays.

I'm in and out of town for the next couple months—it's the holidays.

Or the all time classic: *The business is slow—it's the holidays.* That's kind of two whoppers in one sentence, but that's how you get to all time classic status.

And then in January, it's not as if everyone is hot and ready to go. There's the new justification that January is the charge-up month, get back into town, collect yourself, pick up shifts to make money that you lost by giving up shifts to travel…February. *In February I'm gonna fucking rock!*

I imagine the BHP is not the only place where in January we're in an entire project to "recover" students—the ones who have gone just completely MIA, and those who have returned, but who are bleary-eyed, disoriented, mentally wrecked by too many questions like, *How long are you going to give it?* and *When will we see you on TV?* and *Did you hear your brother just made partner?!* and *Why don't you come home and work in the store?*

So beware the "It's the Holidays" justification. If you find it creeping maliciously from your brain to your tongue in preparation for its escape from your lips and into the physical world of excuses, please stop. And don't just stop saying it, but stop living by it.

"It's the holidays" is an entire mechanism designed to slow you down, check you out, ice you cold. This doesn't mean you don't go see the family if that's what you need to do. But I know I started out at 7-10 days out of town during the holidays, and before I finally had my own family here (the ultimate excuse for no travel to see family), I'd weaned it down to 3 days. So just look at how much time is really necessary and be honest about that— Milton would often tell the story about how he realized his last trip home for the holidays had occurred when his mother asked him to take out the garbage. If I remember the story correctly, he was gone the next day (or was it the same night?) and that was his last holiday visit home.

I remember once looking in on an Orientation class after the holidays, and a young actress who had just done a terrific scene talked about how passionate she was about the play—Shanley's *Danny and the Deep Blue Sea*. She said she had just visited home in NYC to see friends, etc., and turned down most offers to go out so she could stay home and read the play again and again—she was so jazzed by it. I thought this was an unbelievable statement. I mean, how many actors are turning down social this-and-that to stay home and read a *play*? And then read it *again*? Not enough by a long shot. And it can be easier when you're feeling inspired for sure, but inspiration isn't always the state of affairs, and when that's the case you have to seek it, create it, hunt it down and fire it up.

So if you're checking out of town for the holidays, don't check out of your artistic life. Don't ease up on the gas pedal, but floor it instead. Use that time to re-inspire: read plays, see great movies (not just the ones in current release), come up with a list of scripts you're passionate about, roles you dream to play, develop a new line of attack on your career and your development. That way you hit the new year running hard, running fast.

CHAPTER 62

Fuck Improv Training

There. I said it. Why? (And keep in mind I'm talking about the improv-comedy tidal wave that has completely overwhelmed over the training landscape, rather than improvisation as a tool in otherwise "serious" programs.)

1. It reinforces highly superficial tendencies in the actor—the glib, facile responses that are all geared towards generating a laugh. Because *improv* always goes with *comedy*. It never goes with drama. Only *comedy*. So all this improv training is about being fucking funny, you see. And apparently a rule has been passed that funny people are not funny, not fully funny, not *truly professionally funny*, until they take an improv workshop. Improv training has its rules and its guidelines, each program has its technique like any school, but my experience is that no matter what conversations are occurring about "truth" or "character," it ends up manifesting as impatient, microwave popcorn acting for popcorn comedies, and has no real interest in encouraging actors to get down and dirty with the marriage of character to *story*, which historically has marked the skill of a good actor. So for its ceaseless contribution to superficial cheese-ball acting, fuck improv training.

2. As a teacher, it can take a while to get an actor to understand acting, how the writing, the story, the behavior, the inner life all line up, all of the myriad ephemeral little tasks and skills that need to coalesce to make a fine performance, not to mention encouraging the actor to get a grip on their

occasionally chaotic personal lives, get some discipline, take themselves and acting seriously, and take the idea of persistent career administration seriously. Like any artistic training, it can take years, and my experience is that just as we're getting somewhere on this complicated trifecta, the actor takes off to "do improv for a while." Their agents want it on the resume, you see. So for interrupting countless conversations with students who are just breaking through, fuck improv training.

3. There's not a scintilla of evidence that improv training creates a better actor, even for comedies. I've cast my share of projects, and not one improv-trained actor has outshone another traditionally trained actor, and frankly, it's the reverse and by FAR. Most anecdotal feedback I've gotten from fellow directors and writers who have just gone through a casting process, for both comedies and dramas, is that they want to shoot improv training in the head. I've talked to working directors and casting people and asked if they can see a difference and the answer is an emphatic *no*, and that was for the minority who happened to notice this training on the resume in the first place. So for wasting the time of so many casting and directing professionals who have to watch improv-trained actors blow their auditions sky high, even for the comedies that are supposed to be the target market, fuck improv training.

4. It's part of the childish, impatient cultural subtext that is "gimme it now." You don't get anything of value now. You don't become a master at anything by doing ten weeks of "something fun." You get something of value by training your ass off and training hard and training for years. Name me another skill where that isn't true. "Yeah, listen, Madame Violin Teacher, I've been playing my Suzuki method for a couple years now, but I think I'm going to do some improv violin. They say it will help get me work." "Hey, Mr. Carpentry Master, I've been apprenticing with you for a few months now, but I'm not feeling my career coming on, so I'm gonna do some improv carpentry. I'm gonna shoot nails everywhere, just, you know —I need to be free." Medicine. Teaching. Science. The Visual or Per-

forming Arts. Athletics. Standup comics work their asses off for *years* to evolve a voice and consistently good material. No, no— you never would hear something so lame in any of these fields. But in acting—yes. So for its connection to the childish "gimme it now" sense of entitlement and amateurishness that so-called serious teachers fight tooth and nail every day, fuck improv training.

5. Improv training has been marketed beautifully—a completely phantom linkage has been created between "improv training" and a greater likelihood of booking work. I marvel at how it was done. But it's nonsense. There is no such linkage. There are articles in the trade mags each year now about where THEY go to look for comedic actors. THEY are going to this showcase, and then THEY will go to that comedy night. No, no! Oh, no…THEY are not even going out anymore! THEY are staring at the computer screen looking for comic brilliance to pop out at them. It's all frantic bullshit. I maintain that THEY have always sought and always will seek one thing: *talented actors.* A talented actor can find humor where there's humor, and pathos where there's pathos. A talented, trained actor can improvise on the spot, per the request of a director so interested. A talented, disciplined actor will ensure his or her talent is out there to be seen in all forms, on stage, on screen, and online. But this relentless marketing has resulted in agents robotically ordering their clients to "get some improv training," it has led to improv workshops with Levels A through Q, and boy, once you get to Level Q, descending through the clouds will be none other than Lorne Michaels himself, ready to blow you *and* invite you to be a cast member on *Saturday Night Live*. So for its insidious, clever marketing, which has made it seem as if improv training is now the *sine qua non* for an actor's resume, even though if you named the 100 best actors of the last 75 years, I would bet good money that not one single person on that list is improv-trained, fuck improv training.

That is all.

CHAPTER 63

We Just Wanted To Have Fun

And we teachers love you for your wanting to have fun. You know what's really fun? Kicking a scene's ass. That's fun. Putting it all on the line and nailing that sucker. That's serious fun. Sometimes, maybe you don't have the prep time you really needed, and you have to pull it together in a rehearsal or two. You know what's fun? Still kicking that scene's ass, even on short notice, so that we never even know you had to work fast. Excellence is fun. Professionalism is fun.

And here and there, students at the BHP have done a joke scene— something themed to the holiday of the moment, or a special funny presentation for someone's birthday. We love it. No problem. Here and there. One or two scenes in a year's worth. But even then, the best of these "event" scenes are, well, the best of them. When a dozen students got together to rehearse in the middle of the night for weeks to pull off a fully choreographed number from *The Full Monty*, with lights, costumes and a crazy dance routine, as a surprise gift performance for a teacher? *That was fun.*

We all want to have fun. If it's truly the frivolous kind, then go to an amusement park. Play laser tag. You name it, you go for it, have your fun. But don't let the concept of "we just wanted to have fun" become an excuse for shoddy work. A safe barometer for this unique brand of actor's justification is to apply the same to other high-level performing arts or sports contexts: I've had a half dozen serious piano teachers during my adult life, each vastly different from the other in personality and temperament, and I can't think of one of them who'd appreciate my bringing in a "joke" piece to play, or something that was half-assed and stupid, and my telling them, "I just wanted to have fun." Each one of those teachers would have looked at me blankly and moved immediately onto my serious studies.

ON ADMINISTRATION

CHAPTER 64

The Formula

Here it is, folks: **Ability + Administration + Time.**

That's the only formula worth anything in this business. It's not Ability + Parties. Or Parties + Time. Or Marijuana + Ability. Or Ability + Sex With Director. (Well…Maybe the last one. But usually only for a very brief moment.)

Ability comes from good training, hopefully from someone who knows what they're talking about and is good at communicating it to you. At the BHP, good training consists of putting the actor through his or her paces doing what they're going to be hired to do: scenes. Solving scenes. Acting in scenes. So I've come up believing that training should include lots of scenes. Like 100-200 scenes. You're gonna meet a lot of people doing that. A network will emerge, and along the way hopefully you'll be hired, and early on it will be a single scene. As you move forward in your career—more scenes. If you're a star, you're in practically every scene. You're never going to be hired for technical exercises, nor for improv, nor for slating your name, nor for your "camera technique." You're going to be hired for killing the scene, and all the rest will follow from professional experience. But how do you know when you have enough ability? That's tough. Are there more who are, shall we say, *overconfident* in their ability, or insecure of the same? I remember a casting director doing a seminar at the BHP, and he was asked what the most frequent problem was that he saw. His answer: "Ninety percent of the actors who come in for auditions can't act to save their fucking life." So that would seem to indicate that *overconfidence* is the more prevalent issue.

If you have a teacher you trust, they should be willing to tell you honestly whether it's time to go out there and hit the gas on your administration. I'll go out there and say that if you've done any fewer than 50 scenes in a good, challenging no-bullshit class, you're probably not ready. (If you want to fight about that, I don't know what the point is: Are you saying doing 50+ scenes in a good class will be *detrimental?* If you're fighting the number, it sounds to me like a justification for thin training.)

Administration consists of good, old-fashioned diligent hard work. It is usually enhanced by knowing damned well that your abilities are up to snuff, so Administration is best undertaken only once you have ability. I've known plenty of young people who come to town ready to *shred it* with meetings. Their father is so-and-so, and knows Important People, and he's gonna hook them up good! Only one problem: they don't know how to act yet. And then you've blown those meetings. Administration, when the time arrives for it, is a muscle that needs developing like any other skill, at first you'll fumble around and wonder what to do, but as time goes by, you'll develop a rhythm to it, have a longer list of names to hit up, more gigs under your belt, and each gig is more names, and more names mean more gigs.

Time is just time. It's always doing its thing. How much time do you need? Here you go: Minimum five years to put together talent and ability and a basic network of people in town who know you, trust you, bring you in, so that you're hopefully dealing with 50 quality auditions each year. Maybe it takes less than five years, in which case good for you. Maybe it takes more, in which case—no big deal. There's not a career on earth where any less than ten years pursuing it diligently means jack shit. So join the human race and stop complaining about it!

CHAPTER 65

My Agent Said

...that I need to take an improv class.

...that I need to take a commercial class.

...that I need to take an audition class.

...that I need to take an on-camera class.

...that I need to take an improv class.

...that I should stop studying and just do casting workshops.

...that they're going to drop me.

...that I need new headshots.

...that I should drop class and just focus on auditions right now because it's gonna be really busy.

...that I'm not going out because the business is just really slow right now.

...that the business is really slow because of the holidays.

...that the business is really slow because of the election.

...that the business is really slow because of the drought.

...that the business is really slow because of the rain.

...that the business is really slow because everyone's getting ready to leave town.

...that the business is really slow because everyone's out of town.

...that the business is really slow because everyone only just got back to town.

...that the business is really slow because of the economy.

...that the business isn't actually slow at the moment, but it's pilot season and casting offices are only considering "names."

…that I need to have a certain number of Social Media followers to be considered for jobs.

…that I need to take an improv class.

Milton's favorite joke about the actor-agent relationship: an actor comes home to find his wife dazed, beaten, bloodied. Freaking out, he asks, "What the hell happened?" The wife answers: "It was awful. Your agent showed up at the door. When I opened it, he became violent, crazed, and viciously attacked me." The actor then gets very quiet, and replies, "My *agent* was here?!"

Now, I suppose somewhere there's a book by an agent wherein he or she laments that their clients are constantly turned inside out by a ton of "you shoulds," "they says" and "here's whys" from the client's acting teacher. But on this side of the equation, it is certainly a constant source of irritation. And not so much because another industry professional has an opinion about this and that (even if I often think it's a total bullshit opinion), but because actors seem so universally *on their back, on their knees, prostrate*, and *obsequious* in the face of this input.

Opinions about what you "should" do to become successful in this town are the third loudest noise in Los Angeles. First: Traffic and police helicopters. If we could lower that sound to zero, it would be the sound of actors bitching about their lives and careers. If we could lower *that* to zero, it would be the opinions from every corner of this industry about what you "should" do. The fact is, however, that not one of the above statements actually means anything. They're just collections of words put together in an order that secures a certain amount of reflexive, mindless, head-nodding agreement. But there isn't a statistic to be found that any of it is true in the slightest degree, that any of the above will help you succeed, or is the "reason" for anything. What you "should do" as an actor is become competent with the acting portion of the story-telling process.

The following is true:

"Develop your acting ability to the highest degree you are able, via some consistent, challenging training that lasts minimum two years, if not simply indefinitely. Work the career administration in every imaginable way that is tolerable, ethical and professional, and do that for a minimum of five years. Then let's talk about where you are in fashioning a career as an actor."

Tell your agent that your teacher said.

CHAPTER 66

The Three Phases (Plus One)

There are three phases of your average actor's existence in Los Angeles:

Phase One: Prologue

This would consist of the 1-5 years on average that I have observed actors simply to stumble about town without a semblance of traction. If we're lucky, they may be in a class, but the overall discipline is shaky. The actor in early Prologue is often spinning, dazed, and partying, without much restraint. Later in Prologue would be found that person who is getting serious, finds a decent class, and with a degree of focus sets out to assemble their skills as a professional storyteller—but who has yet to administrate. Everyone starts in Prologue, and only determine through their actions and behavior when to emerge from this phase. Prologue is the period between arriving in Los Angeles and becoming a consistently good, professional-level actor who is responsible, focused and ready to leave something behind in favor of being in Phase Two. A lot of actors have said some version of, "Man, I've been in town X years now and nothing's really happened." My response for most is that those X years were Prologue. Those X years don't really count on the clock of "I've been doing this X years." You haven't been "doing this." Not really.

Phase Two: Build-out.

For my money, this is the start point of a career. In Build-Out, by hook or by crook, the actor has gotten himself into a position of acting well on a consistent basis—he/she knows the task, has evolved an approach that works for them, they tell the right story in the right way most or all of the time, they're good group collaborators and have practiced that skill as well. They've probably indulged 1-5 years of Prologue-y gyrations between sloth and chaos in the personal life, are ready to stop the Crazy, and get to work. And work it is. For the next five years or so, the actor in Build-out is serious about his or her administration, works it consistently, follows up all meetings and auditions like a professional, and expands that list of Showbiz contacts. They stop conceiving of themselves as some Special Snowflake simply deserving of regular work because of their talent, and they stop blaming other people for their ills. And they're probably partying less, smoking less pot, writing fewer mantras, and simply working more. A proper Build-Out phase has attention to further development of their abilities, and a goal of 50 actions a week directed outward toward building a network, building the trust that casting directors, agents, writers, directors and producers must have in you as a professional actor. One veteran BHP actor, who has built quite a nice career for himself over 20 years in Los Angeles, recalled to me a conversation with Milton about all this. This actor was wired from birth to be slightly appalled by the notion of naked self-promotion, and Milton replied, "You want a house?" The actor says he thinks of this every week. From his house.

Phase Three: I'm Workin' Here.

Through diligent time spent on build-out, the actor has, we hope, successfully moved to Phase Three, which is marked by more consistent professional work. There are several jobs a year, let's say. You're making your SAG insurance minimum. Maybe you even get to give up your day job. But notice that Phase Three isn't called, "I'm sitting back to enjoy the money I make from acting." It's Work. Still work. Because you have to move the career in the direction you want to go, all the while continuing the actions you did during "Build-out." But you've also learned to ride the ups and downs, the "you're in first position/pinned/on avail" exhilaration that is crushed two days later when they go with someone else who won third prize on a reality show. Your sense of humor remains intact when your agent quits to shepherd goats in Scotland, or drops you and makes you think *you* should shepherd goats in Scotland. You might be able to get away without 50 actions a week, but I would certainly still recommend flawless followup and regular communication (3-4 times a year) with everyone on your list.

(Phase Fantasyland: Struggle? What Struggle?

Some actors, sprinkled in fairy dust, arrive in Los Angeles to find themselves working professionally in no time flat, with nary even a year of struggle *or* study. This is perhaps the most dangerous phase of them all, because the career arrived before the actor knows that careers don't always just *arrive*, before they know that careers sometimes *depart* as soon as they arrive. These actors often have a Phase One lifestyle with a Phase Three career. Very dangerous. These actors can burn out as fast as a mediocre Phase One party animal, and can have trouble getting their mojo back, as they never earned it in the first place. My advice for actors sprinkled in fairy dust is to live Phase Three as if you're in Phase Two, keeping yourself straight, sane, sober, and collecting every damned name you come across, treating them well and true, writing notes right and left, and take that good luck and match it with hard work, make the early career a long-lasting one as well.)

My informal observation is that 80% of actors who land in LA and begin in Prologue never emerge from that phase. They are too addicted to some form of unstructured existence, it's all too chaotic, they just never quite become a professional about it— either from a skills or business perspective. Some brilliant actors can study for years and still essentially remain in Prologue from their sheer obstinacy about the issue of career administration. Of the remaining 20% who enter the Build-Out phase, almost none will be consistent for five years because they get discouraged, or other opportunities for Real Life present themselves and they're happy to pursue those. So, that's about one percent remaining who arrive in Los Angeles and make the full journey from Prologue to I'm Workin' Here! May the Force be with you to be one of them.

CHAPTER 67

A Universal Career Jumpstart

Ask a majority of actors what's going on with their career, and you'll likely get a fuzzy look, the eyes will wander this way and that, some stammering will emerge about needing a better agent, or simply getting any agent, or they did some casting workshop recently. They'll tell you about a note they sent to someone last month, and toss in a few justifications about what "everyone" says the business is like, and of course the improv/on-camera/sit-com/whatever workshop their agent told them to do is a lot of fun, and, uh…well…It can peter out from there rapidly.

Pre-supposing the presence of natural or hard-won ability, a career is then built on relationships—lots of 'em, developed and nurtured over time. Actors can suffer from chronic career myopia, however, with their concept of how it's all going centered on what happens (or not) this week, with this agent, with that audition. Ask about last week and a fog descends, and next week doesn't exist. The sense takes hold that the actor "doesn't know where to begin" on building (or, for some, re-building) their career. This "I don't know where to begin" feeling remains in place even for those who are blessed with talent, worked hard to train themselves, and have a few years or more behind them in the biz.

So, here's where to begin—three pieces of paper (or their digital equivalents), and three lists:

Group One: Every person you've worked for as an actor. For each gig, that would involve the director, writer, producer, casting director, other actors of note. You won't be able to remember all these names offhand, of course, but start with the title of the project (including, e.g., "that independent thing I did in Palm Desert"), and start filling in the blanks as best you can, using IMDb or whatever other resource you need to supplement your failing memory. Agency information is okay, but better overall is the address of their current production office.

Group Two: Audition followup list. For each audition you have, I believe you've met four people—the writer, producer, director and casting director. I don't care that you just had the CD in an office with a camera—they work on behalf of the writer, director, producer, and you have in effect met all of them by reading for the project. They each have names, and you should walk out of the office knowing all of those names, and putting them in Group Two. To start the process, fill in the blanks on the last year's worth of auditions.

Group Three: Those with whom you'd like to work. Write down twenty projects—film, television or theatre—that have rocked your world in the last couple years. It's not about your having been right for any roles, just that the project gave you that feeling of, well…"That's why I got into this nutty business. To do something like that." Find out the names of the writer, director and producer for each of those projects, and get a mailing address or other contact information. If you want extra credit, look up the casting director as well and get their current information. So that's 60-80 names at least.

Now, *work the damned list*. Start writing. A nice note, hand-written when possible. Get yourself some cards/envelopes with your name and contact information—direct phone and email. I wouldn't worry about your photo—they can look you up in three seconds on the web—but you can include a business-card-sized shot, or work a photo into the design of the cards if you wish. The note should be relatively short-and-sweet, sincere and professional. Don't speak from a position as a seemingly lowly actor who's trying to get ahead, but as a fellow industry professional, based on respect and enthusiasm for the work. Don't be cute, clever, joking, political, spiritual or say things like, "…as for me, it's really tough going in this business, but I'm still at it, and learning not to detest myself or others. Yay, therapy!" Don't ask Spielberg to have coffee. Don't try to close some deal with a single note.

For Group One, you're just looking to acknowledge the project, the process, your enjoyment of it, how well it may have done, or what they've done since, or just that it's a nice summer day out. If it's been a while, say something like, "I was just thinking of that project we worked on, and wanted to write you…" That's it. For Group Two, a short thank-you for the opportunity to read, best wishes on the project, look forward to meeting you again (with followups when the project airs, with or without you in the role). For Group Three, a simple and sincere acknowledgment of why their work rocked your world, and how it provided inspiration. You're building the relationship. You're trying to open the door to further communication.

You may well hear nothing back on most of these, and that's fine. This process has little to do with whether individual notes get individual responses, but whether the entirety of your effort to grab onto, develop, and maintain relationships turns a career profit over time.

Add to and follow up these lists. Group Three gets four new names for each audition. Everyone on each list gets 3-4 notes a year, but definitely upon some newsworthy event for either of you. Widely ignored, and yet particularly effective, is your interest in *their* career and accomplishments. Actors have the tendency to communicate from an utterly transparent self-interest, and then wonder why people don't get back to them as they might wish. Proper etiquette and interest in others is noted by them, it's appreciated, it's smart.

Stir with water. Add persistence and training. Simmer for five years, and let's see where you are then.

CHAPTER 68

Build Your Own Door And Walk Through It

My bet is the majority of actors are still operating under the following conventional assumptions regarding their career:

- I will get an important agent and/or manager to rep me.

- I will be sent out on an important audition for a big role / recurring role/guest star/etc. I will book said job.

- Said job will be seen by Someone Important, and I will be brought in for another, more important job, and so on and so on…

- Fame and/or money and/or a career of regular acting work will ensue.

So the actor, even when he or she is trained and has ability (and this is not exactly the norm), is still generally waiting around for the agent to call them for an audition, and their career administration is geared towards improving that agent and networking with casting directors. This is perfectly acceptable, but there's a problem in that warp-speed technological change will constantly chip away at the gates, and agents, casting directors, content-distributors and other gate-keepers will likely find eventually that there is no gate to keep.

Actors must become not only masters of conventional career administration (which, while it is still here, should be chased dutifully), but also far more entrepreneurial about creating content. Milton used to bemoan the fact that he wasn't directing movies any more. He wanted to, but in his mind, directing a movie meant a script being mailed to him, the approval of millions of dollars of expense, and a line of white production vehicles stretching for blocks. I told him once that if he wanted to direct a movie, get a camera, invite his favorite actors to his beautiful home, and start shooting. They could probably improvise something under his guidance that would be better than most scripted films. Hire a guy with a digital editing package on his home computer and some skills, and Milton would have a feature in six months. He looked at me as if I was insane. Ah, well…I think a large part of his frustration was that he wanted validation, he wanted courtship, he wanted to be wanted, he wanted the romance and the money and the various accoutrements that come with "making a movie." But when I suggested he could simply bypass all that and just make a movie, it just didn't hit home with him at all.

I think this is the case with actors as well. Underneath, under much protest to the contrary, there is the irresistible allure of *trailers, money, fame, attention*. We have to get past the idea of millions of dollars—either for film budgets, or for our own compensation. The old-time huge budgets for projects are harder to come by, and are now fragmented over more and more content generators—so the money you'll make will be less. But let's face it—most aren't making any money now! So instead of the dream of $1 million per movie, how about the idea of a steady $20-50 thousand per year, spread over many products? I think this is good, let's see who's interested in telling a story, rather than interested in a Porsche. If you're interested in the art form, in telling the story, in moving people or entertaining people with your performance, then the opportunities are only going to increase exponentially.

The cost of that increased opportunity will be demand for higher responsibility—the individual performer's responsibility to come up with a story to tell. The performer will have to be skilled not only as an actor, but possibly as a writer, as a motivator of others and of organization, and of business, and potentially of other areas of life so they can pull together the rent and car insurance in a regular fashion while they consistently pursue the art as well. The romantic and almost-impossible-to-achieve dream of $1 million a year for your acting services is being replaced by the far more achievable, but you-have-to-work-for-it-and-create-it, $1K-100K for your abilities across the artistic spectrum.

Sometimes when I come up against an actor who's frustrated

about career, I'll posit the following: "Okay. Let's make it really bad. No one will ever hire you to act in film or television, ever. Now what? You're free. No need ever to attend another agent or casting workshop—your employment has been banned. Now what? Are you an actor? What is your *Slingblade*? Tell me a story." And it's amazing how few actually have a story they want to tell. Or a role that comes to mind that would give them everything they've ever wanted to play. To me it's an indication of the habitual passivity of most actors. It's an inertia that must be crushed. No matter how your career is going at the moment, at some point you're going to have to build your own door, and walk through it.

CHAPTER 69

Cynema (or Cinema With A Why)

It doesn't quite work, because "Cynema" and "Cinema" are homonyms. Visually—okay. To the ear, it needs to be "Cynical Cinema."

cynical, adj., 1. concerned only with one's own interests and typically disregarding accepted or appropriate standards, 2. distrustful of human sincerity or integrity

cynema, n., filmmaking motivated by cynical inclinations as to what will move the creators' careers forward, at the expense of coherence, humanity or passion; cynema is often characterized by slavish devotion to a style, it rarely demonstrates any devotion to a focused story, it is marked by poor craftsmanship, improvisation in lieu of writing, a desperate desire to be funny (often by imitating others' humor), emphasis on the "mockumentary" form, hitting visual punchlines, etc.

We've all had enough of it, right? How many invitations have we received to look at Vimeo, YouTube, whatever, to see the latest work by an acquaintance, and you want to throw heavy objects at your fragile computer? If I never see another stupid fucking unfunny mockumentary again in this lifetime or any lifetime to follow, it will be too soon. Stop it! If you aren't going to be funnier than *Spinal Tap* or *Waiting for Guffman* (or that delicious *Extras* skit between Gervais and McKellen about acting), don't do it! And I'll go out there and just say you probably aren't funnier than those films. Those are professionally funny people, and in this business if you haven't been paid to be funny, there's an awfully good chance that if you tried, you simply aren't funny enough to be paid for it.

Each fall we assign the advanced classes at BHP to make their own short films—they get 8 weeks or so, and then we spend a night screening them and talking about the process. I've learned that I need explicitly and repeatedly to ban them from doing stupid comedies, mockumentaries, anything that relates to the industry at all, anything that has as its origination point, "Wouldn't it be funny if…?" And even with those stipulations, one year I had to give an entire class a failing grade and made them do the whole festival over, because almost everything submitted was still in the who-gives-a-shit, thrown-together, bad-sound, stupid-comedy genre.

Even when these web-shorts generate a laugh or two, I find they're cynical. They're thrown together. There's a nastiness underneath it, there's a bitterness, and it resonates throughout like a stuck low note on a piano, its sound regenerated again and again because the hammer is stuck, not damping down the string. They're trying too damned hard to be clever and to hit a tone. The subtext resonates: *We don't give a shit about this, really—we just hope it helps us become successful.* When these considerations override commitment to story, you're heading down the chute to irrelevance. Without story, in its place there is only aimless non-energy, no forward movement, the pace lags, and thus the only thing you have left to elicit a response is *cleverness*, and as result I start feeling ornery, as if I'm being commanded to laugh because…Why? I don't know. Because if I don't, the poor specimen won't make it onto www.funnyordie.com or some such thing. Frankly, I think funnyordie.com should die. How about a site called itsaboutsomethingordie.com? itprovokesmemoves-memakesmethinkmakesmelaughorfuckingdie.com?

All this relentlessly glib, cute bullshit, the cleverness and cynicism, it frustrates the crap out of me because often I know the participants well and I know it is undercutting the real potentials of the talent involved. The question I always have, similar to that of my essay on Shit Theatre: *What else could this person have spent the time creating?* A good rhetorical question to actors: "If someone gave you $1M to make the movie you want for you to star in, what would that story be? And who would you play?"

It's kind of scary how few people have the answers. But I would guess that only a small number would answer, "I would take the $1M and make umpteen cynical mockumentary short films, plus one narrative film about how bad my agent is." I think we'd start to experience a broader story arc, more in-depth character, more dramas would show up to balance out the comedy, the imagination would take flight, the actors would be challenged, etc.

The passion and thoughtfulness that would fuel the feature film you'd make for $1M or more? It should fuel *all* that you do. Five minutes on the web should have the same effort towards quality across the board as would two hours on the big screen. Make it about something. A strong story, believed in by all who are making it, told with humor and compassion and humanity, has far more potential to launch you than a slap-dash, cynical attempt to nail a tone or style that is popular.

CHAPTER 70

Diversity Distress

Diversity.

It's *the word* these days. It's the buzz word. It's an anthem. It's come to be a casting religion.

It's also a dangerous word about which to have a chat with actors, because of its close relationship to various phobias and isms like homophobia, xenophobia, racism, sexism, etc. Diversity aims partly to be the salve for those ills, so it's tough to have a specific talk about diversity in casting without triggering a bunch of trauma and a certain amount of misplaced righteousness about societal prejudice in the affected area.

I think it's important to look at the diversity issue objectively and through the proper lens—there are three distinct issues here: 1) Are enough parts being created from scratch, from writers, at the time of ink-to-page, that represent racial/ethnic/orientation minority characters? 2) Are roles that have *no* specific race/ethnicity/orientation being opened up for casting by minority actors (blind casting)? 3) And #2's corollary: the issue of minority-specific characters being cast with Caucasian celebrities for box office reasons, thus sending minority actors into spasms of social media apoplexy.

Are enough minority parts being written?

There's not a lot you can do here as an actor, other than learn to write well and then write stories that involve characters that are minority-specific in the way that interests you. In a world where "content generators" are more and more in vogue, learning to write well would probably be strongly advised for actors of all stripes. But with the advent of streaming and the resultant explosion in both content and distribution channels, many more writers are out there creating more varied stories and characters. I'd say we're on the right path there. But let's face it: speaking of minorities, there is a minority of scripts that are any good. So if you're in a racial/ethnic/orientation minority, that minority of good scripts is probably even more minor. So you really need to concentrate on writing a *good* script, not just one whose story deals with an historically oppressed group. If you're writing what Milton used to call a "thesis play" in order to lecture the masses about equality and justice, to signal your virtue as an enlightened person, I'm willing to bet you're on the way to a bad script.

Are non-minority-specific characters being opened up to minority actors?

This is probably the question that gets the most action for aspiring minority actors. And it's in a way the trickiest to deal with because it's the one most often mistakenly conflated with various loathsome phobias and isms. It's changing, but I believe writers in the past were simply less concerned with race or ethnicity unless it was specifically relevant as a story point. A scene about Korean immigrants needs Korean actors. A scene where a doctor comes in and looks at a medical chart? Well…They just wrote, "A DOCTOR (mid 30s) enters." I think nowadays writers feel obligated to indicate specific race and/or ethnicity, and I'm cynical enough to think this is done not from genuine interest in minorities as much as it is purely to serve the "diversity mandate." So even though the role has zero ethnic/racial specificity to the story, they'll write, "A DOCTOR (Asian, mid-30s) enters." Everyone is looking to check as many diversity boxes as possible for these roles, and stay out of trouble with anyone who might be considered part of the diversity police both inside and outside of the producing studio.

This is good news for the random minority they may choose to allocate to the role, but not necessarily so for other minorities who now seem to be excluded because someone said this doctor needs to be "Asian." And it completely excludes the notion that the writer(s) in question have any interest in the actual cultural underpinnings of any specific race/ethnicity/orientation they choose to attribute to a character. They probably don't.

But the fact is that casting is far more open to minorities of all stripes than it ever has been before. People can argue passionately about whether that's happening fast enough, or with enough attention to any particular group. But it's opening up. And if I were you, *unless the story point at hand is specifically related to a particular minority*, I would assume the minority attribution is simply a random choice, and you should go for any and all of those roles. That "Asian" doctor can become a "Hispanic" doctor in no time flat if you nail that audition. (My last television job from the acting phase of my career was in fact when I was called in for and booked the role on *ER* of *"Doctor, mid-30s, African-American."*)

You can't be a victim to this stuff. If you're passionate about a specific minority experience, then learn to write, and write the damned story that deals with it on a human level. Make that short film. Write that play or screenplay. Keep a blog. Run for office. In the meantime, do the necessary work to ensure you are the best damned actor you can be, including the ability to turn off any accent (vocal or physical) that presents an obstacle to your being whatever is necessary for the role at hand. I find that too many ignore the efforts *that are entirely under their control*, while still complaining about injustice when it comes to casting. Do your work, administrate with charm and persistence, and as you get those auditions, go in there and kick their asses. Simply be the best actor of any stripe in that room. Soon you'll be able to make the *really* hip showbiz complaints, those that that transcend race, ethnicity and orientation: "They want someone younger," and "They're casting out of New Orleans."

Are minority-specific characters being cast with Caucasian celebrities for strictly box office reasons?

Yeah. What else is new? It's show business. Not show *fairness*. Not show *enlightenment*. So you're the star-bellied Sneetch about whom this movie is being made, and the studio goes and casts a plain-bellied Sneetch who has a "name" or is worth a certain amount of box office traction in foreign markets (and who, in addition, might actually be a great actor). I don't know what the point is to complaining about it. Get to work. You don't want to be a "wictim" in your career any more than in your acting choices. There are two ways to beat it: Build a career impressive enough that your name is worth box office traction here and in foreign markets. Or, as I wrote above, write the short film, play, or screenplay that deals with star-bellied Sneetches, and cast the bestest, awesome-est star-bellied Sneetch you can find, which may well be you, and hope the project is of high enough quality to make an impression in the marketplace. The rising tide will lift all boats involved.

CHAPTER 71

Auditions, Part 1: Before And During

They are the ultimate in "necessary evil." Everyone in town has an opinion on this process, and after a while another opinion seems incrementally meaningless in all the noise. Nonetheless, I shall try. In no particular order, here's what I would offer to help make peace with the audition process, from zero until you exit the room:

You're looking for quantity. You're looking ideally for 50 or more decent auditions a year, not counting commercials. When you get up to this rate, I think the level of neurosis about any single audition diminishes, and you're swinging the bat enough to find a rhythm. At fewer than 20 decent auditions a year, the relative importance of any one of them rises to a point where you are in danger of putting too much pressure and significance on it, and that's problematic. You might mistakenly do enough acting in that room for the *five* auditions you feel you should have had during the month you only had this one.

They're looking for quality. Not just that you're a good actor— that's the baseline necessity, that you know what you're doing. But the quality of the part, which is largely an ephemeral, tough-to-describe aspect of casting. It's something that is mostly actually out of your control, having to do with your look, your energy as a person and whether it seems right for the role. This is particularly the case in naturalistic TV-land, where "character work" seems minimal. You can be objectively fantastic in the role, your choices just *money*, and still lose out to someone who is perceived to have the right quality. That's why on your end, quantity is so important. With more quantity, it's more likely that your specific innate quality will hit the mark on some of these roles.

Don't think too much. Prepare well, as best you can. Listen to music in the waiting room, or just tune out. Then go in and just respond to the situation. I'm of the opinion that once you enter the office to sign in, any specific thoughts about the character, the story, your talent, your nerves, the other actors in the office waiting, the importance of the job, etc. are just useless noise. It's gonna go your way or not, and the thoughts you have once you sign in are not material to that result either way.

Don't memorize, Part 1: It doesn't mean you don't know your lines backwards and forwards. I just mean you should still hold the pages and refer to them. Milton advocated this as part of a subtle communication he thought it delivered: "You think I'm good now. Imagine when I *really* learn this." When you come in and don't hold the sides, the communication becomes: "This is the best I've got," and in a way takes away from the mystery of just how good you can become when they start directing you.

Don't memorize, Part 2: At least half the time I see actors bring in a "memorized" audition, their nerves get in the way and they flub the lines and end up having to look at the script, which is stuffed in their pocket or just completely absent and they have to stop and find it. That's fairly disastrous for you if it happens. Don't let it happen. Just hold the script, look at it now and again—that way, if your memory fails you even momentarily, you'll have it right there in your hands.

No props. Just…No props.

And that's it. Milton said he thought actors went crazy with anxiety about auditions because in some distant past lifetime, the actor was brought before an ornery authority figure who demanded immediate entertainment or the actor would die by the sword. You're not going to be killed for not booking this audition. At best you'll book it, and at worst, you'll walk out of there with some names to put on your list for further administration. Not a bad day.

Auditions, Part 2: After

So…How'd it go?

Answer: Who cares? You book it, or not, and you move on (with impeccable followup, of course).

When good actors go too long without booking, a very dangerous process can start to occur: The actor begins to *think*. And in these thoughts, the actor begins to *diagnose*. And with this diagnosis, the actor begins to remedy what they believe to be shitty acting, which is clearly shitty, demonstrably shitty, it's shittiest shit you've ever seen, and impersonal to boot, not to mention glib, and unfunny, and unconnected, and fucking old, and and and and and and and…Because if it were not so, they'd book the job—after all, they were *perfect* for it.

So let's step out, rise up, and look at this situation from 5,000 feet instead of five inches.

You have your impression of the work you brought into an audition. Okay. That's one. But this may differ from the actual quality as might be determined by a person you trust—a teacher or whomever you rely on in that regard. That's two. It's all pretty bloody subjective. All performers, however, are prone to think they sucked when in fact they did not, or that they killed it when perhaps they've had better days.

Then we have the folks on the other side of the desk—their impression of your work, versus your impression, versus this "objective" truth that could be seen by someone you trust outside the equation. How many have come out thinking they sucked and then gotten the call? So. Three independent realities available to us so far.

Then we have what they said to you about your audition, which may or may not be what they actually think. Maybe they chirp, "Nice job!" to every actor from best to worst. Or maybe they stare at you blankly, even though they thought you were fabulous.

Then you have what they may have said to your agent, versus what they actually thought, and then you have whatever variation the agent definitely said to you. Many famous stories there. Milton had his about telling an agent that the actor was "too streetwise," for a role, and the agent passed along to the actor, "Milton thinks you're too sleazy." Ouch.

And all of that is before you get to the many factors that are out of sight and largely out of your control: The essence or quality you emanate and its suitability for the role, physical factors, nepotism behind the scenes, the veto of a single producer when everyone else wanted you, the advocacy by the same producer when everyone was against you, the "name" who turned it down is now on the phone…There may be issues with how you enter or leave the room that can color negatively an otherwise terrific read, or you could have a terrific off-script personal moment with people in the room that saves a mediocre read.

So you could deliver, by some objective outside-the-equation opinion, an A+ audition. But you think it was a B+ at best, and the casting person stared at you as if it was a Z-, and thus you buy a gigantic ice cream sundae on the way home to compensate while waiting for a call. The casting person in fact thought it was A-, but now the producer wants his niece in the role, so to make it easier, the casting person gets on the phone, and for various reasons of temperament and politics tells your agent C. The agent, thinking they know just what will motivate you to do their brother-in-law's audition workshop for $500, calls you and says D. The actor hears D, opens a box of Oreos, and begins feverish web research on programs for an associate's degree in accounting.

Now—could there be trouble with how you audition? Sure. Certainly a class where you can drill the audition process with input from someone you trust can be valuable, if only for some intensive practice. And even then I've known actors who behave differently in class than they do outside. But yeah, you should feel comfortable with the process in an exercise format within a group you trust, for sure.

After that...Skip it. For an actor to come out of the process not having booked a job, and think they know "the reason" they didn't book it...*Yikes Yikes Yikes.* As one student hilariously put it to me at some point, "I finally realized that maybe I don't have to save my whole family with this audition." My advice: Don't get sucked into this crap. Just concentrate on increasing your overall ability with acting and staying sharp via a decent class, drill the audition process in class so you know you can serve it up in a supportive environment, and then work the administration to increase the number of auditions, and hopefully as well the importance of the roles and quality of the projects. Every speck of brain power that is currently being sucked into the black hole of analysis on how you *think* you did versus what they *said* you did versus what the *agent* said they said about you...Just apply all that energy to creating future opportunities. You'll go nuts otherwise.

CHAPTER **73**

Costaritis

costaritis, n., a disease whereby normally intelligent, talented actors are suddenly reduced to a heap of blithering self-doubt over the inability to manifest the auditions for, and/or book, television co-star roles.

Beware this dangerous and contagious disorder! Watch for these symptoms:

1. Secretly hoping for bad things to happen to your actor friends, who somehow, with magical effortlessness that eludes only you, get auditions for *CSI: Poughkeepsie*.

2. Working for 10-12 hours to prepare fewer than 6 lines of mediocre TV dialogue. *I will not be outworked for this role*, you think, as you frantically pace back and forth into the wee hours, creating an extensive character biography and scintillating arc for your role. Thank God you blew off class tonight!

3. A sinking feeling as you drive 1.x hours to the audition in rush hour traffic…you secretly ban the thought from your head: *Why am I doing this, exactly?*

4. A further sinking feeling, as you leave the audition, that you came off no more distinctly than a can of soup on the shelf, and you ask yourself, *Why the hell are they even auditioning people for this role? Doesn't the director/writer/producer/DP have a friend they know who can just do it?*

5. Later that night after the audition: As you stare vacantly at a reality TV show, you question your life, your choices as an actor, your choice to be an actor, your talent, your acting school, your agent, your manager, your family, your support system, your relationship, the efficacy of those casting workshops you've been attending so diligently…

What is the antidote for costaritis? Two tablets of belief and confidence, and a swig of context. I think part of the costaritic depression that affects so many comes from using so little of the relative wattage of your talent, or trying to apply the full wattage to a role that simply cannot stand the scrutiny. The adage is tried, and unfortunately true—*go for the art of it all.* Costar auditions should be comparatively unimportant little flakes of administration that come your way here and there, while you're dreaming and scheming of far bigger fish to fry. Every time you get that costar audition, prepare as much as necessary (could be 5 minutes or 50—time doesn't mean quality), go do your best for sure—be charming, confident, secure, and bold. Then leave. And go hit a museum, or watch a classic film, or read a good play, paint, make music, go dancing, or…*write a single page of material along the lines of a role you would want to play if they were writing them for you.*

There is nothing so tragic as to watch terrific, talented, bright actors of all ages go into a full outbreak of costaritis. There is no known vaccine, but fortunately, it is easily cured!

CHAPTER 74

Reel Thoughts

Every actor seeks the holy grail of a great "reel." Many who have yet to book a dozen television roles seek to shoot material themselves so as to improve the reel, and I think in general this is a fine idea. But two elements are being communicated with these reels, and most people seem to be aware only of one. The obvious element is that of "how is this actor acting?" But the second element is equally important—and that's the subtextual communication being delivered via the *quality of the video*. And that communication is very important. You simply cannot afford to act well in a video that sucks, quality-wise. I don't know how else to say it. Because the suckiness keeps me from really observing the actor—it becomes a simultaneous communication that is discordant with the acting (assuming a good actor). And quality is easily achieved —there's simply no excuse for sucking. Any excuse you think you have for poor quality is being crushed by the fact that tapes are being created that look and sound great, and your butt is being kicked. You need to make the effort not to suck simply because a bunch of others are out there not sucking. Other thoughts:

Quality, Part 1: Please make sure you look good. You can help yourself a lot by ensuring a makeup person is with you— sounds dumb, but several of these videos had attractive actors with either overdone or zero makeup. It's a balance. I don't presume to lecture on the matter, I'm not a makeup expert. Some actors need very little. But I know when I'm looking at too much or too little—and I'm observing both of these too often on these tapes. I know we live in a superficial society, and the society can be condemned for its superficiality, but you simply do yourself a major disservice by not looking as good as you can on these tapes. I suggest bringing another person because it's just better to have someone you trust in charge of this matter, so you can focus on the acting part. Also—gentlemen, make sure your suit jackets, shirts and collars are checked!!

Quality, Part 2: I'm seeing too many completely static shots, camera on tripod, with waist-up framing—the aesthetics of a police interrogation video. Conversely, one of the audition tapes I saw was a full-on short film in the style of the "Batman" films, conceived and shot for the purpose of the lead actor being considered for any role in the upcoming sequel. This thing rocked. It was a fully-realized piece, written by the actor, shot by a talented director. The camera *moved*, it had some visual effects, it was scored with Danny Elfman-style music, and regardless of any nits you could pick, here's what it communicated: *These are serious people.* They have a love for this kind of film. They had the intention and dedicated whatever resources they had to making this look impressive. They have esteem for themselves and respect for the work that goes into making a good film. I believe that subtextual communication is extremely important. It immediately grabbed your attention from its high quality alone.

The medium-shot waist-up static tripod police interrogation video, however, communicates this: *I know I need to submit a video for this project. Besides, my teacher said I need to "create opportunities for myself." But I don't have any money. I don't have time. I don't really know how all this shit works. I have some desire. What I really want is simply to be cast because…Well, just because. Please like me despite my poverty. I don't know if I have what it takes for the long haul. Frankly, I'm a little depressed.* This is not a good subtextual communication, and it reads loud and clear no matter how well you think you're acting.

Sound: Don't shoot in echo chambers. Too many people are using small rooms with hard surfaces and the camera mic. It's going to sound like shit. Sound has to be good—get a location that absorbs sound and don't use the camera microphone.

Length: Don't shoot nine minutes of material. Part of the quality problem is that people are simply trying to shoot too much, and the quality goes down as a necessity of too much length and too much time wasted getting all that material in some kind of usable condition. Set up a simple shot, move the camera slightly during the shot, have it be a medium or closeup if at all possible, and act the shit out of it for about 2-3 minutes. Done.

Material, Part 1: This gets tricky, since I am guilty of having told a number actors who did a great scene in class to shoot it for their reel or for casting in a project. But look—one of the reels I saw had a scene from *Pretty Woman* on it. I mean…No way. No. You cannot think you're going to compete with Julia Roberts in the role that made her career. No one looking at that tape is looking at this actress— they're looking at their memory of Julia Roberts and that's that. Another had the Walken/Hopper scene from *True Romance*. Forget it— no way. So if you're going to shoot something from very famous material —I'd seriously question that. If it's 2-3 minutes from something not as well known, sure— but stay away from *Streetcar, Forrest Gump, Pretty Woman, Raging Bull*… Anything where the original performance or scene itself is famous. You will not win.

Material, Part 2: If you do have a famous scene or role that you feel strongly you want to shoot for your reel, I would suggest you write a variation that is original, so you're not competing directly with lines that people may be referencing to the source script. The "Batman" riff I keep referring to was a completely original script designed as a short film, but nailed the tone, cynicism and dry humor of that franchise. I think there's a lot more freedom available to you with an original script, and everything is based on everything else anyhow— just write your *Raging Bull* scene sideways and you'll have the temperamental relationship between brothers, jealousy, all of it— without competing with that script. You don't want to give people watching your video an excuse to have their minds wander through cinema history figuring out where they've heard these lines.

Distribution: Do not distribute your video via your personal YouTube channel. One person sent me a link to her audition video this way— carelessly. I won't comment on the other videos that were there next to the three minutes of serious career administration—but it was not a good juxtaposition, let me tell you. So create a separate professional channel for online videos related to career administration. And honestly —I would question putting up personal videos that have you looking foolish or drunk or ridiculous. Almost every applicant for any job is being Google-searched for criminal records and the like, but wanton stupidity captured on video is not something I would want a potential director or producer to see if I could help it. This is the world in the 21st century.

CHAPTER 75

X To 1

Teaching at the Advanced level at the BHP is a blast, because each week I deal with very talented actors doing very high quality work, many of whom are swell personalities to boot. The bad news part is that too many of these talented actors are "not working as much as they'd like to be," as the euphemism goes.

So this begs the question: What's going on with your admin? Answer: Some clever version of "not much." Followup question: Why? Followup answer: Well…They talk about confidence, they talk about "branding," they talk about ineffective agents, they talk about how CD workshops don't yield results, they talk about the alignment of the sun, moon, and stars, they talk about personal problems and relationship troubles and karmic injustice. But what most are not talking about is simply a diligent, consistent outflow of high quality communication and promotion regarding the product.

Outflow equals inflow, folks. And there is an X-to-1 relationship there. There is some number X of outflowing communication/promotion that will yield a unit 1 inflow. If you send out 100 letters and get one in response, then you're a 100-to-1 person. So keep sending out 100 units of outflow. You don't have to *believe* in it, you just have to *do* it. Some people have the admin gods on their side, it's effortless, and it seems that if they merely think about Steven Spielberg, the next day they get the call for an audition for *Jaws 10*. The best possible ratio would be 1-to-1: every single letter or call or what-have-you yields a positive response. That's a fantasy, but it's here just to make the point. Everyone has an X to 1, but very few people are solving for X.

If, like many actors, you're sending out 5 random postcards or half-hearted notes each month when the mood strikes you, when you're feeling "confident" or "inspired" or whatever, and you have nothing coming back to you—then you haven't hit X yet. Your X is higher than 5.

Another dubious phenomenon is the one whereby Joe Actor sends out 100 letters and gets his unit 1 comeback—a single audition. Instead of realizing the 100-to-1 equation, Joe thinks the 100 will now yield many more auditions that have simply had the poor taste not to appear yet. The promotion and admin activity stops, as does, of course, any return flow. Back to base camp and we start climbing again.

It's simple math, daily hard work, and not a complex association of psychology, misapplied corporate branding techniques, chakras alignment or other head games that feel cathartic to chat about in support groups, makes money for those who purport to sell the Magic Pill that will unleash careers, while actually, factually, statistically, doing nothing to change the condition. Outflow. Outflow. It's about consistent outflow. It should be *quality* outflow for sure, specific for sure, targeted for sure. But don't kid yourself that you need to take six months to develop a "quality" piece of promo, while doing zero admin during that time. A hyper-concern for "Quality" can become an excuse for doing nothing, and wraps itself nicely with a perfection syndrome so that nothing ever goes out because nothing is ever "good enough" to go out.

My experience is that whatever your X is, only about 20% of that should be random impersonal postcards, casting workshops or breakdown submissions. My guess is that for most actors, that number is distressingly close to 80% of their output. But look: Casting directors are hired by the producers to do a job for them—before a casting person is hired, a script has been written, believed in by a lot of people, financed, etc. So when you focus your admin on casting directors and the breakdowns they put out, you're hitting only the last 20% (at most) of the entire process that brings a story to life. You need to hit the 80% or more of the iceberg that is underwater: Writers, Directors and Producers. If you're in the headspace of those folks as they create a script and move it towards production, the casting person will be calling you without your even knowing who they are. This does NOT mean you back off the current admin you unleash on CDs, but *does* mean that you have to put out multiples of that number targeting the story creators and movers.

CHAPTER 76

The Branding Myth

The study and attempted application of generalized "Actor Marketing & Branding" techniques have increased in the last few years, and count me as strongly opposed to most of it.

First, since I believe many actors conflate the concepts of "branding" and "marketing," let's differentiate: My shoot-from-the-hip definitions would be that "branding" is the process of clearly identifying the specific features of Badass Product X and linking them with the name Badass Product, while "marketing" refers to the strategy and actions undertaken to let the world know about Badass Product. For your average up-and-coming actor, let's simplify life and assume that "marketing," "promotion," "advertising," and "sales" are pretty much all the same activity: Letting the world know you exist so that producers, directors and casting people call you in for roles.

Asking how you should *market* yourself is a valid question with many simple answers, all requiring consistency and discipline over time.

Asking how you should *brand* yourself, however, is trouble. It's introspective, I think it leaves actors staring at walls trying to get an "A" in wrongly applied corporate-think. It introduces needless complexity to a simple matter: *Are you a good actor? Nicely done, good for you. Now get out there and let people know.*

So a problem has arisen whereby the word "marketing" is used both for the necessary activity of presenting yourself to the Industry, but also the unnecessary analysis of your brand, looking at yourself as a product, and how to distinguish that product from other actors/products. Enter stage left: a cottage industry of entrepreneurs looking to make money on that intro-spection, and sell actors on their "marketing strategies" and/or their highly evolved tools for marketing, which often include excessive "branding," to all of which I say…

Meh.

You're not a can of Coke. You're not a cell phone. You're not a branded commodity. You're red on Monday, you're blue on Thursday, you're sweet one day and savory the next. Ideally you're whatever you need to be to service the story for which you're being considered. The idea that with due attention to proper branding you'll find that special something about your-self that will be consistently valuable to others is, to me, highly questionable. Why? Because these thoughts about The Brand of You as a precursor to taking administrative action have zero use or perceptibility *outside of you.* It's just like the thoughts about The Talent of You as a precursor to acting. There simply is no linkage between those thoughts and the real world. You're going to go out on stage and act regardless of your thoughts *(Am I any good?),* and you should damned well administrate your career regardless of your thoughts *(What am I selling?).*

The whole idea of being an actor is to say to the world, "I'll be whatever you need me to be to tell your story." To worry ex-cessively about branding your specific qualities would seem to be antithetical to this purpose, and all the time spent theorizing about your "branding" would frankly better be spent improving as an actor and simply getting out there. Once we've got the act-ing in shape, it's a matter of being seen in as many professional settings as possible, delivering the goods when asked or hired, and a monastic devotion to communicating regularly with every-one you can think of about what you and they are doing. Give me a good actor who conducts himself professionally, and puts out a diligent 50 pieces of communication each week, and show me where he is after five years. I'll bet he's better off than the one who delays action because they're cogitating on branding strategies as if they are working the corporate job we all swore we'd never take.

And yeah, I get it, if you have a very strong physical type—intensely athletic, supremely nerdy, Vogue cover-worthy cheek-bones and skin—then that clearly identifiable physical type can be marketed to solve certain casting problems. Milton spoke often of the importance of an actor knowing his or her "casting"—the first circle roles where most storytellers would place you based on your look and your manner. Sometimes the gorgeous actress doesn't see herself as the lead because of some inner esteem issue. Sometimes the down-to-earth character actor believes with all their might they should be the romantic lead. A good teacher can help resolve those issues, so you develop more realistic view of your casting.

But even then…Let's say you have a very specific look, the "studious/nerd look" for instance, and you're going to market that look for all those roles. You could take two equivalently nerdy young specimens, and their quality when acting will be completely different. One comes off supremely arrogant, another comes off sweet and innocent. But let's go even beyond that—you may have on your hands the supremely arrogant nerdy actor who through diligent acting study develops his skill and knowledge of story and tone, and who hence knows for this certain script he needs to bring in the sweet/innocent version of the nerdy character, and he ends up booking the job…The variables are insane to contemplate. How do you "brand" the look versus the innate quality versus the ability? (Let me guess: Take the Professional Actors Marketing Workshop/Level Two for $199.95, and they'll let you in on the secret.)

Frankly I think you should just do whatever comes to mind to broadcast the message that you are talented, compliant, sane, humorous, easy to work with. Market the fact that you're a professional, you'll tell the story right and be fun to have on set. Ensure this gem can be found easily through all the various technological means used by those people who cast projects. Introduce this gem in person as much as you can.

Sometimes the hemming and hawing, the misapplied branding techniques, corporate-speak mission statements, convoluted conceptual frameworks— it all leads to occasional frantic appeals from actors to know…*What is my path?* And this is something that seems very discordant to me. As a musician it never occurred to me to ask my teachers, "What is my path?" or "How should I market/brand myself?" Because the answer would simply have been, "Your path is to be the best fucking pianist you can be, and then get yourself heard as much as possible using whatever means possible." Along the way, you will discover many things about yourself and what you're interested in, and where your ever-evolving skills fit in an ever-evolving business.

Part of what drives me nuts about the "marketing" thing with actors is that it is an overemphasis on what *others* are interested in instead of what *you're* interested in. Acting is tough enough in this regard— there always seems to be another person making the decisions about what parts exist, who gets called in, who gets cast, who "they" decide will be the next star…I think each actor's sanity is increased to the degree he or she individually becomes the decision maker. *I like that filmmaker. I like that television show. I like this kind of part. I like action. I like independent. I dream of sitcom. I dream of one-hour drama.* And then you chase that, because it's your passion, not because it's vector-aligned with Marketing Strategy Q476-B (rev. 3).

So to those who have been sold on the idea they need to "brand" themselves via some corporate mode of thinking, or who think there is some elusive and yet highly specific answer to what "their path" is as an actor: At the BHP we emphasize Acting, Attitude & Administration. The answer to questions like that lie in those three areas, and that sequence. Acting—get it in shape, including the underestimated importance of knowing the story, its writer, and its specific tone. Attitude—professional, courteous, on time, respectful, not neurotically insecure or irritatingly know-it-all. Administration— now take the actions necessary to get a quality actor with a good attitude out into the marketplace. Take those actions consistently, each week, regardless of how you feel about yourself or about the business. You'll never go off the rails.

CHAPTER 77

Staged Readings

Don't suck at staged readings. There are people in that room who are trying to evaluate the script, the story, how it might land, how it can be improved, whether it can be improved. You are instrumental to that task. Like it or not, they are evaluating you at the same time. If you suck, it may well be remembered. If you're awesome, that may well be remembered too. So don't suck. Here are some ways not to suck:

- Be on time. That means 30 minutes early. Nothing is more irritating to the writer and/or host of the reading than to spend the last minutes before the reading wondering whether all of the actors are going to show up. They may not say anything about it, but the closer you are to being late, the more loathed you become. Being *actually* late, as in conventionally late, as in the reading starts at 10am and you show up at 10:05am—this is worthy of putting you to death. Your death sentence is not commuted just because you chirpily texted the host at zero hour about *traffic*. Or *parking*.

- Don't be drunk, high, or hungover. (Don't laugh. It's happened to me.)

- Don't look like shit. How many readings have I attended where the actors walk in bedraggled and slovenly? A reading is a professional opportunity, a moment for you to shine. So look the part of a professional, and dress slightly up from the norm. Take off your baseball caps. You could even wear a collared shirt or a jacket or anything other than your Saturday afternoon worst, and people will notice, and appreciate it.

- Read through the script beforehand. You didn't get one? Insist on it. Have a sense of what your part is, which scenes you are in, what's going on in the story. Look up words you don't understand. If there's a paragraph of nomenclature, practice it so you don't trip up on technical terms. This is part of being prepared. A professional is prepared. An amateur wings it.

- Don't read off your damned phone. It's too small, and no matter how youthful and perfect your vision, it's amazing how badly people read when they read from a phone. You might get away with an iPad or equivalent, though frankly the light from those things is irritating as hell, and no matter what device is used, it always seems to suck the actor's energy into it and away from the audience. Just use a paper copy.

- Project your voice. You're not wired for sound. There's no boom mic. The people evaluating the script are not inside your head. They're *over there*. Have a voice. Use it. Send the script, via your voice, *over there*. Your mumbling uncertainty and addiction to naturalism make writers want to kill you. You're not having a conversation with an actor one or two chairs away, you are using your abilities, along with those of the actor one or two chairs away, to *send the script over there*.

- Stay in the reading, both physically and mentally. I've seen actors mouthing cute little jokes to each other *during* a reading more than zero times, which is the only acceptable number. I've seen actors literally fall asleep during portions of the script where they weren't in the scenes. I've seen them flail about to deal with a buzzing (and yes, even *ringing)* cell phone. I've seen them check email, and send text messages. I've seen them gesticulate to someone —*where's the bathroom?*—before then getting up during a reading to relieve themselves. (Those are usually the ones who were late, as in just barely on time for the reading.)

In short, a staged reading is a gig. It's a professional moment. Treat it as if you were onstage for an audience performing a play. Factually, that's what you're doing.

CHAPTER 78

Career Manifesti

Milton advocated that his students have what he called a *Career Concept*, which was a written statement describing what they wanted to achieve, a sense of what it all would look like if the career went as they wished. He's certainly not the only one to have suggested this kind of manifesto—teachers and "career consultants" often suggest his kind of written work. I've read my share of these over the years, which led to my following up with some additional thoughts:

I think writing down, at any length, some specifics about what you're looking to achieve in your career is a good thing. This is why Milton developed the idea and put it early on in *Dreams Into Action*. He alluded to the result of this exercise as certain kind of "Declaration of Independence," and some write-ups that I have read even have DECLARATION OF INDEPENDENCE written on the first page. Okay. I don't give a shit what the title is, but I think it's important to note that the actual Declaration of Independence marking the breaking off of the American colonies from the British was just over 1,300 words. A history-making, country-founding document was 1,300 words. While Milton encouraged writing down as many specifics as possible, he also used the words "lean, mean and concise," and did so for a reason.

I've gotten the subtext when reading some over the years that they have been created for someone else. There seems to be a significant effort to explain not only details about a possible acting career, but political and personal belief systems that are interwoven throughout, as if the actor is trying to communicate some innate truth about themselves, something that is probably clear to them when they look in a mirror, but harder to explain to an outside reader. Why all this effort? There is no need to explain your beliefs, politics, philosophy, or psychological inventory in a career concept.

You can guess where I'm going: These suckers are too damned long. I'm seeing Career Concept documents that are 3000-4000 word, 15-page or longer manifestos that have as separate sections the following: Mission, Purposes, Postulates, Policies, Principles, Affirmations, Personal Assets & Liability breakdowns, Projects, Goals, Plans (broken down into bulleted lists of items under each branch of BHP teaching), Lists, and on and on and on. Now on the one hand this work is often very impressively brought together, it takes time, and it takes a certain confront to look at it all, and I applaud that. But I also worry that the results are possibly too unwieldy, complicated, redundant, circuitous, and beg a giant question after the dozens of hours being spent to create them: *Now what?*

(One thought I had—what if the dozens of hours spent creating these manifestos had simply been spent getting in communication with industry professionals?)

Milton was very concerned with the Now What? question. In the 12 years that followed the publication of *Dreams Into Action*, I was part of countless meetings between him and individual students, as well as witness to innumerable critiques where he might touch on Career Concept. And in each of those meetings and talks, he sought to break down what was usually a highly intellectual and ethereal morass of career ideas into a simple concept. (It would be a very Milton thing to do to have six people in front of him at a staff meeting at his house and go around dissecting the essence of each person in about two minutes—for all six. Many of these little gems could have been adopted as a career concept.)

He often wanted a single sentence. He wanted something you could put on a post-it and affix to your bathroom mirror so that in the morning you woke up, saw this simple declaration, and it moved you to do something that day about your career. I remember one was simply, "NOW." A single word, used to address that particular actor's habitual procrastination about everything. I met recently with a student who was frustrated by his inability to get a regular job-job because he didn't have the proper education/accreditation that employers look for. He's ridiculously talented. I offered this: "Since I'm not qualified to do anything else, how about I actually try to get acting work?" We laughed about that, then wrote down, "It's time." A counter-notion to this actor's idea that he had to "pay his dues" for a few more years before regular work would come his way, which I thought was bullshit.

Ultimately, the Career Concept exists to move you to action, not to get an "A" in Career Concept writing. If it doesn't fire you up, it's not a good concept. If it is bulky and can be used as a paperweight, it's not a good concept. Milton used the analogy of buying a car—quite rightly pointing out that (practically) no one says, "I need a car. Just any car." And through this analogy he's trying to get actors to be more specific than, "I just want to work. You know—any work." And by getting specific with the concept, hopefully it fires you up to do something about it, and target specific people who might line up with your concept of what you want to do.

If you like BMWs, you go to a BMW dealership. If you like one-hour dramas, there are people who write, produce, direct and cast those shows. But no one I know who has ever wanted a car wrote a 15-page manifesto about it, beginning with, "I would like a car with four stunningly round wheels and stylish appearance that sails through traffic with the performance of a Porsche and the economy of a Prius, a car that inspires others to drive it, that inspires others to be as bad-ass and yet ecologically sensitive as my car, a car that resides both in the Hollywood Hills and is also driven to New York where it will have its own garage in a downtown pied-a-terre, where after it books one Broadway Show a year it will also have six TV guest-star appearances as well as being on numerous late night talk shows…"

If you want to free-associate across every facet of your life, psychology, self-analysis, behaviors, *etc. ad infinitum* to create a 15-page draft of a Career Concept—I'm all for it. It may well be beneficial to do so. Every script has as its first iteration a pretty shitty, overlong, overwrought, overwritten first draft. NOW WHAT? Get it elemental. Get it lean. What's it about? Unlike a script, a career concept need not be something that communicates to others. No one else has to get it. No one else has to read it. No one else has to be entertained by it or moved by it. It frankly isn't anyone's damned business but your own. There is no template, and no one should be offering one to you. The idea is that in the middle of an actual actor's day—*get up regretting something from last night, feel discouraged, avoid the breakdowns, cruise social media apps, go to lame job, rehearse scene, feel discouraged, go to commercial audition, feel discouraged, surf the web, flinch on exercising, eat too much sugar, go to class*— that somewhere in that day-to-day reality, you find 15 minutes, or one hour, or two hours, where this concept gets you to *do* something about the career instead of wallow, avoid, or theorize about it.

By the way, I remember another student for whom the entire Career Concept concept was so infuriating, so frustrating, so crazy-making— she was just bonkers on the entire topic, coming to tears in front of Milton about how it simply did not compute for her. Milton's answer: "Forget it. Don't do one. Forget I wrote about it." He took her copy of *Dreams Into Action*, drew a bunch of lines over the entire chapter (in pencil), and handed it back to her—and both of them cracked up. It was the last time she dealt with the topic, and they got on happily to other areas of career administration. So, as with all aspects of technique—it has to work for you, and if you really try and it doesn't—let it go. There are plenty of successful people who probably never wrote one of these out. It's a tool. You should try it as it may help, but it's not on a tablet handed down from Moses.

CHAPTER 79

The Wall of No

My wife once had coffee with a very successful entrepreneur, and he told her he woke up every morning wanting to hear "no" at least ten times by the time he went to sleep. This took her by surprise, so she followed up, and he expanded: "For me to hear a 'no' from someone, it means I had to have an idea or proposal or something, get it in front of someone else for them to evaluate it, and then they thought about it, even if for a second. That represents a lot of good work done. And it's just 'no' for now. Maybe it's 'yes' later on. Eventually, from someone, I'm gonna hear 'yes,' but it's the same work done either way. The main thing is to do the work, that's what lets me sleep."

Soon thereafter I met with yet again another of the fifteen bazillion actors I know who display immense talent and who do pretty much nothing about running the business of getting that talent out there. So I drew a far messier version of this diagram:

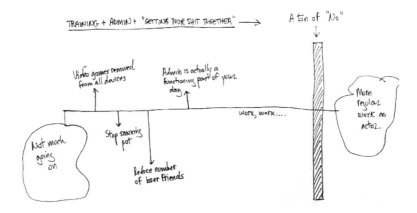

Over on the left-hand side is "Not Much Going On." I think many actors may enjoy sitting there in "Not Much Going On," because, while they know they're completely slacking, there is this very hopeful future out there that will no doubt make itself apparent. At some point. When they choose to start working. But not now. No. Too soon. After all, they have to "get their shit together" first. And then, dude: look out!

Moving rightward, tailored for the subject of my meeting, but no doubt universally applicable, are these targets:

1. Video games removed from all devices.

2. Stop smoking pot.

3. Reduce number of loser friends.

4. Admin is actually a functioning part of your day.

And after those targets are met, and you hustle up for a while, you hit a wall. The Wall of No. That's a great place to be, hearing "no" all day long. Because that means you're out there, you're being evaluated, you're getting auditions, there's some action, etc. And yet hearing "no" sucks to an actor, who, like all performing artists, are sensitive creatures seeking validation. I've known many to hit the The Wall of No and they take off. They quit. Too much "No"! Too depressing. And yet to my thinking, that's exactly where you want to be, because at some point it will be a "Yes," and you build on that. Each "No" represents someone you met, other people who are associated with that project, a whole list of names to contact a few times a year. You just have to learn to ignore the ouch of hearing "no" and stop taking it personally. Not easy—but that's what you have to do. And if you can survive the Wall Of No, you'll find more regular work coming your way.

Frankly, I wish the problem was that of too many actors quitting at the Wall of No. The biggest problem I see is that too many are sitting idly at "Not Much Going On," smoking pot, playing Angry Birds, and hanging out with other people who think this is productive behavior that will eventually get them a career. Because, you know—they're gonna get that agent who will make it happen. Uh huh. As Milton used to say, with some amusing accent, "Fantasyland!"

So get moving. Work your ass off in a class, remove the video games, the smoking pot, the loser friends (or insert here your own particular form of slacking). Make admin a functioning part of your day, and drive headlong into the Wall of No.

CHAPTER 80

Showcases, Workshops And Integrity

Lights up on…An agent showcase. Over the next hour or so, fifteen scenes will be performed, about 3 minutes each. Almost all will be glib comedies with glib acting, no one giving a shit about anything other than whether this so-called "work" will please…*them*. THEY. The all-powerful THEY, who will assess your talent, your look, and then hopefully represent you and get you auditions.

Recently a scene was performed in class. It was a two-and-a-half-minute rather glib comedically-tilted fight between a young couple at a party —an awkward compliment he had previously paid her anatomy was received poorly, she was still stewing on it, and that was the premise. Banter was exchanged, actress walks off in a huff, actor follows, exasperated, and…*scene*.

Turns out one of the actors had written the scene, because they were performing in an agent showcase a couple nights later, and they couldn't find something that would suffice for the three-minute limit. In addition, the omniscient, all-mighty THEY say it's good to do comedy in these workshops. It's what THEY want to see.

How does this situation make me vomit? Let me count the ways:

By trying to reduce your talent to a workshop-digestible three-minute piece of junk food, I believe you are sacrificing integrity vital to your survival. If someone asked me to play piano for three minutes, or teach for three minutes, or write something in three minutes…It's just awful. *Fuck off.* That's my answer. You want me to prove my talent to you in three minutes? "Fuck you.

There. How long did that take?" I think it might be handy for the actor to know that this would be a very nice start point for all issues related to "prove to me you are talented in three minutes." (I'm not being literal. Don't tell potential agents to fuck off. I'm just trying to instill a viewpoint.) The only form of art where I think this three-minute thing works is singing—because three minutes is just about the average length of a song, and so you truly are showing off your talent in the manner and form that will occur if you make it big. But great acting doesn't happen in 3 minute chunks —you may get costars and 5-and-unders to start your career, but this is rarely an actual demonstration of your talent.

Now, I get it: People want to work. Actors want to impress Mr./Ms. Casting Person and Mr./Ms. Agent, they have paid $X to attend this workshop/showcase, and in so doing they have agreed to submit to certain processes, which may include a three-minute time limit on your work. I get it. But I'm sorry, you have never agreed to prostitute yourself during the three minutes. (Paid showcases and workshops have come under attack as being illegal "paid job interviews," with detractors in those who say it's automatic prostitution for the actor. But while they exist, they are an admin tool, and we can't pretend that many don't take advantage of the opportunity, and some do well with them.)

So when they say the three minutes is up to you, you get to choose what you perform...Well. Fucking kill it. Don't bring in a piece of cheese you think the omniscient, all-mighty THEY will like. Bring in three minutes of the best work you can possibly bring. Maybe it's funny. Maybe it isn't. One of the actors in the scene I saw has 10 scenes to his credit over the last 18 months that blew people out of the water. I told him he should do one of those pieces, a stunning piece of character work about a guy with a mental disability, and dare them to cut him off. If they cut him off dismissively at 3 minutes, then he knows they are NOT the person to represent him. The person he wants to represent him ideally will be moved by his work, as we all were, and would never cut him off.

Bottom line: this is about your integrity. The business has all sorts of necessary constructs that force the actor—in showcases, workshops, auditions—to cram their talent into a small room, little time, standing on a spot, looking at a camera, looking at a bored evaluator, working with strangers, working on material that isn't so great, etc. This is all part of the journey, and a professional actor learns to bring their talent to whatever party has been set up for them. Often you don't have much choice in the matter.

But sometimes you do have the choice. And when you have the choice, usually via a monologue or scene that you select to present in any of these settings, or in your demo reel, go for the best you've got in you. Even if it doesn't work out, you go home knowing you put your best out there. Don't bring a piece of cheese just because THEY say that particular cheese is what a different THEY want to see. No matter what *this* THEY says about what *that* THEY wants, I think what is wanted by *all* THEYS is *talent*.

We all go into dark theaters dozens of times a year, each time hoping we will not be betrayed, and that we will be moved, dazzled, entertained by what occurs. We keep going, again and again, even though we've been burned far more often than not. Such is the power of the desire to be transported. I don't care how cynical we can become about the business, about agents and casting directors—I believe they all want talent. (See the documentary *Casting By*...) They want someone to blow them away. So blow them away with the best you've got. Do not lower your level of ability to serve up material you think they want to see, which for some reason ends up being a lot of glib sketch comedy. Serve up some passion, some humor, some depth— whatever it is, but serve up your best.

CHAPTER 81

Textversation

Ten years ago I taught an actress who was then probably around 25, maybe younger. She worked her ass off in class, but at the time I thought her casting was such that she needed to stick it out, get older, and then she'd really be in demand. As it happened, she stuck it out, and has been booking more and more in her thirties. She recently booked her first recurring television job by offer alone, news of which reached me through the grapevine. This textversation followed (edited for clarity):

ME: That doesn't suck.

ACTRESS: Right? Crazy. Wardrobe already called. Script drafts in my email and I'm still like…Did that really happen?

ME: Told you all those years ago: You just needed miles on the odometer.

ACTRESS: Praise be to perspective. Thank God for living with a writer/director. Seeing his side, I'm a million times more chill now. And when my actor friends call me about stuff, I'm like, "None of what you're talking about matters. None of it." I thank you highly for trying so hard to get me to understand. But there were so many things before the things before the things before the things to understand, before I could understand the things you were trying to get me to understand.

ME: What you just said. Yeah. This thing is tricky. Praise be to your sticking it out to find it out.

ACTRESS: Thanks. That's really the thing. Sticking it out. And the "facing your fears" deal. I think about that all the time now. What does a 20-something know about really facing fears? Like really really. When you get to "really really," it's probably not so much.

ME: What would you say is the subject actors talk about, that you want to reply, "None of that matters"?

ACTRESS: Shit, man. For starters—in TV, the lines from the audition are rewritten 90% of the time when you get the gig. So for TV, I've ended up like, "fuck the lines." Sometimes they're purposefully fake, because they don't want to leak the plot of the show. So they're really looking for the quality, the essence of the character, and meanwhile you're spazzing about the lines. You end up tripping over the lines in the audition, but what you're really screwing up is your presence in the room, not the lines. But when you come from theatre, and Arthur Miller took two years to write those lines—those are the lines you fucking learn. But the TV writer who had to write an audition draft at 3am this morning, knowing the draft will be totally different for the shoot? That changes what you put your emphasis on as an actress. But NO WAY you could have convinced me of that in class ten years ago. Zero chance.

ME: Uh huh…

ACTRESS: Also…that we're in the story telling business. Not really the acting business. And they will take the essence of the character, the look, the voice—every time, they will take that over better acting. Because the baseline requirement is that you can act. You can't even get into real rooms until acting well, and with ease, is a given. So let's say we eliminate 80% of the actors in LA because they can't really act well. So now there are still tons of good actors, and they're going in for the real auditions. Once that happens, getting the part is as much about your essence as it is about a specific choice you make. Because this is 2016 and they aren't just looking in Los Angeles, they're looking in L.A., Chicago, NY, London, Australia—and it's all delivered to their email inbox in an office in fucking Burbank. They're going to find the perfect fit for their vision. Whatever that is, because the vision is changing, they're arguing about it even as you audition. There's only so much you control. Not very much at all. So it ends up being…hard work + passion + nurture the relationships with people who believe in you = people who think about you for jobs = auditions = jobs booked. Rinse. Repeat. Just like you always said.

ME: Got it. Just checking. Yeah—we're in the storytelling business, not the "I'm excavating my personal truth" business. Sometimes they coincide, but really not often. And even when they do, the better storytelling usually wins.

ACTRESS: Yup. Actors can be neurotic and self-centered, which I empathize with, it's part of the scarcity and fear about being in this business, I think. But it causes them to lose perspective. They complain and complain. They can barely function well enough to make a good video audition in their apartment. And I sympathize, I was there myself. And maybe I'm a dick, but now I'm like, "Listen, you can't get yourself in shape to tape an audition for a network show? No way are you getting a network show! You can't tell the story if you can't take the time to learn the story, its particular vibe. The vibe of that show. You can't be a lead storyteller without taking someone's story seriously."

ME: In other words, take the story more seriously, and yourself less so.

ACTRESS: Blog entry. Or tattoo. At least one of those.

ME: I'll go with blog entry for now.

CHAPTER 82

They Said I Shouldn't Communicate

Of all the piece-of-crap "they say"s in the business, one of the most odious is "they said not to communicate." Probably a dozen times over the years I've had a conversation like this:

ACTOR: I was at this event, and it turns out the person next to me was the head of casting for a major studio. We hit it off great, and she said she'd be more than happy to introduce me to the casting directors on the lot.

ME: Amazing!

ACTOR: So…

ME: Fantastic! Have you followed up on that?

ACTOR: Well that was what I wanted to ask you…

ME: What? Ask me what?

ACTOR: How would I go about doing that?

ME: What do you mean "how"? Did she give you her contact information?

ACTOR: Yeah, I mean, like, a phone number.

ME: That's contact information.

ACTOR: Right. So, should I just…call her?

ME: Yeah. You call her. Why are you so tentative?

ACTOR: Tentative?

ME: Yeah. Why haven't you called her already? When did you meet her?

ACTOR: A week ago.

ME: Call her immediately. Now. Right now. Why are you waiting a week? This is crazy.

ACTOR: Do you think so?

ME: I know so.

ACTOR: Well, because the thing is I talked to my agent…

ME: Yeah. And…?

ACTOR: And he said not to contact her directly.

Nauseating. Part of this goes to the "My Agent Said" passivity of actors, who are all too willing to give up all of their professional self determinism to "My Agent Said." Another part goes to that mysterious part of our psychology that holds back from following good news where it may lead. And so the "they say I shouldn't communicate," instead of coming off like the ridiculous advice it is, comes off as wise.

Communicate. No one resents thoughtful, professional communication. If you have a lead, follow it. Meet someone? Follow up. Just finished a gig? Follow up. *Meet someone who offers to help you in some obviously beneficial way?* Communicate. Follow it up. I would frankly put on the suspicion list anyone who advises you *not* to follow up a good lead like that.

CHAPTER 83

Fighting Aussies

This is a transcribed critique, edited for length and reading clarity, that I gave in 2013 to an extremely bright, attractive and talented Australian actress. It followed an improvisation exercise and my comments on it, and started with my simple question about what she was working on next in class. Then this unfolded, quite amazingly.

ALLEN: What are you working on, other than tagging along during my rehearsals?

ACTRESS: Uh, maybe *Antony & Cleopatra*. I just need other actors to play with me on some things I want to—

ALLEN: I'm sure you'll have great difficulty in finding that.

ACTRESS: I want to do…*Elizabeth*…Ah, *Game of Thrones*. He wants to do *Game of Thrones* with me.

ALLEN: Can we get some of this shit going?

ACTRESS: Well these people have like six scenes and are really busy so I have to wait my turn.

ALLEN: Yeah, but there are also actors here who don't have six scenes going, and you call them, and you charm them and you persist. And you say, "Cmon, let's get together and read. I'll buy you a Coke." So that you move it along. Because there is this part of you that has this thing. Whether it's shy or self-effacing or "I don't want to impose…" That whole thing that you've got. It's charming, it's fine, but it's not going to get you what you want here in class and then that's a microcosm of what you want to get out there, which isn't going to respond to "I have to wait my turn."

ACTRESS: That makes sense.

ALLEN: We need to alter "I have to wait my turn" and move it towards, "I can get shit to happen." You just met a fine actor, you can find something to do…He's looking for…Charm these people. "Hey, have you read that thing? Hey, do you have a moment?" Instead of "Oh, you've got six scenes? Okay, I'll wait until May."

ACTRESS: But I feel like some of what I want to do is stuff no one else would want to do.

ALLEN: Why don't you try it instead of feeling like—

ACTRESS: Farce, or—

ALLEN: What?

ACTRESS: Commedia…or….

Actress curls up in her chair in retreat from the world.

ALLEN: What is this? You have this bizarre body language. Why are you putting on this shy, withdrawn little-girl thing?

ACTRESS: It's like, I don't know. I don't like acting in front of my friends or family or people I know. It's like with an audience, I don't know them. Does that make sense?

ALLEN: No. Not one word.

ACTRESS: I find it easier to act in front of people I don't know.

ALLEN: That's not the point of this—

ACTRESS: I feel right now very inadequate.

ALLEN: Yeah, we all think you're very inadequate. It's like, "What is she doing in this class?"

Class laughter.

ALLEN: But we've got to cut through a bit of the bullshit here. And say you're a formidable actress. That's already proven by work that you've done. So. You've got to take that formidable talent and then apply it administratively, and in the way you carry yourself, and in the way you deal with situations. To get what you want. And what you want in the class is easy. Compared to getting what you want out there, where it's a bit more difficult. So here is the lab where you get those skills going. "Hey, classmate— here's a script. It's of a certain form. You may not enjoy it, but I think you would be great. Let's read it together. I'll tell you about it, And if it's a style of theatre where you're like well I don't know…" Whatever. But go after it.

ACTRESS: Yeah. But I do get what I want out of class when I'm watching other people. I learn a lot by observing.

ALLEN: Okay, that's fine. But you won't observe your way into a career. That's the problem. It's not going to work. And I have a feeling that this sort of style…It's attitudinal, basically, and it's probably the same out there. *Shy. No offense. I don't want to impose…*But you're a formidable talent. And could have a career here. United States. Los Angeles. Film. TV. Theatre. Whatever you want. But I have the feeling you're not quite going after it. So can we alter this thing you're doing? This little girl thing? Why are you deleting ten years of your life?

ACTRESS: Because I feel like I'm a ripe old age in Hollywood right now.

ALLEN: Yes, yes—

ACTRESS: Expired.

ALLEN: Expired. Put out to pasture. I understand. Yup. You say it as a joke, and then I think there's part of you where—

ACTRESS: It's true, yeah…Yeah, definitely—

ALLEN: You don't look like you're ninety. I don't know what you're talking about.

ACTRESS: Everyone's looking at me.

Actress slumps and starts picking her teeth.

ALLEN: Yeah, everyone's looking at you. They're gonna. Get used to it. Stop picking your teeth. Sit up straight. Better. I've come up with a new exercise for this actress. She's going to have to sit there and fucking command the space and not be like, in this little girl voice, "Don't look at me! I'm just beautiful and talented!" SMACK.

ACTRESS: Sorry.

ALLEN: Knock it off. Stop it. Look up.

Class laughter as she tries.

ACTRESS: Okay, I'm good.

ALLEN: Better.

ACTRESS: I'm sorry! Hold on…

Laughter as she retreats again…

ALLEN: I'm going to do this to you every class. When I do a critique, you're just going to sit there like an adult and look at everybody. You understand what I'm saying?

ACTRESS: Yeah, I do. You're not telling me something I don't know.

ALLEN: So what what in fact is happening with you "out there"?

ACTRESS: I'm auditioning. I'm writing all sorts of cards and things like that.

ALLEN: And how's it going?

ACTRESS: I guess…Fine? I got a reel the other day, and I didn't have any video content because all I've done is theatre before.

ALLEN: Is there a website?

ACTRESS: Well…I don't…Ugh…I'm…Sorry. I'm just predicting what you'll say back. So I shouldn't…

ALLEN: What, it's an Australian thing that you don't do websites?

AUSSIE CLASSMATE: I get it, I get it…

ALLEN: Something about you don't put yourself out there…?

AUSSIE CLASSMATE: People get fucking *slaughtered* who put websites out there. People would be like, "You fucking douchebag, shut up, get that website away from me."

ACTRESS: Yeah, people here tell me, "Don't be so Australian about it." But it's a different mentality here, I'm not used to it. I'll go into a room to audition, and then I'll leave. And my American friends will be like, "Did you tell them you can do this and you can do that and that?" And no, I just went in there and did my work and I left.

ALLEN: You can go in and you can leave, it's not like you have to tell them you're an equestrian biochemist in your spare time. Go in there and do your work and then leave. And then follow up diligently. They should be able to find you easily via the "interweb."

ACTRESS: It's an Australian thing, but you do come across like a wanker if you're caught promoting yourself.

ALLEN: I understand. But Australia is fifteen hours…it's a fifteen hour flight away. I know they can click on it back home and go "What a wanker!" But they're fifteen hours away and you're here. Participating in this society. Where people in this business need to be found quickly, so they can be like, "Who's this? Oh, there's her reel, and look at that." Boom. Boom. Boom. So you need to knock off all the wanker bullshit, and just do it anyway. I don't think this attitude is helping anyone. Are all these people in Australia working? Who call you wankers?

ACTRESS: Yeah. They're all from these shows. They're—

ALLEN: You mean working down there.

ACTRESS: They're working, but it's a funny thing because you can be trained in Australia, it doesn't mean you're gonna get work here. But if you do a shitty soap show, it's gold over here in America.— from that show? Can't act for shit.

ALLEN: Right. This is going live. This is broadcast live over the web.

ACTRESS: They're pretty people. It's a thing.

ALLEN: Can we knock off all this fucking bullshit? I feel like every topic I bring up brings up considerations of what Australians think of you, you're a wanker, you're this, you're that, they want this, they want that, talent is a waste of time...All I'm saying is that it feels like administratively things are kind of happening, but not with enough intention and force. And persistence. All I'm saying is that you should be found easily by people who go, like, "Oh, there she is! Her reel. Thank you." You don't have to put up a blog that says what you had for dinner. Just a place on the web where your reel is found. Through any of the networks. Casting networks, all that stuff. Is that done or not done?

ACTRESS: Uh, casting networks? Like LA Casting?

ALLEN: Yeah, all that stuff.

ACTRESS: Oh, yeah.

ALLEN: And your reel is up?

ACTRESS: I don't know if I can put it up yet. Because the director gave me rushes and it's still in post-production. I don't know if I can release it, I'd have to...

ALLEN: I know but can you CALL THEM TOMORROW? And say, "Hi! I'm just checking on the progress of my reel?" Can you do anything? Can you call everyone you know in the business tomorrow? Can you write cards tomorrow? Can you get six scenes tomorrow? This is what I'm talking about. Every fucking thing I say has a deflecting, dubious response that comes back. "But but but but but but but..."

ACTRESS: Honestly, I don't know if I want to act.

ALLEN: *Oh for fuck's sake.* Shut up. Shut up. I'm not going to get into all that. No one knows whether they want to act. You think you're alone in that thought? Throw a rock, hit an actor in this class and they don't know if they want to do this. You're doing it! What are you going to do, sell insurance?

ACTRESS: Well—

ALLEN: All of this is completely normal. I can pull anyone, start excavating, and I'm going to get, "I don't know if I really want to do this. I don't think it can happen. It's really hard. The business doesn't know me. I've got to crack open a door. I don't have my reel." All of it. *All of it.* And the emotion attached to it. All of it. Completely normal. You're fine. You want to act. There's no question. You don't act the way you do without wanting to do it. I just think you should give the business part, the administration part—give that a bit more of an effort.

Actress cries.

ALLEN: What have I tripped and fallen upon?

ACTRESS: I just don't know if I want to…when I was younger…

ALLEN: *To Stage Manager:* Get me some vodka, please.

ACTRESS: You get to this stage where…And I feel like it's too late to turn back because this is what I do now.

ALLEN: This *is* what you do.

ACTRESS: It scares me. I wake up and it scares the shit out of me every day that I fucking chose this path and I wish I wanted to be a vet or something.

ALLEN: A veterinarian?

ACTRESS: Or something! Something where I could just climb a corporate ladder. Because you put in the hours, and this industry doesn't function like that.

ALLEN: Where's Tim? Any words for her? He just said, earlier tonight, he had a nervous breakdown doing that, working in an office. You're not wired for it. I mean, you would be competent at it, there's no question that you're bright. But you're not wired for it. You're fucked.

ACTRESS: But I just feel like I don't like this industry. I don't like this system.

ALLEN: I know. Poor girl. But I'm telling you: you haven't dealt with the system enough in a conscientious fashion. Not enough to know if you can have the effect you want to have.

ACTRESS: There's no time now…

ALLEN: Yeah, better pack it in.

ACTRESS: Yes, I just want to go asleep.

ALLEN: And then tomorrow, if I were able to conjure it up, "Here's a guest star on some show. It's four days of shooting, it's five thousand bucks, it's a great part, and it's potentially recurring…" You would be happy as a clam. Going to the set and shooting. Happy as a clam. The difference between here and there is a bit more throttle. That's all I'm saying.

ACTRESS: Yeah but I also feel like I get sent for roles that aren't my acting style. And that's hard. I mean I had this…"We need a character archetype that matches some celebrity Asian actress, go in there and be some drippy lawyer and wear a mini skirt…" And that's the shit I get sent out for. And I don't like that system either. Where they have to sell you as an idea and as an archetype.

ALLEN: Right. So? Each one of those you go in for, you know what it means? What it means is a contact. A person. A casting person. You meet them. You do your best. You acquit yourself well. You take some shitty script and act it the way you want to act it. Then you follow up. Twenty of those auditions have twenty contacts. And you work it. You think it's going to be different if you become a veterinarian or sell insurance or do something in the corporate world? It's still who you know, who you fuck, the politics, the nepotism, the bullshit, the doing the things you don't want to do, to try to get ahead. So what do you want to do, go to Mars?

ACTRESS: Yes, I'm just hoping they'll colonize it somehow. I just feel like…The system can't work for me. I just don't know how to work the system.

ALLEN: *You haven't tried enough to know.* That's what I'm trying to tell you. Can you give it a hard, diligent year of work? And then see where you are in terms of opportunities? All this referential stuff to Australia, other people in Australia, if they do shit in Australia they're glorified here, if you do good stuff in Australia they don't know you, the system, the system, the system, the system, the system…You've created quite a formidable machine in your head—calibrated to keep you at the effect of others and their bloody systems. There's a role for you in the business. You just have to work harder at it *despite* all these emotions and all these insecurities, and all the doubts. Give it a real shot.

ACTRESS: I feel like just being here is giving it a shot. It costs a fuckload of money to come here from Australia and not be able to work. I can't work here. I can't get a friggin' *bar job.* And then there's all this ethnic crap, that I only get sent out for stuff that says "Ethnic" or "not Caucasian," and that fucks me up. I don't think my talent means shit. I just don't think the people who are funding shit go, "Oh, well, she's actually a better actor than that person who, you know…"

ALLEN: *You're Goddamned right they will.* Not all the time. But some times. Because ultimately they need their story told right. And so yeah, they might start out, "We're looking for a white girl, and you're Asian and Australian, so…" But you've got to beat all that. All that is just persistence. I can't believe they've gotten you like this. It's pathetic.

ACTRESS: I know that. It's just exhausting…

ALLEN: Oh, self-pity is very exhausting. It's exhausting to indulge in self-pity. It's so tiring. So I get it. And I can be ironic, I joke with you because I know you can handle it. You're an extremely talented and intelligent and charming person. *They're looking for people like that.* Yeah, you've got to beat the preconceptions, and yeah, you've got to beat the system. But you've got to get off the pity party. And the sense of false superiority about it. And just get involved. Day by day. Week by week. Casting director workshops. Agent workshops. Followup. Seven times per—

ACTRESS: Asian workshops?

ALLEN: Agent. Agent.

Huge laughter from class.

ALLEN: Although I think there should be…You may be on to something: *An Asian workshop.*

More laughter.

ALLEN: Day by day. You go after it. Despite all the feelings. You've got to operate *despite* feelings. In the face of feelings. With a "fuck you" towards the feelings. The feelings are going to do what they're going to do. You know what? Your feelings are going to do that if you go to law school. They'll be the same feelings in a different frame. You can do seven years in a law firm and make partner. You know how many law partners I've met, and they're FUCKING MISERABLE. THEY FUCKING HATE THEIR LIVES. I meet them and they're like, "It's horrible." But they're trapped because they built a big house off the money. So you're fucked eight ways to Sunday. But. Good thing is you're talented. So you can make a go of it. You've just got to go do it. Day by day. Let this emotional thing happen. And then…March! And try to remember there are people who have worse problems than you. Take responsibility for the advantageous position you are in, that you get to fight this battle. And not the battle of whether you have food. Or whether some insurgent or terrorist is going to fucking blow you away in Syria. Knock it off. Get to work. You can have the emotions, I get it. And then work. But I think what we tripped on was a gigantic mass of self-pity. And you've got to knock that off. It ain't attractive. It's not effective. So you go home, and you write a note. Any note. Five notes. Just like this: you sit at your desk, and you're sobbing, and you take pen in hand—"I…*sobbing noises*…saw your show *sobbing noises*…and it rocked my world…" Whatever. Your feelings do not have to line up beautifully for you to do the administration. And through that administration there will be opportunity. An agent. An Asian. An Asian Agent. A job. It's going to come. How long is your O-1 visa this time around?

ACTRESS: Next July.

ALLEN: Eighteen months. Work your ass off. Just work your ass off. Do everything that is talked about in Milton's book, two books, my blog, a bunch of networking with people who do stuff successfully. You talk with them, you sit down with Jorge Garcia and you go like, "Hey, tell me about your life. What did you do? Tell me what happened. Now what do you do?" He's a guy who's achieved what anyone would want. Worked his butt off in class, then gets a lead on a hit series for seven years? Shooting in fucking Hawaii? Awesome. Guess what? He's working at it. He's working at it. So even the people who you think have everything you want, they're still working at it. So will you do me that favor? Eighteen months. Can you do that for me? And know that all this is totally normal, it's fine, and you can still take action. Through your tears. You get it? I'll take this way more than all that false modesty…I'd rather have this. It's stark. Raw. Looking straight at it. Gorgeous. I'll take this a bazillion times over the little girl whining sounds. And whatever that weird thing you did with your arms, that was amazing.

ACTRESS: Interpretive…

ALLEN: Yes, interpretive dance. There's the fucking humor. I need all of it. All of it. Okay? I appreciate your honesty about all this. Not easy. What I just did to you is not easy. I mean, I tripped and fell on it. But then we're dealing with it. But you've got eighteen months. Throttle open. For eighteen months, and we'll see where we're at. By then you're sixty five, time to look at retirement homes. On Mars.

CHAPTER 84

Opportunity Knocks, But Doesn't Leave A Note

All administrative activity by the actor is geared towards creating opportunities to show their stuff. And yet actors too often prepare for opportunity only when it wears a metaphorical t-shirt with "Opportunity" written on it: an audition, a meeting, something where clearly a job or new representation is at stake. And outside that, there can be the tendency to check out, head dropped, eyes glued to the phone. Some will check out because they're "with friends" and so the standard of professionalism drops. But I submit that's exactly where the standard should be raised. Opportunity doesn't put its name on a t-shirt. Opportunity doesn't necessarily advertise on Actors Access. Opportunity doesn't require a drive-on pass. Opportunity is often standing right next to you—yeah, that guy who you're ignoring, or the young woman over there who seems shy. You'll only realize it in five years when that person you dismissed, ignored, the person you didn't meet or talk to because you were checking your social media feed, or whose script reading you fucked up by not really giving your all…this is the person who will be in charge of millions of dollars for a project.

Opportunity comes from getting your heads up from the damned phone and participating with your fellows in class, rehearsal, wherever. Yes, you must be social. No, you cannot check out and bury your head. Bury your head, check your "feed" and play video games at home. (I have occasionally banned all phones from the post-class get-together at the local bar, and once quite literally wrestled a student to the ground to try to extricate the phone from desperate, texting hands…) Get this: the likelihood that you will get a meeting with a top-5 director is far less than the likelihood that someone you know right now, who is sitting with you in class, will write, produce, direct, or otherwise be involved in a project, and will look over a class list for possible actors. You need to be in that person's headspace, and you won't be there if you check out. You won't be there if you're late. You won't be there if you're moody at the wrong moment. You won't be there if you are self-involved and non-responsive.

Judgments are being made all the time about you. I had a conversation once with a director of a staged reading, where I had observed three actors who were late, clearly barely participating, joking and checking phones *during* the reading. I didn't talk about that with him, I was asking about the script, and he immediately, quite clearly and irritably named the three actors in that reading, and went off. They were dismissed from consideration for that script, and for all other projects. Will this guy end up doing something really important? We don't know. Can you afford to be wrong about that? Hmmmmm. I don't think so. So I think you'd better bet on *yes*. It's a win-win conclusion. And it's not like that director told them that they fucked up—he was polite, thanked them, goodbye, talk to ya soon, etc. Those actors will never know the opportunities that just disappeared from their future— the opportunities just simply won't exist. Step back a moment from the endless fascination with apps and games and bullshit on your phone, and the obvious may suddenly be dreadfully clear: The damned thing isn't ringing.

ON LIFE AS AN ACTOR

The Social Media Swamp

Picture this utopian vision: You go about your days much as you do currently, but with a massive decrease in the level of distraction, agitation, and chaotic noise. In the place of all that, you will have free space to…Think! Dream! Plan! Write!

How can you achieve this relative nirvana?

DELETE SOCIAL MEDIA APPS FROM YOUR PHONE.

I'm old enough a fogey that Facebook was for years the only social media that I used regularly. While writing this book I've taken a liking to Instagram and its less acrimonious environment. I've never gotten into Twitter, and could barely tell you the difference between—or relative utility of—Tumblr, SnapChat, and the others. I saw a play recently in which a character referred to Tinder as "the apocalypse," and from what I've heard, I would probably agree. (And one must assume that in the years to follow, all of these names will find themselves in the dustbin of tech history.) In any case, at some point, frustrated by the toxic political contretemps occurring on old-fashioned Facebook and its formerly somewhat entertaining NewsFeed, I deleted the app from my phone. And lo and behold…Peace! It wasn't until I deleted the app that I realized how reflexively I checked it during the day, anytime I was standing in line, or during a break in class, or at a red light, etc. And each time I checked I would get irritated about something, or I'd get caught up in reading comments to something I had posted, contemplating my response to this person or that as I went to my next appointment. And even when I wasn't in the mood to light it up on politics, I'd just start clicking the link to some interesting story, which would take me to another link, which would prompt a Google search to "fact check" a bit of what I was reading before...In general my mind would become engaged in all manner of useless activity, taking up a significant chunk of free thinking time.

Ugh. Writing about it now, I'm quite certain a fortune wouldn't be enough to pay me to reinstall the Facebook app.

Among actors of the current moment, you'll hear occasional discussion of the IMDb (Internet Movie Database) Star Meter, which isn't strictly social media, but is kind of a related, wretched device by which actors are supposed to be able to measure their relative *somethingness* in comparison to other actors. You'll see posts from people desperately asking to interact in some way to drive their Star Meter up during an important week of auditions. Fuck the IMDb Star Meter. Stop looking at it. Never think about it again. (I have often half-joked that I would love to find the lowest ranked individual on the StarMeter and buy them dinner, ask them never to change.)

There is a legitimate use of social media for career administration. People have to know you exist in order to hire you, and social media is clearly of assistance there. I understand that. But I think this legitimate use has become a blanket justification for millions of creative people to check out of their lives, and frankly their creativity, for hours every day. These apps are programmed to act like casino machines to feed your brain tidbits of acknowledgment and validation, and create addictive behaviors. Add in the showbiz community's pre-existing condition of insecurity and neediness in general, and you have a formula for epic, brain-exploding levels of neurosis. It's total bullshit. We talk ourselves into the justification that staring at our various feeds for hours on end is equivalent to "working" on promotion. You're not working. Certainly not most of the time. Not even close.

The fact that celebrities have millions of "followers" is somehow taken as a pretext for reverse-engineering success by getting "followers" as a *means* of achieving celebrity and/or success. It's totally cuckoo. The next step of this nonsensical reverse-engineering is the idea that *casting* should factor in both talent *and* social media presence. Here's my take: Those who say they are casting a project based partially on the social media following of the actors coming in—they have succumbed blindly to cult-like social media worship, have no clue what they're doing, do not have a project worth your time, or all of the above. I have had many a writer, producer, director, and actor *all* tell me stories about gigs that were cast using this metric. Often the entire project fell apart immediately; these producers who think casting should factor in the number of social media followers—they seem usually to have very shady, insecure financing. Or the so-called actor with the magic number of followers revealed themselves to be utterly incompetent and ended up needing to be fired.

I'm not saying you need to disconnect from Social Media—heaven forbid! I'm merely proposing that you *remove it from your phone*. (If you're getting jittery at the very thought of this advice, maybe you just take a moment to contemplate that fact.) If you want to engage the swamp, either for personal or professional reasons, then try doing so only through a tablet dedicated to hosting all your social media apps, but which remains located at home. So you get an hour in the morning as part of your career admin, if you feel social media plays an important role for you there. One hour, max. Another hour, max, at night for your personal fix. On a tablet. The rest of the day, going about town, auditions, rehearsals, class, etc.—enjoy being blissfully unplugged from it all. Sure, I use the phone to check the news, the sports updates, deal with email, text, business stuff, that kind of thing. But the massive, mindless social media swamp doesn't get near me, and I have found myself far happier for this fact. Delete them. Trust me. It's a happier, more productive day without them.

CHAPTER 86

Workin' 9-to-5

In case you haven't heard, The Biz is full of gossip. People sleep with each other. Then they break up. They do stupid shit at parties. They get married. They get divorced. They are "difficult." People talk about people. It's a shocker. In another stunning development, because of the many intense, small and ever-changing ecosystems in this business (read: film sets, play rehearsals, and acting classes), you could find yourself in a holy-smokes relationship in no-time-flat, invested fully in any number of ways, discover within eight weeks that this investment was perhaps ill-advised, and yet somehow you keep doing it again and again and again. New people, intense feelings. *New people, intense feelings!* Quite a ride. It's part of The Deal, part of why a lot of people love the business—they thrive off a bit of emotional chaos and the highs and lows of it all. Artists can be manic high-low people, fueled by emotional responses, and it all fits together a certain way.

I'm not judging. Been there myself many times. But the downside: the number of hours of work, focus, administration and creativity utterly lost to the distraction, emotion, and heartbreak that revolve around what is too often just petty stupid fucking gossip.

And nights are dangerous, aren't they? The downside part of the Showbiz Holy-cow Intensity Thing tends to be particularly downsidey as the hours creep. The later it is when you're sending a text, the more trouble you're asking for, right? The emotions, the neediness, the loneliness, the gossip, the ratio of bad decisions per 100—it all skyrockets between 9pm and sunrise.

So, while conceding utterly that Showbiz relationships can be intense, needy, short-lived and overly emotional, I offer the following two Advisable Policies For Life in Showbiz:

1. Keep all business communication (including that regarding class, rehearsals, etc.), and all communication from the new people in your life, to business hours. Set 'em as you wish. 9am-to-5pm. 9am-to-6pm. Whatever. If you're communicating, particularly by text or email, after 6pm—it had better be with your significant other, or someone you've known for years, so (we hope) the trust and the parameters have been established. If you have to communicate outside that group after 6pm, ensure it is utterly dry business communication. All incoming communication from fellow students in class, people who might want to get you in bed, people who are seeking to get you out of bed away from whomever you're in bed with, solicitations to gossip…All these communications go unanswered until 9am the next morning (if even then).

2. Share nothing of negatively-tinged emotional content via text or email, don't initiate or attempt to resolve emotional topics by text, email, social media. You could apply this universally and probably live a much happier life, but let's say this should absolutely apply to anyone who isn't either a significant other or someone you've known for years where, again, the trust and the parameters have been set. I fail on this many times a year, so I know the terrain as well as anyone, but I have learned the hard way to try my best not to communicate electronically about emotional subjects or thorny business issues.

The amount of friggin' drama I have confronted over the years, mostly in relation to class dynamics between students (and too often between students who really barely know each other—the new people-intense feelings "friends" that are so frequent), that has been fanned and set ablaze through overly emotional text and email messages (usually sent after 9pm), has been utterly dumbfounding. Text is good for: "Confirming rehearsal at 8pm?" or "Can you buy eggs on the way home?" It's really, really, really, *really bad* for: "Listen, the way you spoke to me today was very hurtful, and frankly, just speaks to the kind of person I've always suspected you were. And by the way? EVERYONE thinks this about you." Ugh. It's comical. You might think I'm making it up, but I would guess at this moment, a lot people who are reading this essay now wonder whether the NSA has provided me personal access to their electronic communications. That right there is a hybrid of some text/email in the chain of every gossipy junior high school-level blow-up that has occurred in the last ten years or more.

Try it for a month. From 6pm-9am the next morning, the only people you communicate with by text/email/social media are romantic partners, family, or people who have been solid friends for, say, at least two years. And don't get negatively emotional via electronic messaging of any sort.

I think you'll find the emerging quiet a bit more conducive to the work you need to do.

CHAPTER 87

Somebody Said That Somebody Said

…that you're a jerk.

…that you did something horrible.

…that your audition sucked.

…that your relationship is on the rocks.

…that you're a substance abuser.

…that you're no good as an actor.

…that you hopped into bed with so-and-so.

…*et cetera ad infinitum ad nauseum.*

Save yourself a bunch of physical and psychic head trauma by ignoring all "somebody said that somebody said" information. It's not information. It's likely not true, or at best it's only partially true. And on the rare occasions that somebody said that somebody said something positive, that's probably not entirely true either. But let's face it, the somebodies who theoretically said whatever they said to somebody who said it to you are rarely saying something positive. Right? It definitely seems that just about all somebody-said-that-somebody-said information is negative. When you try to verify this information, it's like trying to pull on wet tissue paper and it's a damned mess and you end up with probably zero *real* information, a lot of *contradictory* information, and sheets of wet tissue paper all over you. And chances are good you don't even feel any better for all this mess, and in fact you probably feel a good deal worse.

We learned this back on the schoolyard with that dumb game where you start by whispering "I have a sandwich," and by the end of the line of grade-schoolers it's become "The moon is made of dog crap." And yet in what can be a very gossipy business, full of intrigue and rumor, we sentient mature adults, aspiring to the highest levels of professionalism and artistic achievement, compulsively indulge the habit for somebody-said-that-somebody-said.

Ignore it. Sigh deeply and express boredom. Move on with your life. It may well be that somebody said that somebody said something that you need eventually to handle, but the fact is you don't really have "actionable intelligence" until you observe and hear it directly with your own eyes and ears. If you think the somebody-said-that-somebody-said information is important to rebut or handle in some way, go to the supposed source directly. But you'd better not be bloody accusatory and uppity about it, because I can pretty much guarantee that this supposed source didn't say what somebody said they said, or at least not in the way it was reported, or probably with some entirely different context, and you're gonna have egg on your face by being uppity and righteous before you get the scoop. So if you insist on investigating somebody-said-that-somebody-said, do so cautiously. Or live the happy life by IGNORING IT AND MOVING ON.

And how about this particularly lethal variant: Somebody Heard That Somebody Said. How many times has something like this hit you: "Yeah, I heard so-and-so thinks you're this-and-that." Clearly this falls within the broader topic of somebody-said-that-somebody said, but has that awesome dissociative "heard" word. *I heard that someone said something.* And immediately, this places you, the recipient of that communication, in this position: "Somebody said they heard that somebody said." Impossible to trace. Try chasing that one down! It'll go like this:

YOU: From whom did you hear that?

THE OTHER: I don't know. At the party this weekend. Someone said they heard you were yada-yada.

Did you see that? With a single question, you're now *here:* "Someone said that someone said they heard that someone said."

You can see how completely screwed you are. So again: IGNORE IT AND MOVE ON.

CHAPTER **88**

Get A Grip On Your Finances

Everyone's got money problems, right? It seems that whether you're making money or dead broke, there are still money problems. I know lots of people who make plenty of money, and they still have money problems, so it's not as if making money solves anything if you're clueless about what to do with it. I observe most often two mistakes:

1. No Savings.

2. Quitting job-jobs too soon.

No Savings. Here's the Number One Important Item to Change Your Financial Life Forever (and you don't need to send $19.95 or call an 800 number to get it): SAVE TEN PERCENT OFF THE TOP OF ALL INCOME, AND NEVER TOUCH IT.

This should happen no matter what level of catastrophe you're in financially. Most people don't save because they feel they're in such a fix that they "can't," or don't deserve to, or whatever. But debt shouldn't affect savings—and no, I don't care that the interest being paid on the debt is higher than the interest being earned on the savings. Savings should occur no matter the fires burning around you. You can be fucked up financially and save 10%, or fucked up financially and *not* save 10%. Short term you're still probably fucked up, but the difference is that the saver has decided this fuckedupitude will finally stop. If you owe an ugly world $10,000 and made $100 this week, save $10 and then face the world. It will still be ugly, but the $10 means everything to the future and very little to the present situation.

Those who make the decision to do this and don't flinch and don't pull the savings out to handle an emergency will win. That doesn't mean the converse is true and that those who don't save always lose. I've just observed those who don't save or constantly blow the savings will continue to exist in a month-to-month, year-to-year haze of financial stress, waiting to win a career lottery. On the other hand, those who are able to implement the savings policy will win—defined here as "will get a grip on their finances and stop stressing out about it in fairly short order, usually within 12 months." Period. It's just a statistical observation.

Set up an automatic, recurring transfer from your checking account to your savings account. The transfer should occur once a week. The amount should be equal to roughly 10% of your weekly income. If your income varies from week to week, take an average.

If you get a bigger check along the way, or you have a great week, then you have to transfer an additional amount that reflects 10% of that great week. If you have a regular $40.00 transfer that is automatic, based on $400 a week income, and you suddenly get a residuals check for $1,000—then you must ensure that you save an additional $100 in that week.

Notice that there is nothing here about a prerequisite that you make more than you spend. It doesn't matter. Most people raise their eyebrows and say, "I have $500 a week in expenses, but I'm making $200 a week. I'm $300 in the friggin' hole, and you want me to save $20?" YES. Savings occurs based on income. It's not based on what you owe. It's not based on you making more than you spend. It's based on income. It's based on any incoming money. You made $10 this week? Or you borrow $10 this week? Or you found $10 this week? Cool, cool, cool. Save $1.00, and then move on to your other issues. Pay yourself first.

Here's the kicker: Do not touch your savings account. Ever. Don't touch it. Don't touch it. Don't touch it.

DON'T TOUCH YOUR SAVINGS ACCOUNT.

We were all brought up at some point with the idea of "saving for a rainy day." And this is why most savings accounts are so empty. Many people start the savings action, but the first time the brakes fail on their car, the savings is gone. "Rainy days" come to mean just about anything. Your savings account is not just a "rainy day" fund. Nor is it a new TV fund. It is your FUTURE. The idea is that you will never touch this money. In fact, let's call it your future account, your prosperity account, your some-day-I-don't-want-to-work-this-Goddamned-job-and-be-able-just-to-pursue-my-friggin'-ART account. Whatever we call it…

DON'T TOUCH IT.

Here is the biggest gut check of the whole program: Most are cool to this point, they get all jazzed up to save, they do it for a month or two, and then…A rainy day hits. Dental work. Car repair. What do you do? Well, if you come across a day when you have zero dollars in your checking, $1,000 in your savings/future account, and the rent is due, you will *borrow the money for rent*. This is the hurdle. And once you cross it, you're well on your way, because that means you've finally decided: your future is more important than whatever stupid bullshit is happening right now. (And don't forget if you borrow $1,000, the first thing you will do is transfer $100 to your savings account!)

The concept here is that debt is *managed*. It's a tool. It may go up and down, and we're certainly looking for zero debt in the long term, but the one thing that NEVER stops, NEVER goes down, is your rate of savings. Ultimately, this savings can be transferred to an investment vehicle like stocks, bonds, real estate, a business that provides you income, etc. But for now, it's just cash that sits in that account or CD or IRA and accumulates and earns a bit of interest. Don't worry about investing in non-cash vehicles until you've got about $100,000. I'm not an investment advisor by a long shot—I just assume by the time you've got $100K in savings, you'll have worked hard enough for long enough to know better what to do from there.

As things start cooking, you can raise the percentage that you save. But don't get aggressive, save $500 in one week be-cause you're feeling swell, and then the next week go, "Ooops. I shouldn't have done that. I'm so manic! Part of my charm. I'm just going to remove that $500. That was a mistake." NEVER TOUCH THE SAVINGS. Because if you touch it once, you'll touch it again, you'll go back to thinking that whatever bullshit is hap-pening right now is more important than your future, and then your savings will be gone in no time flat. Handling debt certainly has its place in getting a grip on your finances, but it's simply not as important a priority as INVIOLABLE SAVINGS.

Quitting job-jobs too soon. I have seen the following more often than I can count: The actor has a reasonable job-job to pay the rent. Then they book a national commercial. Or a pilot. Or a movie that shoots in three months, but it's gonna be a good payday. Based on booking the gig, they now quit their job-job, and *without fail*, the commercial doesn't air, they're written out of the pilot, the movie that shoots in three months fails to pull together the financing. The variations on this theme are endless. So your question is, "When can I quit my job-job?" Answer: When you book acting work that pays you what you earn in a full year of the job-job. And that money has to be in your account. Not promised. Not a signed contract. *In your bank account.* Only then can you quit. Sorry.

CHAPTER 89

Doing Shit Theatre

Okay, let me just ask it plainly: Why do so many actors involve themselves with such shit theatre projects? Because we've all been there, where we've gotten ourselves together to go see our Talented Friend in their play, and we are…horrified. Right? About 20-30 hours a year at least go by this way. And we come up with something nice to say at the end, get in the car, and rip the experience all the way home, often with a stop for a necessary drink at a nearby pub. And the most common question is often *Why did my friend purposefully associate him/herself with that shit?*

Consider me serious when I say I don't mean to offend or diminish the efforts of the thousands of people every day who are trundling off to rehearse their latest play. I'm not trying to be cute. I truly respect the endeavor—it's not easy, and much of the labors involved are motivated by a real camaraderie and enthusiasm.

But why…why, oh, why…? Now this gets very tricky. It's all in the eye of the beholder, right? I don't think anyone goes to work thinking, "I'm gonna dedicate myself to creating a complete piece of shit today." And certainly I'm vulnerable to the immediate comeback: "Listen, I've seen some of what you've written or directed and in my opinion it was shit." So let's hold on tight. I'm not talking about a group of primarily dedicated, experienced, professional people who set out to create a story and an experience, and for whatever reason it doesn't work out— and obviously all is subject to The Subjective Personal Opinion of the Beholder. No problem. Nor am I talking about a group of perhaps less experienced, less trained, not-quite-professional-yet people who are doing their level best, but that "best" is not yet developed. Beginning musicians still need to start performing at some point, and while it isn't yet of a professional standard, you'd be an asshole to criticize the effort and thus shut down the possibility of encouraging further growth.

So let me rephrase: "Why do so many talented, professional actors, who should know better, involve themselves with what they know damned well is shit theatre, when they could be doing something else with that time and effort?" Because let's say you've got 5 weeks of rehearsal, 4 hours a day at 6 days a week—plus 6 weeks of performances, admin, invitations, traffic, etc.—let's add that up to a rough 300 hours or so of your life that will go into Play Q. And in my humble opinion, for most of these really talented actors, who could easily be carrying part of a film or all of a good play or really making a difference in their career, that 300 hours is a waste. Now picture putting that 300 hours into training, or even into pure administration toward the film/television/theatre professionals with whom you really dream of working. Because I think if one of those industry professionals actually gets out to see you in this shit play, you'll have done more damage than good. You try to say to yourself, "Well, the play is shit, but everyone will see that I'm good in it." Maybe. But there's this risk: Even if you're the only good thing in a shit play, you will primarily be associated with a shit play, with amateurism. I think you're better to hold off until you have a really good part in a really good play. Too often we have the spectre of Talented Person Y, doing Shit Play Q, spending 300 hours on this thing at the opportunity cost of 300 hours spent on—.

But how do we get around the subjectivity of it? How do you know a shit play from not? How is this whole entry not just an explosion of snobbishness? Well—again, this is directed toward talented, trained, professional actors—and I believe these people *know*. And they know *early*. They knew it was shit *the first time they read the script*. They knew after *one week of rehearsal*. And then they doubled down on the bad investment. Why do I assert this? Because most have admitted the same to me on the occasions when I've felt courageous enough to ask. If I know the person well enough, or if they take extra effort to extract my honest opinion—I'll tell them. And most often they know it, they admit they knew all along, they are sheepish about it.

So it's really not about an external, subjective, snobby viewpoint about my opinion of shit theatre. It's about integrity. I believe the individual actor knows damned well they are diving into shit. But they somehow try to *unknow* this, they use the ol' "Well, it is acting work and all" justification, and I believe they brainwash themselves and violate their integrity for the next 300 hours of that play. So if you believe in the script, in this theatre company, in this opportunity— then go for it. Truly. That's what we all do—we believe in something and then chase it. But if you know damned well it's crap—then know *that*. Act on *that*. Walk away with the knowledge that better parts are coming your way, better scripts, and that your integrity is more important than this particular job. No one will ever have a shit-free career, but you can at least change the percentages. And when you stand up for your integrity—I believe that is part of this whole career advancement trip. (And shhhhhhh: You'll act better.)

CHAPTER 90

A Good Attitude...

...consists mainly of the ability to behave professionally and take action despite your bad attitude.

CHAPTER 91

To Die, To Sleep

An essay written after cancelling a class in 2010:

Milton would often quote (or more likely paraphrase) Gurdjieff in saying "The first job of the teacher is to wake up the student, and the first job of the student is to realize they are asleep." I've been thinking about this during this summer. I'm sure most teachers experience to some degree the summer doldrums that occur between Memorial Day and Labor Day: attendance down, production down, energy down—a palpable sense of dispersion amongst the students. It takes a certain child-like imagination to persist as an artist, and I think that young part of us just wants the summer off to play.

And listen, I don't begrudge some travel, and summer is a good time to do it—getting out of Los Angeles every so often is definitely a good thing to do. But there is travel as reward for hard work done, and then there is just being asleep for 10 weeks or more, like some weird summer hibernation.

This week I cancelled a class for the first time in my 10 years' teaching at the BHP, because the level of scene production has been kind of sucking, and even when I threatened them last week with cancelling a class session, it didn't change, so I was forced to be true to my word. I hated my Wednesday night off, *hated* it. (I hated it even more when I saw on Facebook someone trying to get the students to come over and watch "So You Think You Can Dance" in the gap where class was supposed to be.)

So. "...To die, To sleep..." Shakespeare perhaps most famously linked sleep with death, but I'm sure he was far from the first. And in contemporary parlance, "asleep at the wheel" signifies going through the motions robotically without any real thought or care, with quite a lethal and literal subtext. Sleeping while driving is about the most dangerous thing you can do.

Yet I feel as if too many actors are sleeping and driving in their creative and professional lives. This isn't strictly about scene production in class. But scene production in class is an indicator of an actor's energy level. There are very few people who exhibit terrific energy in class and zero energy outside. And very few who are lethargic in class and are just kicking ass outside. In general, lethargy is lethargy and hard work is hard work. One of our more successful actors, who spent many years on a recent very famous TV series, returned to class three times a week for the better part of a year and knocked out a couple dozen scenes during that time, before, you guessed it—booking another series and he's off to Vancouver for a few months. He was a hard worker before he booked the original series, too. I could repeat the same pattern for just about every break-out student the BHP has ever had —they are hard workers.

So when I have to face slap what is normally a terrific group to wake them up, I'm wondering where else actors are asleep this summer, or in general. Here are some symptoms of an actor's sleepiness:

Snobbery: To me, snobbery is a form of being asleep. For the entirety of my 25+ years at the BHP, I've heard veteran students bemoan that newer students aren't quite with the program, or are mysteriously less talented than in the past. (*Romanticizing the past*—that could be an essay on its own.) Get over yourself. This kind of judgment is a form of sleep—you get to check out, secure in your theoretically superior abilities, it somehow justifies lack of energy, because energy is for those who don't yet know what they're doing as well as you do…Hah!

Coasting: Sort of first cousin to snobbery. This is prevalent in actors who have been at it for a while, whether that means class or the broader career. A sense of "I've been doing this so long I don't need to work hard anymore." "I've got this." "I know how to act—now it's just the career to handle." I've often talked in class how this attitude is unique to acting, because musicians, athletes, dancers, etc—they would laugh at the concept. Just because acting doesn't place a specific physical/technical demand on you doesn't mean you get a pass on consistent hard work on your craft. Blow it off at your peril.

I didn't even know X was happening: My first year in LA, my brother was also here at the USC Film Scoring school. Jerry Goldsmith was speaking to that class, which I was sitting in on, and one of the students whined, "It seems like the business is all about who you know, and how do you beat that?" Goldsmith rolled his eyes and said, "Go fucking know someone." I loved that line. Applicable to many areas. You'll often hear actors who totally missed some activity/audition opportunity/admin idea/seeing a good play, etc. protest that "they didn't even know X was happening." That's because you're asleep. Imagine what else you don't know is happening. So go fucking know something. Be aware. Wake. Up.

Someone else will or should do it: Lack of responsibility. You observe something not ideal, something that needs fixing, something that needs reporting, a person could use a hand, your set is a little fucked up, your class is a little lethargic, and you move on, thinking to yourself, "Well, it's someone else's job to handle that." Zzzzzzzzz.

I didn't communicate because I assumed blah-blah. This entire thing with the cancelled class was a big fuck-up of non-communication. The executives of the class didn't communicate with each other. The students didn't communicate with each other. No one communicated with me, and I sat there assuming it was all handled. And yet, we're in the communication business—all this acting we want to do is just highly aesthetic communication, like music or painting or any of it. And yet…Zero. We stare into iPhones, we text, we socially media-ize, and yet…Zero. It's actually all zero. Because we're kind of asleep during all that. Meanwhile, important shit is happening right in front of us, or there are important people who need to be communicated to in this business—and you're…asleep. Because the people you need to meet can't be just Facebooked or texted or "messaged." It's gonna take more than that. When in doubt, communicate. How many times a year do you bump into an old acquaintance and say "we should get together"? Now, what is the actual number of get togethers with old acquaintances? And those are the easy ones. You're trying to get in communication with people in this business who don't know you exist yet. Don't be asleep.

"The business is dead right now."...*So I can sleep.* That's the full sentence. You never hear "The business is dead right now" as a call to action. It's not exactly material for the St. Crispin's Day speech. It's always a justification for sleep. Always. Never let the words leave your lips, or the lips of those around you. One of the characteristics you'll notice if you study highly successful people is that they work pretty much around the clock for years on end regardless of what their particular business is doing. Google was born out of the tech bust after 2000—all those out-of-work engineers...That's what they came up with.

Seeking inspiration instead of seeking to inspire: *I'm just not inspired right now.* How many times have you heard or said that one? People think they want to be inspired (which immediately hands responsibility for that to other people), when actually it's far more rewarding to inspire (which puts it in your hands). But the idea of "I'm just not inspired right now" is a common justification for...sleep. Fuck being inspired. Get off your ass and inspire others—by definition it is a more powerful place to be.

Oh, the irony: to achieve the dream you have to be awake.

CHAPTER **92**

I Can't Until

I can't book work until I have an agent.

I can't get an agent until I book work.

I can't administrate my career until I handle my shit.

I can't handle my shit until I learn to love myself.

I can't love myself until I learn to love others.

I can't love others until I learn to…aw, fuck it. Fuck love.

I can't express love until I break up with my jealous significant other.

I can't do a scene until I find something that inspires me.

I can't do a scene that inspires me until I find a scene partner equal to my brilliance.

I can't find a scene partner equal to my brilliance until I find a scene.

I can't find a scene until I handle why I don't like to read.

I can't read until I finish level 1,367 of Candy Crush.

I can't finish level 1,367 of Candy Crush until I binge watch all of the shows everyone says I should watch.

I can't save money until I make enough to be worth saving.

I can't get a job-job until I handle my resistance to work.

I can't handle my resistance to work until I stop smoking so much pot.

I can't stop smoking so much pot until I unlock an alternative route to my artistic freedom.

I can't unlock an alternative route to my artistic freedom until I receive the proper counseling.

I can't receive proper counseling until my insurance covers it.

I can't get good insurance until I book more work.

I can't book work until I have an agent.

CHAPTER 93

Are You Being Honest Or Being A Dick?

I got a text one time from a friend of mine. He had seen a one-act festival that the BHP had produced: "Saw one-acts this weekend. Yep. I want my money back...Hope life is great."

Oh, my. What possesses someone to send a communication like this? I mean —it was 9:30pm on a Tuesday, and he picked up his damned phone and wrote that thing. Pressed "send" and all. Now, this is not about defense of the BHP or of a one-act festival. I actually had nothing to do with the festival night he saw, so this isn't a personal beef. And even if it was, people are free to have their opinion, they're free to broadcast it however they choose. *No law in the arena*, and all that. But it made me think of this idea of using "honesty" as a cover for being a dick.

I think somewhere in this guy's mind is the idea that his "honesty" about his opinion becomes some sort of hard-boiled tough love, and he's holding up some sacred standard of work in his mind and anything that doesn't meet it deserves to be criticized. The reverse vector kicks in: *If I don't tell them what I really think I'm being dishonest.*

Meanwhile, on my end, I get this text and I think to myself— "What a dick." In that moment I don't give a shit about his opinion, because the means and style of its expression completely alienates me and makes me want to punch him in the face. There are plenty of opinions I seek out as a means of improving the work, and not one of them would ever deliver communication like this.

You can encounter the same "honesty" from casting people, agents, friends and family members who say the darnedest things about you, the business, the career, etc. "If you aren't reading for series regular parts on a consistent basis by the age of 30, you should pack it in." That's special—that's a recent one an actress repeated to me, quoting her manager, as I tried to scrape her off the sidewalk. I don't care how true the statement may be to that manager, it is simply a completely shitty thing to say to an actor, and it's demonstrably false. When I told this actress I thought it was a shitty thing to say, she replied, "But he was just being honest. He told me he wants an honest relationship." Yeah. Right. *Here's an "honest" reason you should fucking pack it in and assume you'll never succeed.* Awesome. Just what the world needs. (And then, wait for it...*And now that I've weakened you, let me tell you how I can lead you to the promised land. Sign here, and by the way, would you like to have dinner?*)

So don't let yourself be shat upon by those who come to you with their unsolicited, unvarnished "honest" criticism of your play or your career or your age or your current station in life. This "honest" bullshit is often just an accepted cover for acting like a suppressive dickhead, and is reflective of self-criticism within the originator.

If you see a friend in a show and you think it sucks...Hey, look: There's a chapter here entitled *Doing Shit Theatre*—the phenomenon whereby we've all gotten sucked into doing total crap plays or projects despite our early perception about it. So I'm fully cognizant of bad quality and I'm not trying to whitewash or defend it. But if you think something sucks then keep it to yourself and spare the performers and creators your "honesty."

No one has a perfect record here, certainly not I. I have carried my teacher-as-honest-evaluator role wherever I go (assuming it's what you wanted if you invite me to see something), only to find that my cutting loose with this evaluation ended up being quite problematic. I once walked out of something where there were several students in the audience—torn between showing them in a single gesture that I recognized this play was absolute garbage, and showing them I could behave well *anyway*. (When you have three kids at home and just getting out of the house requires significant logistics, the walk-out option becomes more and more viable. *I'll use that last hour of babysitter time to run an errand!*) I remember once seeing something I was horrified by, and apparently the friend I was there to support could see my eye-rolling pain-wracked face from the stage. *Ooops.* (Now I sit further back just in case I lose discipline.) But we can at least aspire to be more supportive of the creative efforts of our friends and colleagues. Find something positive and acknowledge that. Or, if it was *such* a disaster, say, "Look, this wasn't my cup of tea, but I'm here for you and as a loyal supporter I'll be there for you whenever you perform." That's honest, too, and frames it in a positive, friendship-enhancing way.

The place for potentially harsh critical honesty is when it is solicited. Students pay for class to get an honest appraisal of their work, so teachers get to be honestly critical—but I would hope it's critique in the name of growth not just destruction. And if you earn your friendships well, you'll hear this from them: "Listen— I respect your viewpoint and I want to know what you think. Really." If you're burning with something to say and aren't asked about it, you can offer, "Hey, if you want, I have some thoughts about this as an audience member/someone familiar with your work/someone who cares..." And then it's up to the performer to sign on or not.

So: Honesty does not give a license to be a dick. Withholding your harsh critique does not mean you are dishonest.

And watch out for indulging your "honest" negative appraisals of your classmates or fellow actors on a project. Such honesty brings down the morale of many a group on an hourly basis worldwide.

Note to Performers: You need to be smart and considerate as well. Don't robotically ask people what they "really think" without being able to handle an honest response. If you go past the first level of acknowledgment to get to a "what do you *really* think?" level—you can't then throw a hissy fit when they tell you and it's negative. Also: If you receive a polite acknowledgment of your work after a performance, don't jump on that with followup emails asking people to promote your show to their friends and industry contacts—this can be highly annoying, and makes the person having acknowledged you think they should have just gone ahead and been a dick. If they liked your show enough to promote it to their friends, they'll do that without your pleas to do so. You can get away with, "Thanks for coming—so much appreciated, I hope you spread the word." But don't get into: "Thanks for coming— much appreciated. Listen, can I ask you to talk to your agent about seeing it? Call me and let's discuss!"

CHAPTER 94

Joe Is An Asshole

A few times a year I get to have my least favorite kind of meeting—a get-together with an angry student about why they're so angry.

There's a script. It usually goes like this: *Hi Jane, thanks for coming.* I ask generally what the problem is, and Jane responds with a monologue, spilling over with anger about the way certain staff members or classmates had handled some typically fucked up situation. The list of grievances is the usual bullshit that has comprised every theatre tiff in world history: this personality didn't match with that one, a communication was misinterpreted (nowadays with social media and text —holy shit does this stuff get out-of-hand), so-and-so said such-and-such would happen and it didn't, so-and-so spoke to Jane in a *certain way*. Yawn. I mean, YAWN! Most of it revolves around a specific person. His name is Joe. Joe sucks. Joe's bigoted. Joe is tactless. Joe can't handle authority. Joe is the worst fucking person. And many people think this, by the way. It's not just Jane. Ask around. Joe has been an asshole for ages. Jane can't believe that Joe's many failures have not been reported to me before.

Then my part: I ask her to tell me the story again, but with the caveat that she can't mention Joe, at least not so negatively. Jane has to tell me what she did wrong, not what Joe has done wrong. Milton's definition of responsibility: "Here's what I did to screw up, and here's what I'm going to do to fix it." *Ouch.* That's a bitch, right? Well, generally Jane won't be having much of that, will continue to go after Joe the Asshole, and I will keep stopping her and asking to tell the story without mentioning Joe. Jane will short-circuit. Jane will cry. Jane will get extremely defensive.

Finally, after all this, the best I will get is a version of that distinct brand of non-responsibility, which goes like this: "I take responsibility for not recognizing earlier that Joe was a total asshole." There are innumerable variants of this non-responsibility version of responsibility, but that's the bottom line of all of them.

Taking "responsibility" for not seeing earlier how Joe Asshole was an Asshole is not really taking responsibility. It's just using the word *responsibility* in a sentence full of blame and victimhood. It's clever, but empty. Just take a moment, try to think of what you could have done better along the way. It's difficult. Milton wrote his famous chapter *Blame Heaven*, and yet he could be the screamingest, yellingest blamer you've ever seen. I'm not on a mountain regarding this stuff, either. But working the muscle of taking responsibility will never be the wrong way to go, even when Joe *really is an asshole.*

CHAPTER 95

I Gotta Get My Shit Together

Ah, yes. *I gotta get my shit together.* It's not exactly a new expression, but I dearly wish it would expire, like *I gotta shoe my horse* or *I gotta go to Strawberries and get the latest LP.*

I gotta get my shit together. I need a break. I feel dispersed. I'm uninspired. I need to go make money for a bit. I need to go to Joshua Tree. It's all of a piece. The Grand Justification. Because, of what is this "shit" comprised? Money, relationships, car repair, dental work, I'm-writing-a-script, spiritual advancement, a place to live, the new job…On and on. There's nothing in the world that won't fit under the generous, welcoming umbrella of *I gotta get my shit together.* And no one is immune. Not a human walks the face of the earth who doesn't have some shit that needs getting together.

The one activity that appears not to be part of *I gotta get my shit together* is disciplined, daily, hard work at both craft and career. IGGMST is almost always used as the "reason" one must take a break from that hard work, because until IGGMST is handled, you see, Aspiring Actor will simply not be able to take the world by storm. But when the shit is handled, well, brother, look out! Then, and only then, will class have its proper relevancy, and the scene work will take off, qualitatively and quantitatively. Then, and only then, the concentration will be there, the commitment, the money, the time to do the administration that is being blown off at the moment.

Is there an acting teacher out there who hasn't grown to detest summer? Summer. *I gotta take summer off to get my shit together.* Summer is the great season for getting one's shit together, apparently. Two weeks of travel next month becomes the reason for eight weeks off from class. "Why do you need eight weeks if you're only traveling for two?" Answer? Yeah. You got it. There's a whole category of shit that gets together...*before Labor Day.*

But in 25+ years' association with BHP, I've noticed an unmistakeable pattern: The vast majority of those who leave class under the IGGMST umbrella? I bump into them on occasion some months later, years later...*They're still getting their shit together.* They're still getting their money together. They're in a brand new, shiny, fucked-up relationship that's driving them nuts the way the old one did. They're still smoking pot every week. They're still working on that script. They're on Level 14 of Positivity Seminar X, and the next level, Level 15—that's where the shit really gets handled. Or, often, they've just quit.

And most whom I've witnessed to have made the blessed journey from Aspiring Actor to Working Actor—they've been studying and working at it the whole time. It's not 100% of course, I'm not trying to say that if you're not in a class you won't make it. But definitely a high percentage of those who make that transition— they've been in class the whole time. And of the ones who do make the transition, post-study —the vast majority were the ones who spent *years* hacking it out on a stage a couple times a week.

The linkage here is not that a class provides some magical elixir that leads to work. It's just that it represents an intention on your part. You're going to part with some cash and a night or two a week in dedication to that which you want to achieve— good acting, and a career to match. A class provides structure, accountability, you'll see something that inspires you, which is pretty good. Better, you'll get to inspire others (waiting for inspiration takes a distant second place to inspiring others). The tidal pull towards that unique actor-ly blend of bitterness, cynicism and superiority—it might not pull you so hard, you might get your ass hauled by the teacher in the way it needs to be, in a way that leads you to actions that break some logjam in the acting or the career. To me, class serves the very purpose of getting the aspiring actor's shit together.

So this is not a sermon from the mount, it's not as if I can look at life and say that I've got all my shit together. As I said, *not a human walks the earth*...The point is to discourage the idea that IGGMST is a reason for...*anything*. It's not anything. *IGGMST is the shit.* The game is to do what you need to do, work the way you need to work, persist the way you need to persist despite the fact that there may in fact be some shit that needs getting together. IGGMST will be eternal. What's immediate is your ability to chase a dream and take the actions necessary to achieve it.

CHAPTER 96

On The Care And Feeding of Playwrights

It's an unfortunate responsibility to have any affiliation with a playwright. The necessary support level is high. It's like having some exotic pet. Or a boat. Apparently they say the two happiest days in a man's life are the day he takes ownership of a boat, and the day he sells it. In the performing arts community, there is a perilous ongoing dance between obligation, desire, responsibility and friendship that can have some severely negative consequences if someone's foot flattens another's toe. So let me offer some thoughts on this dance from the playwright's perspective.

In my opinion, playwrights are on the line for their work in a way more closely aligned with painters, composers or novelists than screenwriters, even though many playwrights also work as screenwriters. Just as with every note you hear in a piece of music, or every word you read in a novel—every word spoken in live theatre is controlled by the playwright. I think it was Coppola who said that most movies are written on the hood of a car—lines are improvised and changed between "action" and "cut" over multiple takes, and that's after several writers were hired over many drafts. In the theatre, the words have been dissected and doubted, tossed aside and resurrected, agonized about over a couple years by one writer in solitary confinement. It takes at least two years to develop a decent play, and many great plays out there have taken far longer than that.

I think of the writing process as a spectrum, and at one end, there I am at my computer typing away. At the other end, I may well stare vacantly into the void of ESPN, with some small percentage of my brain still working on the script in the background. I've practically come to tears while playing tennis certain afternoons, not from the poor quality of my tennis, but because I can't figure out the play I'm working on (so it's no wonder I keep framing the ball sky-high into neighboring backyards). But throughout the spectrum, there is the torture of doubting whether you might have anything worthy to say, there is thought, trouble, and inspiration, quietly (or not so quietly) acting out scenes while you drive around town. Finally, a staged reading with feedback: You've invited some big brains to hear it, you've asked for their suggestions, and as you hear them you want to punch them all in the face. You learn to listen anyway. And rewrite. Another reading—more feedback. More rewriting. Casting, rehearsals— notes from the director. And rewriting. It's at least two years per play. Maybe some of us move quicker—but many move slower.

So you get to the end of this arduous process, it's opening night, and what do you want? A full house. Some great reviews would be fantastic as well, but mostly you just want people to see it. It's all been designed for the moment when the story, real live actors, and real live audience members interact in a way we thought all along might be worth the effort. The experience is nicer obviously when people like it, but mostly I just want everyone to see it, to have the chance to see if this alchemy takes place on any given night. And if you're a friend, neighbor, associate, student, co-worker of a playwright, this is where you come in: Seeing it, and behaving well while seeing it. If you don't see it, or you don't behave well, you're going to damage severely that relationship. And that may be fine—I'm not trying to argue that a relationship with a playwright is more important than any other. I'm not trying to say every playwright is deserving of adulation from his network of friends and associates. I've seen adulated plays and wanted to bang my head against a radiator, and I'm sure people have seen mine and been similarly inclined. But there's adulation and then there's simple support. I'm just letting you know that if you have a playwright in your midst, and you happen to be interested in maintaining the relationship, it can get completely fucked up by not coming to the play, or from poor behavior while seeing it. In your world nothing has happened, and over there in Playwrightland it's *toast*, it's *over*.

A play is our version of a novel, but one with a 4-8 week

timer on how long it can be read before it goes away. That very intense investment along with a timer on the chance to experience it makes for a bigger deal in terms of desired attendance. We clock it. We track it. We memorize every face that has walked in, and check it against those we know who have not walked in. (I think the reason many actors in particular may not quite understand this fully is that they may do 3-4 plays a year, or several appearances on television or film, and so each one has seemingly less importance—though I'm a big believer as well that if you are connected to an actor, you should check in once or twice a year to what they are doing.)

And now the behavior part. The Broadway composer Jason Robert Brown once told a harrowing story about being invited to an opening of a Sondheim musical, which apparently had not gone well, and then, along with one of Brown's friends, having an after-show dinner with Sondheim. Wanting to avoid the topic of not having liked the work, they self-consciously and awkwardly spoke of other topics, before an exasperated Sondheim finally asked, "So, uh, did you like it?" Dinner didn't end well. More on that later.

I've been on the receiving end of some pretty interesting behavior at my plays for sure. I shared the more vivid examples of this behavior with a few other playwrights I know, to see if it was just me, and they each immediately emailed and called with several stories of their own that matched or exceeded my own. One humorously blamed me for two hours of work with her therapist to handle the years of repressed trauma and resentment sparked by this conversation.

So here's a little top ten checklist for the care and feeding of playwrights:

1. See the play. And I know—if it's one weekend anything might happen. But most plays run for at least 4 weeks. I've had supposed friends who have missed 45 performances of a play. A couple have missed 90 performances of two plays over two different years. Going to the correct theatre is always good. Being on time, all that.

2. Acknowledge the opening somehow. Acknowledge the closing. Acknowledge a re-opening. Say something. Make us believe.

3. If you're a student of a playwright (I have lots of these), and the play runs a while—see it twice. The performances and quite possibly the script will have evolved, and you can learn from that. You're thinking it's some weird obligation, and it's actually a chance to learn. In the meantime, my actual struggle is to have students see it *once*. (Another memory of Milton: His insistence we all see the film *The Red Shoes* for one shot: that of the dance students rushing up the stairs of the theatre, boundless in their enthusiasm for seeing new work...)

4. Say something nice. Write a nice email. If you're being insincere, don't worry—we know, we can tell. But the etiquette is appreciated while the truth will still be known. When you say nothing, we remember that, too. It's all clocked with astonishing detail and recall.

5. Don't leave at intermission. Ever. That's instant death to the relationship.

6. Playwrights aren't box office staff, and it's depressing to be treated as such. Don't ask about ticket availability, or comps, or how to get them.

7. Don't ask when it's closing. That information is usually a mouse click away. When you ask that question, the playwright hears, "How long do I have to fulfill this stupid obligation to see your stupid play? I'm so disinterested that I can't even look it up."

8. If you say you're going to show up on such-and-such a weekend or performances, be good to your word. If you can't, then let us know. Because we remembered what you said. We're waiting to hear.

9. Don't offer your critique unless it's asked for.

10. If you see the playwright on the way into the theatre, and he/she sees you on the way into the theatre, then make sure they see you on the way out. If that's not possible, then the acknowledgment of the play needs to happen fast. Like, a text on the way home, followed by email later or next day.

And now you're thinking, "Uh, that's crazy. I have to do all that?" Nope. Not at all. Life is busy, and again, I'm not saying a playwright is more important than anyone else. We are exotic pets, and perhaps you're regretting the maintenance. But if you have one, if you're interested in keeping that relationship, then you'll do your level best. As one of my friends wrote me back regarding the draft: "If you have a playwright friend, and you don't see his play, you're not his friend. If you see the play and respond poorly, you're not his friend. You are the death of creativity. You are fucking mold. You ruin shit and you make people sick." So. That's the angrier version. He's younger than I am. I am more wistful, I have more miles on the odometer, I know well I've misbehaved myself a few times for sure. There's no one who can't to some degree be called a hypocrite on the matter of support. But these days, there are few worse feelings for me than that of a friendship drifting away—friends seem harder to make, easier to lose, and this issue of support has been part of that drift more often than I'd like. And while this essay has been written from my personal angle, I'd bet good money that most in the creative fields have their own version of what I'm talking about.

Back to Jason Robert Brown's story. He was advised to call Sondheim the next day and apologize, which he did. Here's his memory of what Sondheim told him: "Nobody cares what you think. Once a creation has been put into the world, you have only one responsibility to its creator: be supportive. Support is not about showing how clever you are, how observant of some flaw, how incisive in your criticism. There are other people whose job it is to guide the creation, make it work, to make it live; either they did their job or they didn't. But that's not your problem. If you come to my show and you see me afterwards, say only this: 'I loved it.' It doesn't matter what you really felt. What I need at that moment is to know that you care about me and the work I do to tell me you loved it, not 'in spite of its flaws,' not 'even though everyone else seems to have a problem with it,' but simply, plainly, 'I loved it.' If you can't say that, don't come backstage, don't find me in the lobby, don't lean over the pit to see me. Just go home and write me an email or don't. Say all the catty, bitchy things you want to your friend, your neighbor, the internet. Maybe next week, maybe next year, maybe someday down the line, I'll be ready to hear what you have to say, but that moment, that face-to-face moment after I have unveiled some part of my soul, however small, to you: that is the most vulnerable moment in any artist's life. If I beg you, plead with you to tell me what you really thought, what you actually, honestly, totally believed, then you must tell me, 'I loved it.' That moment must be respected."

CHAPTER 97

X-Shaming

Teaching sometimes feels as if it's getting more difficult, and that's because it seems the very notion of a teacher advocating a student change in order to achieve a goal (much less just to be a better person) is looked at negatively as being judgmental or intolerant. The weakness that I as the teacher would like to identify in the student seems more and more to have been enshrined as a sacrosanct reaction to some previous trauma. *Don't touch that weakness—I earned it, it's mine!* Whatever behavior pattern you would like to advise as being non-optimal has now been deemed acceptable, and if you criticize it or advise it to be changed, well, then you are X-shaming them. Sigh. I happen to think shame can be a useful tool in human relations.

shame, n., a painful feeling caused by the consciousness of wrong or foolish behavior.

"Consciousness of wrong or foolish behavior." What exactly is wrong with having that consciousness, or the pain caused by it? But like so much nowadays, everything is upside down. Free speech is oppression, and the use of violence to stop people from speaking is the exercise of free speech. Bad behavior isn't worthy of shame, but those who would label it as so are judgmental assholes. The ancient idea that shame can be useful when it comes to monitoring or altering bad behavior has been flipped, and shame the noun has been tossed for shame the verb. Shame is no longer a negative feeling of consciousness by *you*, it is a negative activity of judgment by *others*. And yes, I understand that people can shame others for stuff out of their control—body-shaming and all that. But there needs to be differentiation between actions in and out of your control. Regarding the former, it seems these days that if as a teacher you want to point out some bad behavior, it's at your peril, because you're now an asshole who is *this*-shaming and *that*-shaming and *the-other*-shaming, as if it is all a function of prejudice and intolerance. I had a discussion with one student about a pattern he might change, he became defensive, said that I was X-shaming him, and, exasperated, I came back with the notion that all this X-shaming came down to shame-shaming, and that the Entitlement Society has flipped language upside down so as to lock in as *precious* any freaking behavior pattern that can be justified by your upbringing, be it entitled or shitty.

It ain't what happened to you, it's how you respond to what happened to you. We generally don't admire those who behave badly, no matter what the justification for it. We greatly admire those who behave well, and particularly so when you find out later there was some horrific trauma they overcame, and they never mention it, they just rose above it, identified a goal, and pursued it with vigor, generosity, dedication, and professionalism.

CHAPTER 98

The Do-Not-Say List

Here are the Top Ten gems that actors should simply stop saying, to themselves, to teachers, but most importantly in any actual professional communication whether in person or in writing:

1. This business is so tough.

2. I've got a lot of personal shit going on.

3. It's been a tough day.

4. I don't even know if I want to continue acting.

5. I'm feeling overwhelmed/really tired.

6. Well, I had plans to travel just then.

7. Let me tell you about my new diet. At length.

8. My phone died.

9. Los Angeles is so superficial.

10. I'm working on this in therapy.

CHAPTER 99

Velleity

It's pronounced "vell-EE-itee," it's a noun, and it means "a mere wish, unaccompanied by the effort to obtain; volition in its weakest form." As in: *The notion of being a professional actor intrigued me, but remained a velleity.* I sheepishly admit that even with my fancy education, I was ignorant of this word when an old friend and longtime BHP student texted to say I should write about it. (CUT TO: Allen quickly looks it up on his phone, then texts back: "Interesting! Yes, of course, velleity!")

He had been at a party of some sort with other actors roughly in his age range, but from outside the BHP universe. It struck him how passive they were, while being arrogant at the same time. They dressed the part, modeling their looks off of Sean Penn, Johnny Depp, etc.—only the coolest will do. Yet none of them had much going on with their careers, it seemed almost entirely aspirational, there was no *action*. When my friend would ask what they were doing to make it all happen, there was just a curious, amazed response. *Take action? Career Administration? What's that? Why do it?* He told them some of what he does on his administration, and they were stumped. *You really do all that?* As he told me the story, it reminded me of one of my first days in Los Angeles, which was as a visitor my senior year of college. The friend I was staying with had an old high school acquaintance over, an actor, and, damn, did he come off cool. Way cool. Super cool. I could only aspire to this level of coolness. Uneducated as I was about what questions to ask of actors, I took the old "So what have you been in?" approach, which of course betrayed me as rookie-beyond-belief in these discussions. Nonetheless, his answer stuck with me: "I don't know. Ask my agent." Even as a hopeless undergraduate rookie, I was able to think to myself, *ask your agent what you've been in?* Was he just annoyed by my question? Was I too uncool to answer directly? Was there in fact no answer, because he hadn't worked? Did he think I asked him what auditions were coming up? It was so weird and reflexive, I knew something was up but didn't know what word to use to describe it. Velleity, rare a word though it is, now comes to mind. It wasn't annoyance, nor a misunderstanding—the actor's answer betrayed a far worse problem: Entitlement. *Ask the agent. The agent knows. The agent is in charge. I'm not in charge. I have an agent, and that's that.* I recall that this actor's father was a big-deal Hollywood producer at that moment, and so the situation was compounded by the unique sense of entitlement that can often enshroud and suffocate the children of Hollywood elites.

Entitlement is the dark force behind a lot of velleities—you probably know it all better under the term "laziness," and you don't have to be a child of the Hollywood elite to suffer from it. Milton used to say he didn't believe in "laziness," and that being lazy was just another means of saying "lack of confront." My take is whether velleity is better known as "laziness" or "lack of confront," it's all linked to entitlement, and as a result far too many actors are spending a lot of time on their couches smoking pot, binge-watching various television series, congratulating themselves on how clever they are, how informed their various opinions, and that shit needs to change if anyone expects to get anywhere.

I remember one actor who gave me one of the clearest statements I've heard regarding entitlement, which is a monstrous attitude problem increasingly common to actors and their career administration: "I'm both a victim and I have an ego. I feel like I'm unable to do what I need to do to be successful, nor should I have to."

WOW. Now that's pretty damned brilliant. It's also totally sick, but when you're looking at a monster and how to defeat it, it's handy to be able to describe it precisely. I share this because we all have our velleities, the phenomenon exists to some degree in all of us, yet I had never heard it described so starkly as that. "I feel like I'm unable to do what I need to do to be successful, nor should I have to." Holy shit. Beware.

CHAPTER 100

Art And Practicality

It may be apocryphal, and I can't remember for sure it was about Kurosawa, but I remember a story that at some point an enthusiastic acolyte asked him how he came up with some amazingly brilliant framing for a certain shot in *Ran*, and Kurosawa's answer was that if he moved the camera half an inch to the left there was an electrical tower, and half an inch to the right a Sony factory. Substitute any filmmaker, any film you admire, and I can guarantee a story similar to that. Often the higher aspirations of true art are willingly read into that which was merely practical at the time.

I would offer that practicality is in fact the necessary onramp to artistry. There is a lot of completely unrealized artistry out there in the hopeful minds of actors, writers and directors of all ages. At some point, a likely small minority of that number will take the practical actions to realize some of what is flying around their brains. Once the real world gets to play its role in your story, which is to throw Murphy's Law daggers your way as often as it can muster, practicality will become your new religion. *What can we actually achieve, given certain financial, technical and temporal limitations?* As you answer that question, again and again and again, day after day, the exercise of solving practical problems becomes a part of your artistic technique, equivalent to a warmup or stretching regimen for athletes, or diligent practice of scales for the musician. It puts you in the position of finding the art within limitation and constraint, and let's face it: art *only* exists within limitation and constraint. *We only had two hours in a certain location, so we had to rewrite two scenes into one, and eliminated everything unnecessary that was in those scenes. We only had so-and-so available for two hours, so we shot all her footage, and because we needed a bunch of reactions from her to stuff we hadn't shot yet, I just rolled on her face for a minute asking her to let everything she could imagine affect her. And it was from that footage we found the perfect, most emotional "response" that we cut to later. We couldn't afford the awesome DP, but for less money I got the most eager to do particularly well, and that ended up being worth way more.*

A million variations exist on this theme. Solve the practical problems, and you'll be amazed by how much art emerges, including some that you never intended to be read as artistic at all.

CHAPTER 101

Slouching Towards Bitterness

Oh, the perils of turning 30 while in the pursuit of acting!

I have now watched many young students to whom I had a strong connection close in on and cross the dreaded 30-year-old threshold. And that's when it often starts to happen...The slow, inevitable, creeping bitterness...*The career hasn't moved as hoped. Some other classmate's career has moved, and well, he/she isn't nearly as talented as...No, no. Don't have that thought! That is an unsupportive, mean-spirited thought to think, but damn it I factually am better than so-and-so and where is the justice?...Why did my teacher just suggest a scene where I play a young parent for chrissakes?...The trips home are becoming more painful, the parental apprehension more palpable...My college friend just bought a five-bedroom house, and I still can't afford to fix the brakes on my car...The audition last week for that under-five corrupted my soul. That thing where I was up for the part that would have changed my life but then it ended up going to Fading Film Star was straw last. I can't take it. My agent quit the business to become a Yoga instructor/real estate agent one week after telling me this pilot season was gonna be mine mine mine...Am I going to get to 40 and then quit the business, having screwed up my chance for 20 years' career advancement in the business world?*

Now, it's not rocket science to observe the classic phenomenon of 20-something actors who hit Los Angeles (or wherever) full of vim and vigor and ready to take on the world, and then hit the wall. The wall of jadedness. The wall of cynicism. The wall of bitterness. Nor is it necessarily negative that the older someone gets while chasing a dream, the more there may be a certain urgency to it all. That urgency may be a very well-needed kick in the ass to get off the general pattern one might find—that you can spend your 20s fucking off, but after that it starts to cost you. Urgency, good. Bitterness? Not so much.

If one were to generalize, students in their 20s are ambitious, eager, free-wheeling—as one might expect. Those north of 40 are often thoughtful, talented and diligent students in their own right, and have some mileage on the odometer that gives them blessed perspective and maturity that can enlighten the acting and perhaps ease the spirit. Many of this group have returned to acting after time off for family/job, or perhaps are coming to acting later in life. And some have been at it all along, and simply made an artistic existence work within the framework of their evolving and particular life. The trickiest group? Ages 28-38, with a very tricky, sticky patch at 30-35. There seems to be a particular bitter flavor to the thirty-something variety of creeping doubt.

So how does one take the obvious generality that a thirty-something artistic striver becomes more negative and turn it into a specific action to counter the trend? I think The Bitterness has to do with the feeling of low self-worth, strongly attached to the subset of low financial worth, a sense that one can only live in poverty for so long via the choice to be an artist. As your twenties recede into the distance behind you, desires for a better material life, or marriage/family, etc.—are often thrown into prominence, not the least by seeing friends seemingly surge "ahead" of you, even if only by those metrics.

I question the idea that "success" as an actor can only be defined as "acting is the only thing you do in your life, producing the only income you'll ever need to maintain your life." That certainly is the best case scenario, but to say you love the arts enough to pursue them professionally not only means an absorbing dedication to your abilities and your career administration, but also to designing a life that can handle very nature of an artistic existence.

The theedy-wheedy Oprah-cology part of this is that you need to "stay positive," and "believe in yourself," read *The Secret*, and all the rest. I'm not against any of the positive psychology cures, but I think one of the best means of overcoming The Bitterness comes primarily from good financial policies, and being a valuable person outside the realm of your artistic pursuit.

I believe the student who wants a life in the arts more than ever has to have the entrepreneurial instinct, the ability to put other talents to work for money, or at least the recognition that there is honor in working a job-job for rent money—everyone does so, whether artistic or not. There are many professional actors who have long and fulfilling careers, who also supplement their income from other sources in ways that might surprise.

So here is my anti-bitterness prescription:

1. Sound financial policy. My experience is that almost all actor-related bitterness has financial stress as a strong harmonic. See *Get a Grip on Your Finances*. The biggest lie regarding money is that you have to have a bunch of it first, and then you will be good with money. So people who essentially have zero net worth do nothing about creating sound policies to build the future, because they feel they don't have the means by which to create a future. "I can't save money because I don't have enough money for my life as it is." That is a vicious circle that must be demolished.

2. Be a valuable person, and not just on set. Actors tend to romanticize that their best behavior will appear on set, because only then are they fulfilling their artistic purpose. As a result, the 99% of their life spent off-set is on autopilot, without due attention to being of service, being responsible, helpful, on time, etc. So I don't care if you're working the lunch shift at a fast-deteriorating Wendy's to pay the rent, you should be the best server in Los Angeles during that time. Be the valuable friend, the best employee, the stellar member of an acting class or theatre company. I've often said to the students at BHP that it is far more likely that someone in their class will get them an acting job than it is that a famous director will—so treat them right. The old saw goes, "Don't seek a lover, be one." Well, take the principle there and apply it across the board.

3. Remain part of an artistic group. I run a class, so obviously I can say enthusiastically that I believe a good class can provide continuity, a place where for a few hours of each week creativity and storytelling rule the day. Sometimes the class is the only place where that creative spirit gets its exercise

during the time a career is being built up, or is experiencing a trough. But often The Bitterness will result in a superior attitude about your class or theatre group, "It's not the same as when I started," or "I'm so much better than most of these people," or, "It doesn't inspire me anymore," blah, blah. Perhaps you rationalize that you no longer need it as much as you might have earlier for technical ability reasons and so why spend the money and time? Well, don't seek inspiration from the group, seek to inspire it. You stay part of a group because it helps keep your responsibility level up, and your sense of value, the sense of being accountable. You stay because there's a good chance you may well be the one who should get off your high opinion of yourself and help the new person. You stay part of a group because it's great networking, because passion projects that can themselves alleviate The Bitterness tend to emanate from those groups. And no matter how swell an actor you've become via a class or group, you always need the gym.

4. Break a sweat from physical activity of some sort at least 2-3 times a week.

5. Keep 1-4 in place even when successful as an actor. For those who hit some sense of the jackpot, I've witnessed they will abandon some (or all) of the policies that got them there, and then the series is cancelled, the movie wraps, the play closes—and they're out in the wilderness, where The Bitterness lurks and bites them hard just when they thought they'd moved past it.

One has to watch for that jaded bitterness that can take hold like devil grass. I like mowing my own lawn (with a manual mower at that—oh, do the jaws drop from passersby), and few months after moving in to our home, I noticed this damned weed growing like a horizontal vine over large chunks of the lawn. And once I developed the eye for it, I could see the slight color differential between the weed and the grass, kneel down to pull it up, and marvel at how three feet or more of this stuff would come off the lawn when I hadn't noticed it before, and under it the grass having suffered for lack of sunlight. And thus a metaphor for The Bitterness that creeps up and takes over many actors in the

30-something range. Develop a feel for it—the discoloration, the jaded commentary, the lessening tolerance, the cynicism, the odd sense of superiority, the nodding, knowing apathetic justifications for no action. If you're worried about money, *do* something about it. If you're feeling the career blahs, *do* something about it (including projects of your own origination). If you think you're so awesome, then share some of that with people who might need a dose themselves. Think your job-job sucks? It's an honor to work, so be the best at whatever you do. If you feel the need to excel at something else and you think this is in total opposition to the continued pursuit of an acting career, well—consider the idea that there is no shame in developing an idea for business, or a love of books, or cooking, or what-have-you and doing that concurrent with a diligent pursuit of acting. Because the thing about acting is that you just never know, do you?—what phone call may come, what opportunity arises that leads to a chunk of blessed cash and a sense that it is possible after all. You have to stay in the game, and keep the weeds off the lawn.

CHAPTER **102**

The Dedicated Channel

Jesus I suck why the hell do I continue to pursue this when I could go get a masters or apprentice for a producer or something or go back home where people are real and there's actually weather okay shut up already you need to be positive you need to channel your confidence this is what your therapist has been talking to you about this endless tidal pull towards insecurity where did that come from my parents or an early piece of shit love affair there's no need for it I need to grow the fuck up and stop dramatizing my pain except I'm an actor aren't I isn't that the point to dramatize my inner pain for the world to recognize as their own pain this makes my pain infinitely more noble and in fact it's my duty and my responsibility to feel my pain and parade it for others like a freaking pain peacock but holy shit I'm nervous and I'm not sure my pain is what is needed at this moment because fuck it's a stupid fucking comedy and I hate reading for shit like this it's not what I work on in class why am I taking a class anyway stupid fucking waste of money I hate being part of a group anyhow and now I slept with a classmate which I swore I wouldn't do and it's ugly they're now in love and I'm not or I'm now in love and they're not the balance has been thrown it's not fun I should do improv and have some fun that's what my agent says is that everyone is doing improv I need improv on my resume or just casting workshops are they even legal or not I can't understand that whole deal because I'm good enough I know I'm good enough to book work but I just need a friggin' chance why won't someone call me in to give me a friggin' chance I need to do more workshops okay SHUT UP and focus you're about to audition you're about to go

on in a play you're about to get called to the set you're about to
perform a scene and all these thoughts are really not useful to you
you have to focus and get personal man get fucking personal I'm
gonna be so fucking personal I'm gonna connect so awesomely
the connection is going to be like a warm light emanating from
us outward into the holy shit my rent is due next week I feel
like I just paid the rent and I don't have the rent because my
job friggin' sucks and am I really going to be doing this all my
life like in middle age will I be going to auditions and sitting in
a room looking at people who are my age now and regretting
every choice I made am I going to be alone all my life am I really
going to be with this person the rest of my life should I have just
committed to that other relationship for the rest of my life won't
I ever have kids shouldn't I have had kids I secretly sometimes
dislike my kids shouldn't I be more involved in like what's going
on in the world I have all these opinions I should march more
I should read more I should proclaim more how I'm a virtuous
person with the right beliefs and wait hold on a freaking second
why doesn't my teacher just tell me to quit why does he validate
me why does she believe in me teachers must lie all the time
about *STOP IT STOP IT STOP IT* focus on the scene focus on the
scene focus on the scene get personal have the moment before
have the significant other have the son have the dog have the
physical state have what the history is own my sexuality don't
hide don't fucking hide I'm so not going to hide Jesus I hate this
actor I hate his preparation I hate her questions I hate the way
he covertly directs me I hate the way she overtly flirts with me
do I hate it no I don't hate it how can you hate someone flirting
with you SHUT UP STOP IT okay just quiet your mind quiet your
mind find your peace find your bliss find your gratitude find your
fucking blisstastic feeling of awesomeness find it find it I can't find
it but someone posted something about mentally strong people
and what they do and this doesn't feel mentally strong and is he
writing this about me specifically and while I'm at it I'm hungry
I want something to eat I want an infinity of something to eat I
want to eat nonstop until next week but at least it won't be just
burritos maybe a kale salad and some gluten free cookies in there
as well I can't believe I'm thinking about what food I want to pig
out on when I'm supposed to be getting ready to act what I really
need is to smoke some fucking weed man get some fucking meth

man I need some pot some meth some X some K some lucy some molly I need something I should probably stop smoking so much fucking pot right it's really not making me exactly sharp as a tack I wonder if your thoughts are actually important I mean I'm about to go out there and shit the bed or maybe I'm going to be fucking brilliant and people will laugh and cry and give me compliments and I can never tell the difference between sucking and killing it but in some weird way there's nothing better than going out there and doing my thing why does it have to be such torture and I can't get my mind to have the thoughts I want it to have about the scene about the moment about what's going on but maybe in the end it's not so freaking important what thoughts I have before I act while I act after I act and these thoughts are simply a 24/7/365 dedicated channel of nonstop streaming shit brilliance genius healthy doubt anticipation nerves fear excitement dread that has absolutely nothing to do with execution it's just a channel that exists and it streams and it's not linked to acting at all it just exists and it always will exist and anyone who says they don't have their dedicated channel is a fucking liar and what life as an artist is about is the ability to co-exist with the dedicated channel to function without listening to it so much holy shit did they just call my name did they just call going up did they just call places did they just call first team in did they just call sound and camera they did this is it just go in there just fucking go out there just...and...uh...

Curtain up. Action. They'll see you now.

Epilogue

I have dreams.

Not general ones. Not those dreams of success in its various manifestations. No, no. Specific ones. "Milton is alive" dreams. They started shortly after his death, they recur several times a year, and all have the same general pattern: I report in to some aspect of my current daily life at the BHP, and I find Milton there. As if he never passed away. Or I'm teaching a class, and I glance over to find him sitting in the front row, watching me. It's two hours into class, and I somehow hadn't noticed he was there. Or the phone rings: *ring-ring, riiiiinnnnnnnng…*

"Hello?"

"Yeaaahhh."

"Milton?!"

"Listen, where's my shit?"

"Your…?"

"At my house. Where's my shit? It's fucking empty."

I'm summoned to his house for a meeting. Now, in my waking life, I've been invited to this house for the occasional party in the years since by its subsequent owner, who has done massive renovations on top of Milton's massive renovation. The only trace of its original DNA as the modest, small home to which I first reported all those years ago? Milton's office. But in the dream, the new owner is gone. The house is indeed empty except for Milton's old desk and the chairs in the office. He's livid. Where's all his stuff? I'm called upon to explain all the events of the years since I last saw him, and he's, well…not happy. (To be fair, sometimes he is charming. In some of these dreams, he sets me at ease, and I find myself relieved to speak with him. He nods gently as I explain it all, and the passing years have mellowed him, and he admits having made the first few years after his death unnecessarily hard on me. He'll sometimes say, "You did a good job, man.")

The most recent was several days prior to my writing this. I was in class, but I sat in the audience, and Milton was in "the chair," teaching. Apparently I expected this; it was well into the class and he was meeting my students and being charming, and the vibe of this version of the dream was that all this was expected. No problem. Of course Milton's there, teaching. Why wouldn't he be? It's not like the man died years before. He was just away for awhile, now he's back. As I'm sitting there watching him, it hits me: *What the hell did I think I was doing writing a book?!* How could I possibly think to write and release a book about the BHP, about him, and about acting without his approval? Without even telling him I was writing it? How could I have managed not to tell him anything about it for an entire year, during which I spent every day working in some fashion on the book (and that's after half of it already existed in rough form from years of writing for the blog).

These dreams tend to go on a bit after the big reveal. You'd think once I "woke up" inside them to the realization that the situation was ridiculous, they would stop, but they don't. Instead, seemingly hours later, having spent all that time in the bizarre reality of the dream, pondering the absurdities of various "Milton's alive" plot developments, my eyes will open for real. It will take several minutes of being awake for those vivid plots to wear off, and for me to face a new day in the Oasis of Insanity.

I look forward to each of those days, and the varied traffic that hits me in the course of running the school and its 80+ year old building. Since having purchased it, I've done a lot to improve the place, and there's rarely a dollar I prefer to spend than one spent on improving some aspect of the theatre, in both function and appearance, and the students' experience there. I look forward to the periods I set aside during the week, outside of class time, to help students with their scenes. I look forward to interacting with my staff, almost all of whom were brought on by me since Milton passed on, as we laugh and banter and fight and disagree and then agree again on how best to pursue this crazy business of training actors. I look forward in some way to each nutty situation that might present itself with a student. I look forward to rehearsals for something I might be directing. I look forward to the writing sessions on whatever play I'm working on. Most of all, I look forward to teaching on my nights to do so. Those moments where beforehand, outside, the voice would show up to whisper in my ear that this is the night I'm to be proven for a fraud—those moments are more rare, but Milton's first critique still pops into my head: "Why wouldn't someone listen to you? You seem like a bright enough guy to me." I walk in, and almost every night, there is work that cracks me up, inspires me, moves me—sometimes it's based on notes that I have given previously, but my favorite is when I had no direct impact, when it's a scene that just kills without my having already given notes. I explained this at some point to someone, saying it's interesting that as a teacher your favorite moment is the student "doing it" without you, because when they don't need your guidance to excel, then you've really done the job. This person replied, "I hate that you say they did it 'without' your guidance. They didn't do that work without your guidance, but *because* of it."

After one of those great scenes, I'll stand outside the theatre, watching traffic pass by on Robertson Blvd. I reflect upon all that has happened. A nervous November evening outside the Skylight Theatre in 1990. Al Mancini brings a green, overly-intellectual me in for a landing. Meeting Milton during rehearsals for La Bohème. An almost accidental sixteen-year apprenticeship. Inheriting the business, and then having to save both it and the building from Milton's mess of an estate plan. Improving the building. Starting the blog. Coming up with our "Project X" free theatre concept. Bringing onto the teaching staff those who Milton knew back in the day as young students, but who've stuck it out, grown up themselves. They're older, mature, some married, some are parents. Shit, I have three kids now—last he saw, my oldest was just 18 months old, and he was signing a copy of his book for her three days before he left. The cultural shift away from his fearsome, mercurial, authoritarian style. Even the revised emphasis regarding certain elements of the technique. Story. It's got to be about the story. It's been a busy 27 years. The traffic on Robertson hasn't changed, though. A siren echoes in the distance; the fire trucks are heading north toward me from their station south of Pico.

"There's no way Milton wouldn't be completely psyched that we're still here," I think to myself. "No way he wouldn't be really happy that the kind of work demonstrated in that scene I just saw is still going on here without him." No. Not without him. Because of him.

I look forward to each of those days.

About the Author

Allen Barton has over 25 years' association with the renowned Beverly Hills Playhouse acting school, and currently serves as its owner and principal teacher. He is also a playwright, director and classical pianist. His plays, including CIRCLING, DISCONNEC-TION, YEARS TO THE DAY, and ENGAGEMENT, have been performed in cities across three continents. He earned many years worth of L.A. stage, television and film credits as an actor, and has directed over a dozen stage plays and short films. As a pianist, Allen has recorded five compact discs (available at Apple Music and other streaming services), performs solo recitals regularly on both coasts, and in 2010 was made a Steinway Artist. A native of Boston, he lives currently in Los Angeles with his wife Tiffany, daughter Zoe, sons Reed and Henry, and black Labrador Retriever Milo.

Index